# WALKING THE
# SOUTH COAST
## OF ENGLAND

A Complete Guide to Walking the South-facing Coasts of Cornwall,
Devon, Dorset, Hampshire (including the Isle of Wight),
Sussex and Kent, from Land's End to South Foreland

# DAVID BATHURST

summersdale

WALKING THE SOUTH COAST OF ENGLAND

Summersdale Publishers Ltd
46 West Street
Chichester
West Sussex
PO19 1RP
UK

www.summersdale.com

Printed and bound in Great Britain

ISBN: 978-1-84024-654-4

# WALKING THE
# SOUTH COAST
# OF ENGLAND

## DAVID BATHURST

# Contents

# About the author

David Bathurst was born in 1959 and has enjoyed writing and walking all his adult life. He has walked all the major long-distance footpaths of Great Britain including the South West Coast Path, the Pennine Way, the West Highland Way, the Cleveland Way, the Southern Upland Way and Offa's Dyke Path, and his guide to all the official long-distance footpaths in Britain, *The Big Walks of Great Britain*, was published by Summersdale in 2007.

By profession David is a solicitor and legal adviser to magistrates sitting at Worthing and Chichester. He is married to Susan and has a daughter, Jennifer. While not writing or walking he enjoys cycling, the works of Gilbert & Sullivan, the plays of Alan Ayckbourn, classic British sitcom, teashops and *The Times* crossword. His most notable achievements have been the recital of the four Gospels from memory in one day in July 1998 and the complete works of Gilbert & Sullivan from memory over four days in August 2007.

# By the same author

*The Selsey Tram*, Phillimore, 1992
*Six of the Best!*, Romansmead, 1994
*Financial Penalties*, Barry Rose, 1996
*Around Chichester in Old Photographs*, Sutton, 1997
*Here's a Pretty Mess!*, Romansmead, 1998
*Magisterial Lore*, Romansmead, 2000
*Poetic Justice*, Romansmead 2001
*Walking the Coastline of Sussex*, SB Publications 2002
*Best Walks of Sussex*, Summersdale 2003
*That's My Girl*, New Theatre Publications 2003
*Let's Take it From the Top*, Romansmead 2003
*Walking the Disused Railways of Sussex*, SB Publications 2004
*Once More From the Top*, Romansmead 2005
*Sussex Top Tens*, SB Publications 2006
*Walking the Kent Coast from End to End*, SB Publications 2007
*The Big Walks of Great Britain*, Summersdale, 2007

# Acknowledgements

I would wish to thank Jennifer and Anna at Summersdale for their invaluable help and encouragement; Alison, Chris and Vicky Barber for their splendid photographs of the south Devon coast; and Susan and Jennifer for their constant love and understanding.

# Introduction

In 1980, I read a truly inspiring and life-changing book. I don't mean Norman Vincent Peale's *How To Win Friends And Influence People*; nor Richard Bach's *Jonathan Livingstone Seagull*; nor even Barbara Windsor's *Book Of Boobs* (that was in 1979). The book I'm referring to is *Turn Right At Land's End*, written by John Merrill, and it describes his successful completion, in 1978, of a walk round the entire coastline of Great Britain. It is a tremendous story of human endeavour combined with a wonderfully succinct description of our 7,000 miles of shores. Although John Merrill was the first to complete the walk round the entire coast, others have followed, including Richard and Shally Hunt whose excellent account of their adventure is described in *The Sea On Our Left* (also published by Summersdale, incidentally). But although their achievements have been both amazing and enviable, most of us would have to accept that it's not going to be practically possible to emulate them.

However, a walk along the entire length of the south (English Channel) coast of Great Britain is certainly much more of a possibility for those who relish both a challenge and the opportunity to get better acquainted with our coastlines. A challenge it certainly is – from end to end, including the Isle of Portland, the Isle of Wight and Hayling Island, it measures over 725 miles – and, if you will forgive a line or two of management-speak, meets the SMART objectives of being specific, measurable, achievable, realistic and timeable. It will also be a hugely enjoyable experience, as you get to discover a phenomenal variety of landscapes, from spectacular cliff scenery fashioned by nature over millions of years to vast expanses of beach and shingle, from cosy and picturesque villages to cities of immense historical and cultural significance, from yachting centres populated by millionaires to cheerful resorts, from creeks beloved of smugglers to naval bases of massive strategic importance, from nature reserves to power stations and state-of-the-art lighthouses. You may decide to undertake the challenge for a number of reasons: perhaps as a retirement project, a source of fund-raising, a sabbatical from work, a wish to lose a few pounds (you'll certainly have lost a lot of both types by the time you're done), or exasperation at the quality of daytime TV. You may decide to try and do the whole thing at once, or to do it in bits, as I did – it's your decision.

The purpose of this book is to provide a concise and easy-to-follow guide for those who are contemplating a walk along all, or indeed any, of the south coast of England, from its start at Land's End in Cornwall to its finish at South Foreland just east of Dover in Kent. (The described route actually goes on to the next village of St Margaret's Bay, but the south-facing coast ends at South Foreland.) It will meet the needs of the end-to-end traveller, and many 'asides' throughout the book are directed at those who are seeking to undertake the complete task in one go, but is equally useful for those deciding to walk it in sections, or for visitors to a particular part of the south coast who fancy walking a small piece or pieces of coastline but aren't sure where, or indeed whether, to start. And for those who aren't able to walk, it provides the perfect introduction to the south coast for the armchair traveller, developing on from the magnificent BBC *Coast* series which has captured the imagination of so many. It does not pretend to provide absolutely all the information you'll need – you'll have to check other sources for details of accommodation and public transport timetables – but it gives all necessary route information, descriptions of places of interest on the route, and an assessment of difficulty and quality of the respective day sections. A separate section at the end provides a range of important practical advice. You may choose to use the book as a manual, dipping into it as and when needed, or as a continuous narrative and an unfolding story of a pilgrimage from one corner of our fascinating and beautiful island to another.

No particular level of walking experience is assumed. I anticipate this book will be enjoyed not only by hardy trekkers who think nothing of 20 miles per day, but also more sedate ramblers who are content with barely a third as many and who have no aspirations towards the complete end-to-end walk. The day sections suggest roughly an average of 17 miles, but there are huge variations depending upon availability of public transport and accommodation, as I have tried to start and end each section with a place offering significant availability of both. For those who want to plan shorter walks, cumulative mileages for the individual sections are given in brackets within each section. (Note: the three islands of Portland, Wight and Hayling are all included in the cumulative figures for completeness, but of course it's for you to decide whether to walk them. If you have the opportunity, you should, because they provide long sections of proper coastal walking that you will otherwise miss.) The sections do vary hugely in terms of difficulty: some are extremely easy, and even the most inexperienced walkers will have little problem in reeling off quite a high mileage in the course of them without great effort, but others are very testing indeed and in bad weather even the best equipped walker might hesitate before setting out to tackle them at all. (I say a little more about equipment below.) For this reason, it's very hard to tell how long the walk will take you from end to end, although I would suggest that you should expect to set aside between six and seven weeks in total. I have divided the route into 47 day sections, including a few light days here and there for hopefully obvious reasons.

What is described is, as far as possible, a true coastal walk from west to east, taking advantage of assistance of the prevailing wind. On a number of occasions you will meet river crossings which to walk around would require substantial forays inland, and where ferries are available, they are incorporated into the route description. John Merrill eschewed all mechanical aid, but he was a man of extraordinary physical fitness and had many months at his disposal. The South West Coast Path national trail, with which my described route coincides almost exactly from Land's End to the Sandbanks ferry just south-west of Poole, does make use of a number of ferries, and you shouldn't feel any compunction about doing so too. It is important to note that many ferries are seasonal and I strongly advise you to time your walk along the relevant sections to coincide with times when the necessary ferries are operational (see appropriate sections of text). Sometimes it is physically impossible to stick to the coast itself because certain areas are in private ownership, or have fallen victim to erosion which sadly is an ongoing problem. In such cases, I have endeavoured to offer a route as close to the sea as possible, always using designated rights of way, often overlapping with other named long-distance routes, not just the South West Coast Path. Please note, however, that there are occasional logistical problems along the way that are quite separate from the river obstructions. Some sections are owned by the Army, and if they choose to be firing on the day you were hoping to walk them, you may have to detour some way inland. Some sections are dependent on the tides being favourable, and for those sections it's not always practicable or possible to remain on the foreshore when the tides are high. A separate section at the end of this book provides a list of contact numbers which should help you plan for all contingencies, and high tide alternative routes are included in the relevant text, but even the best laid plans can sometimes go awry through no fault of yours. Local tourist information offices should be able to provide tide tables and advise you of any particular difficulties that you may encounter when tackling a particular section; for example, extreme weather conditions or coastal erosion may cause rights of way to be closed at very short notice.

A word about the day section headings. I begin with the mileage for each, based on the recommended route set out in the text that follows, and then in brackets the cumulative mileage for the whole route is shown. After the mileage I give a difficulty grading of easy, moderate or strenuous. An easy walk may still be a long one but will generally involve straightforward terrain which casual walkers and ramblers can cope with easily. At the other extreme, a strenuous walk may involve a good number of hard climbs and descents, and, especially in bad weather, may prove beyond the capability of those with inadequate levels of fitness and equipment. There then follows a one to four grading based on my personal opinion of how good a walk the day section is, grade one equating to largely unrewarding and disappointing terrain and surroundings, and at the other extreme, grade four equating to a really good walk packed with fine scenery and/or interesting features along the way. Lastly are listed what I consider to be the three 'highlights' of the day section in question. This information should assist all users of this book, from the end-to-end walkers to holidaymakers wishing to sample the odd piece of south coastal walking but not quite knowing which are best suited to their needs and capabilities. The numbers in brackets after place-names in the text state the number of miles to that point from the start of the day section. This will help you to plan shorter walks along the south coast.

If you are contemplating the complete end-to-end walk, or indeed substantial numbers of day sections in one hit, it should go without saying that you must be physically extremely fit and properly equipped, with decent properly broken-in boots, waterproof clothing (it WILL rain at some stage on your end-to-end walk, whatever the time of year), ample supplies of food and drink, and emergency equipment including mobile phone, first-aid kit (including blister treatment) and access to funds at short notice. It is recommended that you equip yourself with an Ordnance Survey map of the area you're walking: the Explorer maps are the best. Accommodation and other amenities are plentiful throughout, and virtually all the day sections have plenty of accommodation and food opportunities en route as well as at the start and end. However, the scale of the task should not be underestimated. It is a mammoth undertaking, well over three-quarters of the length of the complete walk from Land's End to John o'Groats, and you should not attempt the whole thing – or even several day sections – over successive days unless you have previous experience of a significant number of consecutive days' walking without discomfort. You should certainly read this book carefully and see for yourself just how tough a lot of the walking is, especially if the weather is bad. By contrast, if you have in mind discrete day trips on sections shown as easy in the text, the amount of equipment you need, especially if the weather forecast is good, will be negligible, and light-fitting clothing, trainers and a day-pack may be all that's needed. However long or short your proposed walk, one thing is still the same – ALWAYS HAVE A SUPPLY OF WATER WITH YOU, AND DRINK PLENTY OF IT. Thirst – or dehydration, which is the same thing – is one of the most demoralising conditions a walker can experience, but even on the hottest days you can avoid it completely by drinking water at frequent and regular intervals throughout your walk, and not waiting till you're thirsty before doing so (it's too late then). The other thing to avoid is hunger, and you should always have an emergency supply of high-energy food with you – bananas and dried fruit are particularly suitable – because you can't always guarantee when the next cafe or shop will be available. On sunny summer days, you should also guard against sunburn, and either apply sun cream or wear light long-sleeved tops and trousers rather than T-shirts and shorts. And be sensible in your planning, bearing in mind the vagaries of public transport and the need to modify your itinerary if the weather turns bad. Sometimes it's best to swallow your pride and accept the need for an unexpected rest day rather than battle through pouring rain with negligible reward.

But to end this introduction on a positive note, providing you get the planning right and have the necessary levels of physical fitness, you will enjoy a truly stunning experience. The south coast offers walking that is of a very high quality indeed, with some truly wonderful and diverse coastal scenery. Standing on a clear day on the Lizard, Golden Cap, the Needles or the Seven Sisters, when the views stretch seemingly for ever, gazing up at the stupendous Spinnaker Tower as your ferry glides across the harbour waters of Portsmouth, spreading clotted cream on freshly-made scones in the delectable old village of Portloe, standing on the Cobb at Lyme Regis with angry storm clouds rolling in from the south-west and the sea smashing against its walls... there are times when you will not want to do anything else but continue with this amazing walk, packed with variety and interest from beginning to end, and completing it, whether all at once or in stages, will rank as a significant and worthy life achievement. If you're wavering, my advice is – get out and do it. You'll love it.

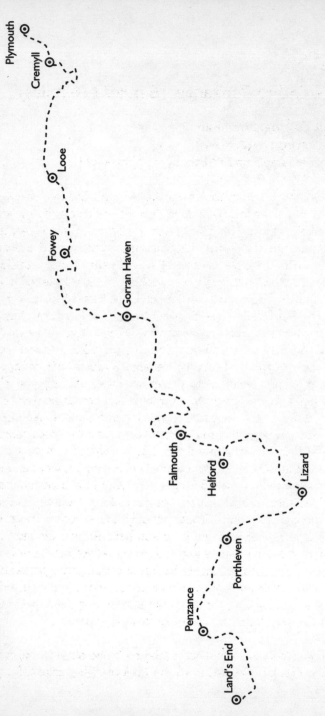

**CORNWALL**

Plymouth

Cremyll

Looe

Fowey

Gorran Haven

Falmouth

Helford

Lizard

Porthleven

Penzance

Land's End

# Day 1
# Land's End to Penzance 16 miles (16 miles)

**Difficulty rating:** Strenuous
**Terrain rating:** ▲▲▲▲
**Highlights:** Land's End, Porthcurno, Mousehole

So, the big day has come. You've made it to Land's End and, unless you happen to live in the locality already, even getting that far by means of wheeled transport may be regarded as something of an achievement. It's a big challenge, and perhaps it's best not to think too hard about just how many miles there are to do: on the South West Coast Path alone, which you'll follow as far as Poole in Dorset, you will reel off a little matter of 380 miles, and that is not much more than half the task. How you choose to mark your stepping out towards St Margaret's Bay, on the other side of Dover in Kent, is a matter for you. If you have spiritual leanings, you may offer a prayer. If you're practically minded, you'll take a swig from your water bottle, reminding yourself of that sensible advice that drinking water when you're not thirsty will help you avoid dehydration. If you're anxious to emulate Wainwright at the start of the Coast to Coast, you'll want to dip your toe into the sea, although as it's 60 feet below you, that may not strike you as either practicable or sensible. Whatever you choose, this is it. You've been photographed with 'the' signpost, the developed article providing a lasting reminder that at this point you were 257 miles from your local branch of Asda; you can reassure yourself you've not got as long a journey as those starting the walk to John o'Groats (although there's not as much in it as those superior beings might have you believe); you can gaze into the teeth of a severe westerly gale and smugly reflect that this will push you effortlessly eastwards, and as the bus or car that brought you here recedes into the distance, your mind is concentrated and focussed by the fact that nothing but your own efforts are now going to get you to the next Cornish clotted cream tea or family-size pasty.

Land's End is certainly a distinctive and romantic place to begin any walk. If you look out to sea from the 60-foot-high granite cliffs, you may be treated to a range of sea life you will be unlikely to witness anywhere else on your walk, with dolphins, porpoises, basking sharks and occasionally seals being sighted on the currents off the headland, and gazing up into the sky you can watch for fulmars and herring gulls. The romance of the place, enhanced by the intriguingly shaped rocks with equally intriguing names like Carn Bras and Kettle's Bottom, is only partially spoilt by the infamous theme park and amusement complex, which in any case is not the only great headland on your journey to have this treatment. From the famous signpost you walk downhill to cross a footbridge, round Pordenack Point then round the next headland as far as Mill Bay. You descend again to a footbridge, ascend and take the second path on the right, proceed to Carn Les Boel and go forward to Gwennap Head – just before which is the fine headland of Tol-Pedn-Penwith – then descend to a road at Porthgwarra. This village boasts a snug cove with a beach of sand and bladderwrack flanked by sheer cliffs of granite rock; look out for the narrow cleft in the cliffs, just one example of the grotesque rock formations which make this early part of the coastal walk so fascinating. You continue along a track off the road end as far as a junction of paths, then bear left. Now there's a climb, a descent to St Levan's Holy Well, and another ascent to the headland of Pedn-men-an-mere, from which it's a short walk to the open-air Minack Theatre, just inland of which is Porthcurno (5). The Minack Theatre, with its Greek-inspired design and with the sea forming a dramatic backdrop, has to be one of the most spectacularly-sited theatres in the country; holding its first production in 1932, it has seating for 750, and continues to be a major attraction for summer theatre-goers today. Don't be tempted down onto the beach, but stay on the cliffs, where you will see a white pyramid marking the spot where an undersea cable was landed in 1870, effectively the terminus of a worldwide network of cables, and there is in fact a Telegraph Museum nearby. And talking of diversions, there's also soon the option of a detour to Logan Rock, a granite block estimated to weigh about 65 tons but which 'logs' or rocks at the slightest touch. In 1824 it was pushed over the cliff by some sailors, an action which caused such a kerfuffle that the ringleader had to reposition it at his own expense.

Back on the coast path, proceed through the gorse to and around Cribba Head, descending to Penberth. Penberth Cove is described by the National Trust as the most perfect of Cornish fishing coves, with its rose-covered cottages, scattering of stone houses and handful of fishing vessels. Beyond Penberth there's a climb, and you need to look out for a signed right turn and an ensuing zigzag descent to Porthguarnon, followed inevitably by a steep climb, helped by steps, up the other side. Keep going on a good path, watching carefully for and taking the signed right-hand turn for Lamorna, and descending to St Loy; there's another important right turn here, just beyond a house and garden, with a descent to a crossing track beyond which you reach the shore of St Loy's Cove, in a beautiful wooded setting. Beyond the cove, look out for a path taking you back up on to the cliffs; there's a descent to Boscawen Point followed by some up and down work culminating in a good track which takes you forward to the Tater Du lighthouse. It's rocky going now as you continue on to Lamorna Cove, dropping down to the houses at Lamorna where in the nineteenth century ships loaded granite that had been gathered from the nearby quarries. Squeezed between granite headlands, the village – a popular base for divers exploring the local reefs and wrecks – boasts a pub called the Lamorna Wink, its name signifying in the days of smuggling that contraband spirits were available here. Beyond Lamorna you rise again to the Carn Du headland, then descend once more before ascending through the charming woodland of the Kemyel Crease Nature Reserve; there's more up and down work past Penzer Point before the path arrives at a road onto which you turn right, passing the Wild Bird Hospital. Just beyond Lowenna turn right and then bear left to reach the centre of Mousehole (12.5).

Pronounced 'Mowzel', this is a pretty fishing village, once in fact the centre of Cornwall's pilchard fishing industry, with a fascinating maze of grey granite houses, many boasting tiny courtyards and semi-tropical gardens beside a little harbour; the oldest house in Mousehole, Keigwin House, dates back as far as the fourteenth century, and was the only house in the village to survive when the village was burned by the Spaniards in the 1590s. The village made tragic headlines in December

1981, when the wreck of the local Penlee lifeboat in treacherous seas claimed many lives. On a happier theme it is also famed for its brilliant Christmas decorations which might include dancing reindeer and multi-coloured serpents. Just before Christmas fishermen gather annually to eat Stargazy Pie in commemoration of a local fisherman whose catch once supposedly saved the village from starvation; it is made with whole fish whose heads poke out through the crust. Perhaps the thought of deep-fried hake and chips wrapped in yesterday's *Daily Star* isn't so bad after all.

Now it's very easy going, as from the Old Coastguard Hotel you simply follow the road signposted Newlyn and Penzance, a path running parallel with it as far as Newlyn. Although the maps might suggest that Newlyn is simply a suburb of Penzance, it does in fact have a character of its own, with a large fishing port – the largest in Cornwall in fact – and an annual, very popular, fish fair; its cobbled streets and profusion of flowers and palms have traditionally attracted many artists, some of the most prominent of whom formed the famous Newlyn School. Beyond Newlyn there's a good promenade waterside path all the way to Penzance (16).

Penzance will seem positively metropolitan compared with what you've seen thus far, and, with its excellent public transport options, it's the first realistic opportunity for you to decide that the whole thing was a bad idea and that the line-up of contestants on *I'm A Celebrity Get Me Out Of Here* will in fact provide a more alluring form of entertainment over the coming weeks. A town did exist here in medieval times, Edward III granting Penzance a weekly market in 1332 and Henry VIII giving Penzance a charter in 1512 which allowed it ship dues on condition that the town maintained the quays in repair. However, all traces of the medieval town were obliterated by the Spaniards in 1595, and what you see now – or could see, were you not so anxious to get your first night's accommodation sorted – is mainly Regency and Victorian. Formerly important in the tin trade, Penzance developed with the growth of tourism from the early nineteenth century, and further expansion followed the arrival of the railway in the 1850s. Among buildings of interest are the pillared and domed Market House, the museum of the Royal Geological Society of Cornwall, the flamboyant Egyptian House in Chapel Street, opposite which is the seventeenth-century Union Hotel, and some fine galleries including the Penlee House Gallery in Morrab Road which houses the country's largest collection of works of the Newlyn School. The most westerly town in England and boasting a ferry link with the Scilly Isles, it has a mild climate in which palm trees flourish, and subtropical plants are grown in Morrab Gardens. Arguably Penzance's most famous resident was Humphrey Davy, inventor of the miner's safety lamp, and a statue of him, dating back to 1836, stands outside the Market House. Amateur operatic buffs, meanwhile, will doubtless be reminded of Gilbert & Sullivan's perennially popular work *The Pirates Of Penzance*, the opera perhaps partially inspired by the fact that pirate raids were occasionally experienced by Penzance in the seventeenth century.

# Day 2
# Penzance to Porthleven 13.5 miles (29.5 miles)

**Difficulty Rating:** Moderate
**Terrain Rating:** ▲▲▲
**Highlights:** St Michael's Mount, Rinsey Head, Wheal Prosper

From Penzance to Marazion the going is very straightforward, initially using a cycleway between the railway and the sea wall; beyond a car park on the far side of the level crossing and Station Restaurant, you walk beside the coast road to Marazion, with a parallel path on the shore-side available a little further on. Marazion is an attractive but unremarkable village, burnt by the French in 1549, and until the nineteenth century, tin and copper was exported from here. Of far greater interest to the visitor is St Michael's Mount and its chiefly fifteenth-century castle, accessible from Marazion on foot at low tide; according to Celtic legend, the mount was built by a giant who supposedly forced his wife to carry heavy granite boulders to the site. A Celtic monastery was in fact said to have existed here from the eighth to eleventh century, and subsequently a Benedictine monastery was built here between 1135 and 1150, the community being suppressed in the early fifteenth century. The present buildings, owned by the National Trust, include a gallery with a wealth of weaponry and trophies, a restored buttery and, at the top, a battlemented chapel, while sub-tropical planting was added in the nineteenth century.

You leave Marazion by way of Fore Street and Turnpike Hill, then beyond the Mount Haven Hotel you turn right down the lane giving access to Chymorvah East. Before reaching Chymorvah East, bear left, descending to a field and then to a shore, bearing left here and climbing onto a low cliff to round Trenow Cove. There's a slight (signed) diversion inland here, but then a swift return to the coast and a walk past Boat Cove on to Perranuthnoe. You cross the road linking the village and beach, then proceed along a low cliff path followed by field paths past Acton Castle, an eighteenth-century castellated mansion, and on to the headland of Cudden Point, the rocks off which have claimed many ships. Here you swing from southwards to eastwards, passing two tiny coves and reaching the village of Prussia Cove (7), named after the local inn The King of Prussia; this in turn got its name from the eighteenth-century landlord of the pub, John Carter, who used the cove for smuggling activities and modelled himself on Frederick the Great of Prussia. The remote Cornish coves were indeed perfect spots to land contraband goods.

You turn right onto a track, right again and downhill to a ford, then climb again to round Kenneggy Sands, crossing a stream and going forward onto Hoe Point; there is hereabouts plenty of evidence of previous tin and copper mining activity, in the form of dumps of the now disused mine. Continue through extensive vegetation to reach Praa Sands (9), descending to the beach. You ascend steps and bear right over Praa Green, then left and right through scrubland and forward to a road; turn right to walk through the private Sea Meads estate, then beyond the estate bear right to where the road ends, and ascend to Rinsey Head, looking out for Wheal Prosper, a restored nineteenth-century engine house of another disused tin and copper mine. Rinsey Head is a splendid spot with waves pounding the granite cliffs and fulmars nesting on the rock face. At the fork of paths bear right; there's a descent followed by a climb, the path rounding. Trewavas Head, and then there's a left fork to pass old mine buildings, a descent and yet another climb, passing the Megliggar Rocks. In due course you descend to the sprawling village of Porthleven (13.5), bearing right when you reach the road and proceeding round the harbour. Porthleven used to be the outlet for tin that was mined in the locality, and has traditionally been a busy fishing port; it certainly boasts some quite impressive constructions, including the eighteenth-century Harbour House and the nineteenth-century West Wharf. But with 13 miles of golden walking ahead of you, and – according to one quick glance at the map – downhill all the way, you can be forgiven for pulling your boots back on and pulling away as quickly as you can. That said, it does enjoy a great selection of pubs and places to eat.

# Day 3
# Porthleven to Lizard 13.5 miles (43 miles)

**Difficulty rating:** Strenuous
**Terrain rating:** ▲▲▲▲
**Highlights:** Mullion Cove, Kynance, Lizard

You exit Porthleven by passing the clock tower at the pier at the south-eastern end of the harbour, walking up Cliff Road and then proceeding along Mount's Road as far as the car park at the end. Bear left here along a coast path which proceeds on to Loe Bar, a sandspit with its white cross erected in memory of over one hundred lives that were lost in 1807 when a frigate, *HMS Anson*, was driven onto the shore and pounded to pieces. This is quite a tough walk, more demanding in some ways than cliff-top walking! Bear right at the next path junction to pass Gunwalloe Fishing Cove, then beyond the cove continue along the obvious cliff path past the magnificent Halzephron Cliff. You have to descend to Gunwalloe Church Cove, the 'church' part of its name deriving from the fifteenth-century church of St Winwalow, whose detached bell tower, actually the tower of an earlier church, is built right into a nearby rock. It certainly is worth leaving the coast path to see it; having done so, and crossed the stream either by footbridge or beach, continue past the car park along the road to the sandy Poldhu Cove. Don't pass the cafe but bear right up onto the headland, passing a rest home (once the Poldhu Hotel) and bear right again onto a cliff path passing the Marconi monument that was erected in 1937 to mark the spot where the first transatlantic radio transmission was made by Marconi in 1901. A radio station remained here till 1922 and it was utilised as a vital link between Britain and the United States during World War Two.

Descend to a footbridge and make your way on to Polurrian Cove, a popular surfing beach, passing below the Polurrian Hotel, bearing right onto a rough road and then bearing right again, rising to a cliff path. This leads shortly to a descent into the village of Mullion Cove (7); join the road past the Mullion Cove Hotel then descend by steps to enjoy a wonderful walk round Mullion Cove and its harbour. Also known as Porthmellin, Mullion Cove is justly famous for its amazing outcrops of giant greenstone rocks, and Mullion Island offshore is a nesting site for guillemots and kittiwakes. Now you really can start to enjoy some of the finest cliff scenery of the south coast, as you leave Mullion Cove by following the road from the cafe, bearing right onto the signed Coast Path and continuing uphill along the superb Mullion and Predannack Cliffs, past Predannack Head. The coast path is undulating but magnificent. There's the option of a detour to Vellan Head, but the South West Coast Path cuts across the headland to pass Soap Rock and then go on to the quite delectable Kynance Cove, descending to the little cluster of cottages. Although it's irksome to have to lose so much height which you know you're going to have to regain, this is a place of stunning beauty. The rock formations are quite astonishing; caves nearby include the Devil's Bellows, transformed into a spectacular blowhole by the surging sea, and other caves here have weird and wonderful names including Ladies' Bathing Pool and Devil's Letter Box. There's an island off the cove, accessible at low tide, called Asparagus Island as that vegetable grows in abundance upon it, and one of the giant mounds of rock is known as Albert Rock after the Prince Consort visited here in 1846. The sheer grey-black cliff faces at Kynance, 200 feet high in places, are streaked with olive-green, purple, red, yellow and white from the magnesium rich serpentine rock. It was at the Rill, just north-west of Kynance Cove, that the Spanish Armada was first sighted in 1588.

From Kynance Cove you then rise again, passing above Pentreath Beach and now heading resolutely southwards along the cliff-top, effectively the west side of the Lizard peninsula, to reach Lizard Point. There is just so much to marvel at as you walk; while to your right are the amazing cliffs, to your left is a quite remote and unspoilt wilderness of heather and grass, and the ground and cliffs around you are rich in plant life which includes bluebell, dropwort, harebell, bloody cranesbill, Cornish heath, spring squill, summer pinks and yellows of thrift and kidney vetch, prostrate juniper, and the so-called Hottentot Fig, a showy South African succulent fruit with white and pink flowers. Having reached Lizard Point and realised you can go no further south, you then turn sharply left along the cliff-top, passing the twin coves of Polpeor and Polbream and a road giving access to the nearby Lizard village (13.5).

Here is the gimmickry – the Most Southerly House and the Most Southerly Café – and the lighthouse, built in 1751, which really can claim to be the most southerly point on the whole south coast walk. Don't think this is any cause for celebration, as you're barely a quarter of the way through your first county! But, yes, there is real splendour here: as well as the cliffs of 'lizardite' – a mineral and basic silicate of magnesium which is a type of serpentine – there are rugged chasms and caves hollowed out by the sea, a host of sea life that includes grey seals, bottle-nose dolphins and basking sharks, and a huge variety of birds such as fulmar, kittiwake, Manx shearwater, gannet, shag, kestrel and great black-backed gull, and butterflies that include the grayling and pearl-bordered fritillary. The most spectacular feature of all – and one to watch for in every sense – is the Lion's Den, a huge hole in the cliff-top near the lighthouse, created in the 1840s by the collapse of a sea cave. Very fortunately, the Lizard hasn't suffered the same fate as Land's End in terms of blatant commercialism, the Most Southerly Café being probably about as brash as it gets. So push the boat out, do, and be content to enjoy your most southerly bath, your most southerly full English breakfast, and your most southerly application of Mrs Bridges' Fragrant Foot Embrocation Cream.

# Day 4
# Lizard to Helford 23 miles (66 miles)

**Difficulty rating:** Strenuous
**Terrain rating:** ▲▲ ▲▲ ▲▲ ▲▲
**Highlights:** Cadgwith, Beagles Point, Dennis Head

From the lighthouse you turn left again in preparation to start heading up the east side of the Lizard peninsula. You descend steps to cross a footbridge and pass in front of Housel Bay Hotel, looking out onto Housel Bay, where there's another Marconi connection, namely the fact that the great man had a bungalow by Housel Cove. You pass the Lizard Wireless Station, Lloyds Signal Station and National Coastwatch Station at Bass Point, your direction of travel just south of east – it is only beyond Bass Point that you really start to pull away in a more northerly direction – then after following a track beyond a house you bear right, passing a lifeboat station and chute at Kilcobben. You descend steps to reach the houses of another Church Cove, then bear left and shortly right uphill towards Cadgwith. You turn inland round an old quarry, pass some fields, then descend to walk through a valley of gorse, rising again but then continuing through a further valley and going forward past the Devil's Frying Pan, a funnel-shaped depression leading to a remarkable rock arch between two cliffs. You bear left to pass through a gate then right to follow a lane that brings you into Cadgwith, using the obvious path to take you down to the harbour; Cadgwith is almost the definitive Cornish fishing village with its busy harbour of boats for lobster and crab fishing, and whitewashed thatched cottages. Join the road that takes you past the Cadgwith Cove Inn, turning right onto the signed coast path, proceeding in front of a row of cottages. Turn left at a little hut with a chimney, ascend and continue along the path past fields and areas of scrub, passing Kildown Point and Enys Head then descending to the cove at Poltesco, site of a former serpentine works. Then up you go again, passing Polbream Point and dropping again to follow a road to the very popular Kennack Sands, complete with rather unsightly caravan park. The coast path doesn't go down onto the beach – although it may be worth it to attempt to get sightings of seals, sharks and dolphins that have been viewed here – but rather follows the path above it.

Beyond the sands the path goes forward to Eastern Cliff, heading uphill through heather and gorse, and proceeding now in a more easterly direction. Progress! Between Kennack Sands and Black Head, the next major headland, the going is magnificent but tough, with a succession of steep drops and climbs. You pass the Carrick Luz headland and drop particularly steeply to the mouth of Downas Valley – this is an especially gruelling descent, and the slippery serpentine stone makes it hard to maintain footholds – then regain the height you've lost with a climb to the delectable gorse-clad Beagles Point, with tremendous views all the way back down the east side of the Lizard Peninsula, and the Lizard lighthouse just visible in the distance. It's then a fine cliff-top march past Treleaver Cliff to Black Head with its coastguard lookout and nearby trig point, 250 feet above the sea. At Black Head, where you say farewell to the Lizard lighthouse which is now lost to sight, you swing sharply north-eastwards, along the top of Chynhalls Cliff; you bear right, downhill, to Porthbeer Cove, then at the beach bear left and uphill again. You then reach the once-fortified headland of Chynhalls Point, which the South West Coast Path planners decree that walkers of the national trail should include on their journey, and woe betide walkers with a keen conscience for this sort of thing if they find, several miles further on, that they have missed it. Jutting headlands may indeed test the conscience of the south coast walker, but it is your decision and yours alone whether you feel obliged to follow slavishly round the very edge of each one, with the state of the weather, the condition of your blisters, and the number of miles from the nearest pub likely to be the deciding factors. From Chynhalls Point you continue northwards, going forward through what in spring is a magical tunnel of fragrant cow parsley and blackthorn, to a road that takes you to the village of Coverack (11) with another headland, Dolor Point, immediately to the east of it. Coverack is a pretty village of thatched and lime-washed granite cottages, with fishing for bass, crab, mullet, monkfish and pollack and sightings of dolphins in the waters hereabouts, and indeed it was once a busy pilchard port. Coverack is traditionally acknowledged as the halfway point on the South West Coast Path; in fact it isn't, because since the addition of Portland to the official route the halfway point won't come till Helford, some 11 miles further on. But you may see some walkers, complete with bulging rucksacks, performing a dance of delight round the village, and this might be the reason. Or of course they could just be very odd people.

Walk through the centre of Coverack along the harbourside road, then when the main road turns inland you continue along a minor, coastal road which duly peters out. At its end you join a track then bear right along a rougher and potentially very muddy path which becomes less well defined and muddier – there's also a stream to cross using granite slabs – as you head towards and then round the aptly-named Lowland Point. It certainly won't be the high point of your day's march in any sense. You then come to Dean Quarries and you need to follow the footpath signposts carefully through the quarry and be aware of blasting which may take place at any time between 10 a.m. and 6.30 p.m.; the area has a long and proud heritage of traditional industry, with stone being shipped from the nearby shores until as recently as 1972. You drop down to Godrevy Cove, proceeding along part of the beach with views to the infamous Manacles Rocks which have seen many shipwrecks, then are forced inland, uphill, along paths through fields and woodland to arrive at the road at Rosenithon. Turn right onto the road, right at the next road junction then bear left as signed through a field, descending to another road which takes you through Porthoustock (14.5). You follow the road uphill out of the village then when it bends right, you go straight on along a track and then right along a path as signposted, uphill through fields, reaching another road which you follow to the hamlet of Trenance. Turn right at the road junction here, going forward to a further junction and straight on from here along a path; this goes forward to reach a road that brings you to a cider press barn and yet another junction. Turn right to proceed into Porthallow, a picturesque village with a small sandy beach and a cluster of cottages round a harbour. Now you can sigh with relief as the messiest and most uninteresting part of this section has been completed. Note that some guides may refer to the existence of a coast route between Porthoustock and Porthallow, past Pencra Head and Porthkerris Point, but although this is not the official South West Coast Path at present, you should watch for possible route alterations in future. The pub at Porthallow displays relics of a ship called the *Bay Of Panama* which was wrecked off the coast here in 1891.

Walk along the beach at Porthallow then follow an obvious coastal path through bushes and then bracken, passing Nare Head and continuing northwards to reach Nare Point, from which there are excellent views to Gillan Harbour which lies immediately before you, and, further north, Carrick Roads and Helford River. All three will present you with potential logistical challenges during the next day or two. Now you swing sharply west, crossing over a small wooded gorge and proceeding along Trewarnevas Cliff; you climb through woodland, then turn right down steps to reach the shores of Gillan Harbour at a little cove. You continue up a concrete ramp and proceed behind The Tower House, then follow a path through quite thick vegetation to arrive at Flushing Cove, and from there walk along another path through bushes to arrive at a junction of paths. The low tide route goes straight ahead via steps to the shore where stepping stones or the tidal ford (normally one hour either side of low tide) can be used to cross Gillan Creek to the village of St Anthony-in-Meneage. At high tide, there may be a ferry available, but in the absence of a ferry wading is out of the question and you will need to take an inland route which is as follows; turn south-westwards, up a concrete lane, then beyond the house called Dolton, turn right and follow field paths again in a south-westerly direction to a T-junction with a road. Follow the road to the head of Gillan Creek, just beyond which is a road junction; turn right here to follow the road to St Anthony-in-Meneage and be reunited with the low tide route.

St Anthony-in-Meneage is a pretty place in a pretty setting; the final syllable rhymes with 'haig' to make 'menhaig' if you're lost and you need to ask your way to it without sounding too much like a visitor – or 'emmet', as locals are pleased to call them. The Norman church here is said to have been built in thanksgiving to a local saint for saving some seafarers from drowning. Follow the road through the village past the church, walking uphill, reaching an iron gate at the top and bearing right to join a path that strikes out onto Dennis Head, concluding your negotiation of Gillan Creek. There are superb views from Dennis Head northwards to Falmouth, St Mawes and St Anthony Head lighthouse; you can see how strategically important this headland could have been, and indeed it was fortified against Spanish attack in Elizabethan times. From Dennis Head you are almost immediately forced inland again, along the south bank of Helford River, the first of many big river obstacles you'll be faced with on your walk. It is, however, straightforward and extremely attractive going, through predominantly wooded country with fine views to and across the river, and a couple of coves are thrown in for good measure. At length you reach Treath where an uphill climb to a road bend is followed by a descent; from here you bear left onto a path, passing a sailing club and joining a narrow road that takes you to the centre of Helford village (23). Helford was once a busy port from which tin was exported in the eighteenth century, but now is a classic tourist honeypot with its lovely whitewashed thatched cottages and exceedingly popular Shipwright's Arms.

Clear signposting takes you to the ferry point and your first ferry crossing of the journey; it is not cheating but very much a part of the South West Coast Path and, believe me, you will not want to make the detour on foot. The ferry, across to Helford Passage on the north side of the river, only runs from April to October and if it isn't running your best bet is to take the bus round to Helford Passage. The ferry crossing is great fun, in a small boat and across surprisingly choppy waters; when I crossed, the boatman said that if conditions demanded, he discouraged older people from making the trip, so if you want to make progress a certain lying about your age is to be recommended. But however old you are, make sure you follow the instructions to alert the ferry, displaying a brightly-coloured disc (mine was orange) to indicate your wish to utilise it.

# Day 5
# Helford to Falmouth 10 miles (76 miles)

**Difficulty rating:** Moderate
**Terrain rating:** ▲▲▲
**Highlights:** Rosemullion Head, Pendennis Castle, Falmouth

From Helford Passage you bear right onto the riverside path heading eastwards, through fields and further woodland; it's easy, gentle walking, quite a contrast to the tough Kennack–Coverack section of the day or two days before. Just before the village of Durgan – more famous for the magnificent Glendurgan Gardens than anything in the village itself – you arrive at a road which you follow through the village, avoiding the beach, then look out for a right turn up the hill as the road turns away from the river. This right turn is onto a path which now proceeds past fields and pines and across a small beach past a boathouse, heading south-eastwards to the mini-riverside headland of Toll Point. Beyond Toll Point you swing north-eastwards past the village of Mawnan with its fifteenth-century church that stands in the lovely National Trust owned Mawnan Glebe, then proceed through woodland and scrubland to arrive at Rosemullion Head, at the northern mouth of Helford River. This is the best bit of your walk from Helford Passage to Falmouth, with extensive views to Falmouth itself, its bay and what is a fascinating array of headlands and inlets; the headland on which you're standing provides a dazzling display of wild flowers in spring. Beyond Rosemullion Head you swing north-westwards then northwards past further woodland and Bream Cove, going forward through a landscape of scrub and bush to reach a road that brings you to the little village of Maenporth.

Follow the back of the beach past the village, then regain the coast path, passing behind the Beach Café and going uphill, heading north-eastwards along a path enclosed by hedges and then bushes as far as Pennance Point, keeping a golf course to your left. You swing left, descending through woodland to arrive at a road, turning right onto this road to reach Swanpool, at the southern edge of Falmouth. Beyond Swanpool continue along a tarmac path past Gyllyngvase Beach, going forward to Cliff Road onto which you turn right. Now it is easy and obvious going along tarmac to reach Pendennis Point, and of course the famous Pendennis Castle, indisputably Falmouth's most romantic and historic building in a magnificent setting. It was built between 1544 and 1546 and boasts a number of very interesting features including a very Italian outer gateway, a drawbridge, a portcullis, walls that are 16 feet thick in places, and a circular keep which holds a collection of cannons. The gun deck regularly sees battles being re-enacted, so hope that one of these doesn't coincide with what you have planned to be an early and slumberous night. At the headland enjoy the fantastic views, then swing north-westwards along the road, now heading directly for the centre of Falmouth (10). You reach a roundabout immediately south of a railway bridge; turn right at the roundabout under the bridge and almost immediately bear left to follow a road that leads through the town centre to reach Custom House Quay.

Falmouth was no more than a fishing village until the construction of Pendennis Castle, but its prosperity was assured when it became the chief base of the fast Falmouth packets in 1688/9, speeding mail and bullion to the Mediterranean and the Americas; it was the anchorage of the *Cutty Sark*, the last surviving tea clipper, until as comparatively recently as 1938. In fact the town's economy was so buoyant that at one time it was nicknamed 'Pennycomequick'. Falmouth developed as a resort after the arrival of the railway in 1863, and during the twentieth century it became effectively a full-time tourist resort, with a major branch of the National Maritime Museum, including a Flotilla Gallery, opening here in 2002. Other attractions in and around the town include an excellent art gallery, a set of 111 steps known as Jacob's Ladder which lead to a fine view of the surrounding coastline, Arwenack

House which is of Tudor origin, and a number of seventeenth-century buildings including the church of King Charles the Martyr. The town is a lovely place to linger and enjoy not only these delights but also the waterside walks, the restaurants and cosy cafes; in fact you may have a better opportunity to sample them than you expected, for if you arrive on a winter Sunday you'll find there is no scheduled Sunday ferry service available to St Mawes across Carrick Roads (although please see below regarding the possibility of a water taxi service). To attempt to walk round will involve a 32-mile walk, taking you well inland, and well outside the scope of this book, so calm your conscience, relax and enjoy a well-earned day off. You're now over halfway through your first county, and that must be worth celebrating… mustn't it?

# Day 6
# Falmouth to Gorran Haven 21.5 miles (97.5 miles)

**Difficulty rating:** Strenuous
**Terrain rating:** 🔺🔺🔺🔺
**Highlights:** Nare Head, Portloe, Dodman Point

The ferry to St Mawes may run from either the Custom House Quay or Prince of Wales Pier, but having located it and successfully completed the crossing, you're immediately confronted with another river obstacle; the Percuil River, which separates you from Place where the South West Coast Path walk officially resumes. There is a ferry but only from April to October and if you arrive at St Mawes outside that time you need to consider alternatives. One possibility is a relatively new venture, a water taxi service linking Falmouth with Place, and contact details are included in the Useful Information section at the end of the book, but this can't be guaranteed; it will depend on weather conditions and availability and willingness of the operator. Going round by road is certainly possible, yes, by following the A3078 out of St Mawes north-eastwards via St Just-in-Roseland, crossing the river at Trethern Mill and then turning right along a minor road to Tregassa, turning right again here onto a minor road via Gerrans and Bohortha to reach Place. But it's 6 extra miles and a taxi may be preferred, perhaps after a potter round the castle which, like Pendennis, was built on the orders of Henry VIII between 1539 and 1543 and has some of the best examples of decorative stonework of all his fortified works.

From the ferry landing stage at Place you walk inland along a road signed for St Anthony's Church then turn right along a path past the church; it's actually a lovely church, dating back to the twelfth century, and worth a quick browse if you've time in your schedule. You arrive at a track and turn right to follow it, then left along a further track and a field path towards a lighthouse, but before getting to it, you turn left up a metalled path then bear second right up another metalled path and then steps to arrive at a narrow road. You turn right here to arrive at St Anthony Head, bearing left to follow the cliffs round to Zone Point where you can look with satisfaction back to Pendennis Point and return to some walking beside the open sea, swinging resolutely north-eastwards.

It's very easy and straightforward walking now on an undulating low cliff path with no great drops or climbs, past Porthbeor Beach, Porthmellin Head (which will figure largely in views down this section of coast for much of your walk to the Dodman), then past Towan Beach and Greeb Point to the pleasant but unremarkable village of Portscatho (6). Unlike some coastal villages which are seen from far away and all but beckon the walker to come in and sample a freshly baked pasty or bowl of finest Cornish ice cream, the village isn't seen till the last moment and, to quote my favourite phrase from the official South West Way guide, 'always seems to take longer to reach it than one thinks it should'. To exit the village you follow North Parade which goes forward to become a path along the cliffs; you drop down to Porthcurnick Beach then walk up a concrete slipway and road, turning right at a gate to access the cliffs once more. You pass the coastguard station on Pednvadan Point then continue along the cliffs before descending a wooded slope to Porthbean Beach. You bear left and left again, but soon bear right along a path with thick vegetation beside you; you cross a footbridge and ascend awhile before dropping through more woodland at Treluggan

Cliff. Again you are directed left, inland, at Pendower Court, then turn right to follow a road down to the Pendower Beach House Hotel and cross a stream by a footbridge. You continue across an area of Pendower Beach then leave the beach by means of stone steps, at the top of which you turn right onto a road then right again; however, soon you are directed left, round the inland side of the Nare Hotel to join a road onto which you turn right. As the road swings left to climb steeply, you turn right onto a field path which now proceeds south-eastwards to Nare Head. Although this looks straightforward enough on the map, this is the toughest walking you'll have had since Falmouth, with a long climb through bracken, a huge descent to Paradoe Cove and then another climb to Nare Head; pause here to enjoy the superb view and train the binoculars on Gull Rock, to the south-east, as this is a nesting site for kittiwakes and guillemots. You round the headland, swinging north-eastwards on cliffs that are over 300 feet high. Staying at the head of the valley you proceed over Rosen Cliff, go round Kiberick Cove, then ascend to a smaller headland, the Blouth; there follows a really steep descent through woodland then you climb again, in zigzag fashion, over some footbridges and up steps between hedges, before descending to Portloe (13) and its little harbour.

Portloe is an absolute gem of a place with not only a tiny harbour but attractive whitewashed stone cottages, many with lovely gardens; at the time of writing there was a pub and cafe here as well. If you have time, you could detour a little inland here to visit Veryan, 2 miles to the west, with its most unusual thatched and whitewashed circular cottages which date back 200 years. Back on the coastal route, you walk up the road to exit Portloe by Fuglers, turn right down a road, bear right once more between an old boathouse and former chapel, then go left, right and left again up steps as indicated. You now follow the coast path to Tregenna, enjoying lovely views both eastwards and westwards, and descend through trees into a bracken-clad valley to go over two footbridges. You ascend and head away from the coast but soon bear right and go downhill through an area of gorse, the path steepening, then go forward to descend steps to the lovely little village of West Portholland and its footbridge; from here you proceed to its equally charming twin, East Portholland, either along the sea wall or the road. Leaving East Portholland you continue along a zigzag track, turning right and proceeding round fields to arrive at a road onto which you turn right and which you follow, with Porthluney Cove to the right and Caerhays Castle to the left. The castle, built in 1808, was the work of John Nash who was also responsible for Brighton Pavilion and Buckingham Palace; it enjoys a stunning woodland setting, boasting a world-famous collection of camellias, magnolias and rhododendrons.

A little further on along the road past Caerhays Castle the coast path leads off to the right. You ascend, aiming for the corner of a wood ahead, then bear right, proceed beside a fence and enter an area of woodland, ascending steps before descending through fields and down steps to Lambsowden Cove. Beyond the cove, past Greeb Point with its astonishing rock formations, you follow a rough path along slopes clad with bracken and outcrops of rock, then continue along the cliffs through fields before dropping to the lovely and totally unspoilt Hemmick Beach, and turning right onto a road. Very soon, however, you turn right again and now begin your final assault on gorse-covered Dodman Point, or the Dodman as it is known; this is an even more impressive headland than Nare-Head west of Portloe, and one of the major headlands of south Cornwall. There is a strenuous climb followed by a descent past a cove, then another climb to the granite cross on top of the Dodman, nearly 400 feet above the sea. Believed to be the work of a giant, and the site of an Iron Age fort, this headland is a fantastic spot, with views which on a clear day will extend back as far as Nare Point south-west of Falmouth and possibly beyond that, and in a forward direction you will see ahead past St Austell Bay to Gribbin Head, which you will reach in another day or two, and beyond. The cross was erected in 1896 as a seamark to reduce the danger of shipwrecks, although two warships sank hereabouts only a year later.

Gorran Haven is your next objective and you may well have opted to stay in the village. Seeing it marked on the map as being just the other side of Dodman Point, you may think it's just a simple stroll to reach it from the headland. Beware – it's further than you think and may seem even more so at the end of a long day. As at Nare Head, you swing from south-eastwards to a more north-easterly direction, passing Penveor Point and Vault Beach then negotiating another headland, Maenease Point, before veering north-westwards to drop down to Gorran Haven (21.5) and its harbour. Gorran Haven was formerly a crab fishing village and known as Porthjust; it is a useful place to stop for rest and refreshment but is not the most picturesque village you will meet on your Cornish coastal walk.

# Day 7
# Gorran Haven to Fowey 20 miles (117.5 miles)

**Difficulty rating:** Strenuous
**Terrain rating:** ▲▲▲
**HIghlights:** Charlestown, Gribbin Head, Fowey

To leave Gorran Haven you walk up Church Street then bear right onto Cliff Road and right again following the sign for Portmellon, then enjoy a quite superb cliff walk, with beautiful views and a real sense of calm. Passing Penhaver House, you ascend then drop to a footbridge, rising again to the little headland of Pabyer Point before descending to Turbot Point and walking round the edge of Colona Beach. You cross a little road leading to Chapel Point, unavailable for public access, then swing north-westwards beyond the Point and continue close to the cliff-edge to arrive back at the same road. You turn right on to the road, descend, then bear right again to enter the village of Portmellon where, as a defence against the sea, houses are protected by stout shutters and fronted by concrete walls that are 3 feet thick. It is significant for you in one respect: you have now completed 100 miles since you started from Land's End, and although there's still a long way to go you can feel a little bit proud of yourself.

You continue along Portmellon Road, rising steeply and then dropping down into Mevagissey (4), making sure you take the road turning through the park in order to access the village. The well-known architectural historian Sir Nikolaus Pevsner, famous for his series of books, *The Buildings of England*, describes Mevagissey as a 'little-spoilt fishing village', which, alas, is not entirely accurate; it gets terribly crowded in the summer, and even back in 1968 my mother in her diary was moved to comment that it was 'spoilt by too many gift shops!' Until the nineteenth-century fast ships were constructed here, used for transporting fish but also contraband goods, but this village with its picturesque harbour and narrow alleys of fishermen's cottages of traditional slate and cob is now primarily a tourist honeypot. Walk to the head of the harbour and, heading for the museum – a late eighteenth-century building which was once given over to the construction and repair of smugglers' boats – look for a narrow signed path leading off to the left, above the harbour, and proceed up steps to the coastguard lookout. This is the start of a really tough section of the walk, one of the toughest so far, with a lot of stiff climbs. Now keeping the houses on the outskirts of Mevagissey to your left and the cliffs to your right, proceed a little west of north then veer more north-eastwards, descending to a valley and rising up steps. You round Penare Point then veer west of north again, descending and rising once more, passing the ruins of Portgiskey and arriving at a road. Turn right onto the road and follow a path parallel with it, soon reaching the village of Pentewan, regrettably more memorable for its huge caravan park than anything else, and turning right onto the village street. Although it's hard to believe today, Pentewan once had its own harbour and a thriving port which in the eighteenth century exported local stone and was later used for shipping coal, timber and clay.

You ascend steeply from the village square, then turn hard right along The Terrace and pass the village church, then when you get to the end of the road you join a path and very shortly bear left up steps. Route-finding along the coastal path is now straightforward but the path itself is very tough, with some steep climbs and descents. You descend into a wooded valley and bear right to pass Hallane Mill, then continue along past the little peninsula of Drennick, past a rushing stream and waterfall which I witnessed in the middle of a drier than average summer, and even then it still looked spectacular. Just ahead of you is Black Head, a promontory which faces south and the circuit of which the South West Coast Path omits – a matter for your conscience and the condition of your blisters, perhaps – but the views from it, notably to Mevagissey Bay, are tremendous. Having headed mostly north-eastwards from Pentewan you now veer northwards and then north of west, proceeding along Ropehaven Cliffs then descending into woods before an ascent to reach a road just north of Trenarren. Turn right onto the road then right again onto a path which returns to the cliff-edge and negotiates a massive switchback descent and climb, then drops down to Porthpean. This marks the end of a very tough section and heralds much easier walking all the way to Polkerris beyond Par Sands.

You pass in front of the Porthpean Sailing Club then proceed down a slipway in the direction of the beach and walk along a concrete wall; from here you ascend steps and continue rising through woodland before dropping again, with the houses of Duporth to your left, and further woodland around you. It's now a straightforward stroll into Charlestown (10), previously called Porthmear, which boasts a charming main street lined with beech trees and Georgian cottages. Charlestown is named after the entrepreneur Charles Rashleigh who in the early 1790s began work on a harbour here for the purpose of exporting the china clay deposits in the area. The harbour was actually planned by John Smeaton, after whom a tower on the Hoe at Plymouth, which you will encounter further on in your south coast journey, is named; it was duly completed in 1801 and right up to the 1990s it was used for shipping clay, but today its curiosity value is in the old-fashioned square-rigged sailing ship that can be seen *in situ*, and there is also a shipwreck and heritage centre. Walkers who are film or TV buffs may recall it being used in the films *The Voyage of Charles Darwin* and *The Eagle Has Landed* or the worthy BBC series *Poldark* and *The Onedin Line*. But if as you limp round Charlestown after the bruising walk from Mevagissey you're unable to remember the village featuring in this way, you can simply plead fatigue as an excuse rather than being forced to admit you were watching *On The Buses* on the other channel!

Walk right round the harbour and at the far end turn left onto a metalled path. You proceed alongside fields then bear right to follow a cliff path overlooking what when I passed was the massive, and massively ugly, holiday complex of Carlyon Bay. The going remains straightforward but somewhat uninspiring as you continue beside a golf course and aim for the china clay works at Spit Point, turning left along a metalled path beside the perimeter fence of these works. Although it's undoubtedly an eyesore, it remains a vital part of Cornwall's economy, with a flourishing export market for the clay to Western Europe, especially Scandinavia; looking inland, you may observe the huge spoilheaps from the china clay works, known somewhat ironically as the Alps. Just before the railway you veer sharply right to proceed parallel with it, soon reaching a road onto which you turn right and which you follow under the railway to enter the village of Par (14). At the road junction of Par Inn a short way beyond the railway arch, you turn right over a level crossing, go under the railway again and follow the road straight ahead to the next road junction; it's all quick, easy walking, but awfully disappointing after what you've been enjoying most of the way to this point. At the junction you bear sharply right, along a path that takes you to Par Sands (described pithily in *Brewer's Britain and Ireland* as 'somewhat clay-ey'), then proceed along a track behind the back of the beach, past another huge caravan park, to a car park at the south edge of the little village of Polmear. Passing the Ship Inn, you now take a sharp right (southwards), and proceed above the eastern fringes of Par Sands, ascending then dropping to the village of Polkerris and its harbour, walking all the way down to the beach. I have to say I found Polkerris one of the most overrated Cornish coastal villages, the view from the harbour really spoiled by the china clay works, and in summer, when the place is crowded and the queue for cheesy chips is six deep, your first thought will probably be to get away from it as rapidly as possible. You bear left, inland a little, then bear right and climb up steps and a zigzag path through woodland to return to cliff walking again, and straightforward and delightful it is too, taking you almost due south to Little Gribbin.

Beyond Little Gribbin you veer more south-eastwards, still on the cliffs, to reach Gribbin Head with its distinctive daymark, a red and white striped tower 84 feet high (effectively serving as a daytime lighthouse) offering magnificent views back to the Dodman round St Austell Bay; in fact on a clear day you can look back from the headland over much of the work you've done since you came off the Dodman. Saying a last farewell to St Austell Bay, which has been varied in character if nothing else, you now make your way round the headland. Veering north-eastwards, you drop to the beach overlooking the delectable cove at Polridmouth, bearing right as directed and, after passing another beach, a house and stream, bearing right again through trees. Not far north of Polridmouth is Menabilly, the home of the novelist Daphne du Maurier and the fictional Manderley in her most famous work, *Rebecca*, while Polridmouth itself was where the eponymous heroine of that work met her watery end. A superb walk along an undulating path now follows, including a descent to the beach at the rocky Coombe Hawne, and another climb and a wooded descent to the beach at Readymoney, the unusual name deriving perhaps from a complimentary comment on the quality of the land; it's here that you come to a remnant of the sixteenth-century St Catherine's Castle, yet another defensive creation of Henry VIII, and the mouth of the River Fowey.

At Readymoney you join Readymoney Road which takes you into the town of Fowey (20), your first town since Falmouth. During the fourteenth century, Fowey was Cornwall's major south-coast port, and one of the busiest in England; as well as shipping large quantities of tin, the port fitted out ships for the Crusades and in the reign of Edward III, 47 vessels were equipped by the town for the siege of Calais. The town was burned by the French in 1457, but following the building of St Catherine's Castle (see above) the town flourished once again and became the major port for the shipping of china clay. Indeed, china clay quarried around the town of St Austell is still shipped from Fowey today but, as in so many Cornish towns and villages, tourism is the prevalent industry, the river dotted with pleasure boats. Fowey is full of interesting features, including the splendid church of St Fimbarrus, the Ship Inn with its Elizabethan panelling, Place House largely rebuilt in the early nineteenth-century in Gothic style with high walls and battlements, the sixteenth-century Merchant House, and further sixteenth- and seventeenth-century houses in North Street, Union Place and Lostwithiel Street. The popular Cornish novelist Sir Arthur Quiller-Couch was town mayor here in 1937 and fictionalised Fowey as Troy Town; the astrophysicist and Nobel laureate Antony Hewish, who discovered pulsars, was born in the town; and the town hosts an annual Daphne du Maurier festival in honour of the authoress who, as we have seen, lived close by. The town, with its picturesque old streets and air of prosperity, is similar in character to Padstow on the north Cornwall coast, and the two places are linked by a 26-mile walk called the Saints Way, providing in fact a link with the North Cornwall section of the South West Coast Path. Just in case you fancied a quick early morning stroll before continuing your coastal walk.

# Day 8
# Fowey to Looe 12 miles (129.5 miles)

**Difficulty rating:** Strenuous
**Terrain rating:** ▲▲▲▲
**Highlights:** Pencarrow Head, Raphael Cliff, Polperro

It's time for another ferry crossing now: the ferry to Polruan on the other side of the River Fowey runs daily, all the year round, so this one will be the least of your worries, with no danger of a 12-mile detour by land unless you arrive at a truly extraordinary time. Polruan has a charming waterfront, quaint narrow streets, and by Town Quay there's a fifteenth-century blockhouse from which, once upon a time, a heavy chain was connected to Fowey to seal off the river mouth. You begin your exit from Polruan by ascending from the quay, with a choice of road or steps; now bear right along West Street then left along Battery Lane, going past the Headland Gardens, and alongside a car park. Passing the National Coastwatch Station, you now continue along the road, soon bearing right to join a proper coast path and embark on one of the finest stretches on the whole of your journey along the south coast. For the most part it's cliff walking in its purest form with no roads and hardly a house to be seen; if the fates decree you are to be allowed only one fine sunny day on your pilgrimage, you should really hope that it is for this walk.

This splendid walk begins with an ascent along the cliffs past Blackbottle Rock to a grandstand view of Lantic Bay. As you make your way round the bay and its twin beaches of Great Lantic and Little Lantic you descend, then instead of dropping down to the beach you bear left, uphill, and once again drop down as you approach Pencarrow Head; you round this fine headland, with tremendous views extending as far back as Dodman Point, once more taking care not to be drawn down onto the beach. You pass an isolated house that was once employed as a lookout, and is just about the only house you'll see close to the path between Polruan and Polperro, then begin to round Lantivet Bay, heading north-east on what is justly described in the *Cicerone Guide* as a 'roller coaster'. There's a steep plunge into West Combe and then a footbridge crossing above a waterfall, and, looking to your left, there is a lovely view to the little Welsh-sounding village of Lansallos with its prominent church tower; the church, dedicated to St Ildierna, is worth a detour if you have the time, and is notable for its Norman font and 34 bench ends of the early sixteenth century with carved arms and heads.

Back on the path, to your right you'll see the delectable Lansallos Cove, surely one of the most picturesquely situated beaches in Cornwall, and boasting a rock-cut path used by farmers to facilitate the transport of seaweed from the beach. Watch for a left turn then a hard right turn, followed by an ascent, a descent and a footbridge crossing, then beyond the crossing you rise once more, going past another daymark. As you walk up this path, the only sounds you're likely to hear are those of the sea caressing the shores and a bell-buoy warning of the danger of an offshore rock; the views remain superb, and on a clear day you will see past Pencarrow Head and Gribbin Head all the way back to the Dodman. The path continues to undulate as you proceed, high above the sea, heading just south of east alongside Raphael Cliff, with its splendid natural rock arch. Then, swinging gently just a little north of east, you head for Chapel Cliff, with a steep drop and then a really tough climb; although the going is not easy, there is no difficulty with route-finding and the views to the sea are simply fantastic. You will feel a real sense of remoteness as you walk this section, despite the fact that you are nearly at Polperro, the next staging post on your journey. Following an exhilarating promenade high above the sea through bracken and gorse, you enter a wooded area and emerge to enjoy a splendid view down to the harbour; as I wrote in my diary when I walked this section, it's a 'thrilling climax to an unforgettable walking experience'.

Bearing right at the viewpoint, you join a metalled path which goes downhill to reach the harbour and the village of Polperro itself (7). In the 1850s, two thirds of the population of Polperro were engaged in fishing, with pilchards the staple catch, and smuggling was also rife in and around the village. Now its charming little harbour with simple Georgian houses, the Heritage Museum of Smuggling and Fishing, the famous House On Props (actually wooden stilts), the tightly packed white-and-cream cottages lining the narrow streets, and the river Pol which passes through the village make it one of the principal tourist magnets of east Cornwall, and if you visit the village during the summer months, you will certainly know it. Pevsner sums it all up beautifully: 'There are plenty of teashops and places for buying Cornish ware, not always manufactured in Cornwall.'

Make your way round to the head of the harbour, and turn right to follow The Warren towards Talland Bay. Now climb away from the village along this road, which continues as a path, then when the ways divide, bear right along the path signposted for Talland. This path can get astonishingly crowded in the summer – when I walked along it there was a bus timetable actually on the path itself – and you may find yourself jostling for space with shall we say rather slower walkers with a rather less demanding itinerary. But as you will so often find as you walk the south coast, once you've got about half a mile beyond the nearest convenient car park, you're likely to find yourself on your own. Until you get within half a mile of the next car park, that is. You drop down towards Downend Point, rounding this modest headland and going forward, north-eastwards, to a road; follow the road then when it turns away from the sea you bear right on to a path, bearing left and then shortly right to arrive at Talland Bay, overlooked by the thirteenth-century church of St Tallan. You continue eastwards along a road then bear right, again following a road, to reach a cafe. Now, for a while, the going is straightforward; you follow steps to reach a path that provides fine airy walking as you head south-eastwards past Hendersick to the rocks above the Hore Stone, from which there are fine views to St George's Island. This island, which will remain visible on and off for the next 60 miles, is also, and rather less patriotically, called Looe Island. It was once the site of a Benedictine monastery and during World War Two had the misfortune to be bombed by the Germans who believed it to be a warship; nowadays, it has a bird sanctuary with one of the country's large breeding colonies of black-backed gulls. From the rocks above the Hore Stone you swing north then north-eastwards, keeping Portnadler Bay to your right, and the going is easy and straightforward until you arrive at a road at the south-west tip of Hannafore, the gateway to Looe. You have the option of following the road or a parallel strip of grass round Hannafore Point, and you now simply veer a little west of north to follow the road to the seven-arched bridge over the river separating West Looe from East Looe (12). If you felt very lazy you could use a ferry over the river, but best not tell your sponsors; while the ferry over the Carrick Roads from Falmouth to St Mawes, avoiding 32 miles' inland tramping, is forgivable, a ferry just to save the time it'll take to eat a Wall's Magnum ice cream is morally somewhat questionable. Then again, so is a Wall's Magnum ice cream.

# Day 9
# Looe to Cremyll for Plymouth 20.5 miles (150 miles)

**Difficulty rating:** Moderate
**Terrain rating:** ▲▲
**Highlights:** Battern Cliffs, Rame Head, Mount Edgcumbe

Looe, despite its lavatorial name, is a pleasant place to potter around. If you will pardon the pun; there are in fact two Looes, no Lautrecs. West Looe and East Looe are linked by a bridge which replaces a magnificent thirteen-arched bridge built between 1411 and 1418. As early as 1800 crowds were being drawn to the resort, no doubt enticed by the availability of the first bathing machines, and the arrival of the railway in 1879 enhanced its popularity. The old town of East Looe still has quite a picturesque High Street and an Old Guildhall which now contains a museum but which used to house a magistrates'court and jail cells. Nowadays the only captives in Looe are likely to be the tourists, but the town does enjoy a strong fishing tradition; it touts itself as a shark-fishing centre and the quays overlooking the harbour are stacked with crates and lobster baskets. Having crossed into East Looe, make your way to the Guildhall via the harbourside or along the main street, then proceed from Fore Street to Buller Street, turning left into Castle Street and climbing on to East Cliff on a metalled path. At a fork, bear right and proceed along a gravel path, then descend via a further metalled path; you continue beside houses then walk along a road to reach Plaidy Lane. Turn right onto the lane and walk towards the beach, but rather than continuing onto the beach you stay on the road, going away from the beach and uphill. Look out for a metalled path going away to the right, which you follow uphill and then when you reach the top you keep going along the road. Now you need to look out for concrete steps going down between houses, and having descended these you go forward to a path leading to Millendreath Beach, described in *The Rough Guide to Devon and Cornwall* as a 'crescent of sand and shingle'. Again, you don't get on to the beach but follow a road away from the beach, ascending once more.

In due course the road ends, but you continue along a path through woodland, arriving at a road by a campsite. Turn right to follow this road briefly, then bear right again onto a signed path headed for Seaton, one of two Seatons you'll meet on your south coast walk (there's a Seatown as well, but don't let's get technical). The path undulates through a mixture of open spaces and pleasant woodland, arriving at a road; turn right onto this road and follow it down to the unremarkable village of Seaton, bearing right again to cross a river and follow Bridge Road. From here to the neighbouring (and it has to be said, equally nondescript) village, Downderry, you can proceed initially on the sea wall then the beach, but if the tide is in you may be forced to follow the road. On reaching Downderry you will need to leave the beach (if you've followed it from Seaton) via a slipway and Beach Hill to join the main road through the village and be reunited with the road route from Seaton. You continue eastwards along the road past the church, then as the road bends sharply left you leave it by following the signed coast path eastwards, uphill, towards Battern Cliffs, bearing right near the top to follow a wall along the cliff-top. This is excellent walking with fine views, but make the most of it, as things will deteriorate not too far ahead. Undulating walking, close to the coast, brings you to Portwrinkle (8), the route bearing right along a road to reach the harbour, which once saw extensive exports of cured fish in locally made hogsheads to Ireland and the Mediterranean. Although its harbour is pleasant enough, Portwrinkle sounds more quaint and charming than it actually is; I would venture to suggest it vies with Polkerris for the title of the most disappointing village on the south Cornwall coast, with a sprinkling of houses, a large car park, and when I visited, just a takeaway cafe.

You stay on the road beside the shore as far as the Whitsand Bay Hotel. At the hotel the road turns inland and you leave it, joining a coast path which goes up steps then past a golf course where you need to keep an eye out for low-flying golf balls, and on to Trethill Cliffs, where your problems begin. Directly ahead of you is Tregantle Fort and its military firing range; if firing is taking place, you will be forced to the left to walk beside the B3247 road, then when you reach a fork in the road you bear right and follow the road round to the point where it arrives at the coast again at Tregantle Cliff. If you're lucky and no firing is taking place – during August and alternate weekends (whichever those are) – you may be able to stick to a coast route through the ranges. The lucky and unlucky routes reunite at Tregantle Cliff and you now follow a signed path parallel with the road to Sharrow Point. From here you now have to walk beside the road past a seemingly endless line of holiday cabins at the village of Freathy, and not far beyond all that is a huge holiday park to the left; this really is depressing, especially in poor weather, and a big anticlimax after the glories of Lantic Bay and Raphael Cliff. Beyond the holiday park you are signposted right onto a path going roughly parallel with the road, but there's no escape – yet – from the cabins as you follow an undulating course. At one time the path threatens to rejoin the road, but a right turn takes you away from it again and into more open country. Beyond Captain Blake's Point you are forced briefly inland to walk round the eastern side of Polhawn Fort, but beyond the fort you swing south-westwards and now enjoy your best walking this side of Looe, as you stride out to reach Rame Head, the most prominent headland since Gribbin Head, and the site of a beacon that was kept blazing to guide ships into Plymouth. A hundred years or so ago a local farmer ran herds of sheep and donkeys on Rame Head Common, and actually carried on a donkey hire business; his customers were mostly fellow farmers who collected sand and seaweed from the beaches for fertiliser. You can enjoy good views to Hendersick and most of what you've walked since Looe, for what it's worth, but Plymouth remains tantalisingly hidden from view. There's the possibility of a detour to the ruins of the late-fourteenth-century St Michael's Chapel, but whether you exercise this option or not, you now need to swing eastwards along the clear and unerring coast path, providing your most enjoyable sustained walking for many miles. You arrive at a road and follow this to the next headland, Penlee Point, from which there is a superb view to Plymouth up Plymouth Sound, the area of sea onto which that city looks out. You then swing north-westwards through woodland, following a road interspersed with sections of track, emerging at the delightful village of Cawsand, its name thought to have been derived from 'cow sand', since cows were once a common sight on the beach here, especially in summer when they waded into the sea to escape the flies.

The village is joined onto the equally charming village of Kingsand (17), and having reached the Square at Cawsand, you simply follow Garrett Street to reach Kingsand; both villages, with stone colour-washed stone cottages and narrow alleys, provide one last delectable taste of Cornwall.

At the post office at Kingsand you bear right, passing the beach access route, then bear left just before you reach The Cleave and go right into Heavitree Road, going uphill. Having gained some height, you bear right to enter Mount Edgcumbe Country Park and follow a clear coast path, initially through open country and then into woodland, emerging at a road and turning right to follow it. Shortly you turn left along a path and continue along a section of the one time Earl's Drive, but shortly after going under an old stone arch you turn right, then following the signs, you proceed through a principally wooded landscape to arrive at the foreshore. Almost immediately you are directed away from the foreshore, continuing to a classical summer house, then pick up a concrete driveway which you follow around the Barn Pool bay. Go forward from there into the Formal Gardens, emerging by the Orangery restaurant; having refreshed yourself here, you may wish to enjoy a wander round the landscaped gardens which are famous for the camellia, of which there are 600 different species here. The big house, although Tudor in appearance, is a 1962 reconstruction of the original sixteenth-century building.

From the restaurant you pass through an arch then bear right through the park gates to reach the ferry slip at Cremyll (20.5), where a ferry takes you to Stonehouse, on the western tip of the city of Plymouth. Although a regular daily service is provided today, and takes just a few minutes, in Victorian times both its comfort and speed were sources of dissatisfaction; it was in January 1877 claimed with some irony that the 'special express ferry starting at one o'clock almost always succeeded in reaching Stonehouse Hard by half past two'. Whatever time your ferry leaves Cremyll, you can look back with immense satisfaction at the passing of the 150-mile mark, and the completion of your first county. Land's End seems a very long way back indeed.

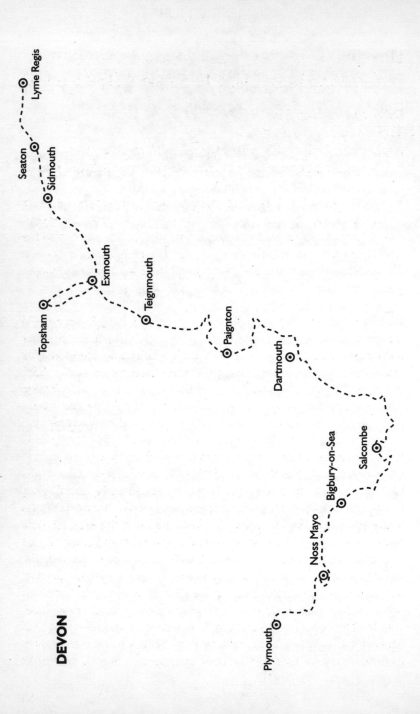

DEVON

# Day 10
# Plymouth to Noss Mayo 13.5 miles* (163.5 miles)

**Difficulty rating:** Easy
**Terrain rating:** ▲▲▲
**Highlights:** Plymouth, Great Mew Stone, Wembury Church
* mileage pre-supposes ferry across Cattewater is NOT used

Your walk along the Devon coast starts with the fiddliest piece of walking you will have to deal with on your south coast pilgrimage, namely the walk through Plymouth. That said, you will surely find the walk fascinating and, particularly if you are on a tight timescale, you will almost certainly leave the city feeling you'd have liked to spend longer there.

Plymouth, previously a fishing community named Sutton, has a noble history. Naturally blessed with one of Europe's finest deep water anchorages, its patronage by Sir Francis Drake and Sir John Hawkins established the port's supremacy in the sixteenth century. It was in 1588, the year every schoolboy knows, that Drake sailed from here (having finished his game of bowls – although the state of the tide wouldn't have permitted him to depart any earlier even if he'd wanted to) to meet the Armada, and in 1620 the Pilgrim Fathers left here for the New World in the *Mayflower*. Later, Captain James Cooke was to launch voyages of discovery from Plymouth, in the nineteenth century convicts doomed to transportation departed from Plymouth for Australia, and Charles Darwin set sail from here on his *Beagle* voyage. The Royal Fleet was stationed here during the wars with Spain, and with the establishment of the Royal Naval Dockyard here in the seventeenth century it was to evolve as a naval port of massive strategic importance, guarding the western approaches to England. Inevitably it was a target for German bombs during World War Two and the city was devastated, but it was rebuilt and revitalised and as well as remaining an important naval base, with the Devonport dockyards continuing to be a mainstay of the local economy, it is now an international ferry port with regular services to Roscoff and Santander. A number of important historic landmarks remain, notably the Hoe, the prominent hill overlooking the Sound on which is Smeaton's Tower, a red and white lighthouse built in 1759; it once stood on the treacherous Eddystone Rocks and was subsequently reassembled on the Hoe. Next to the Hoe is the Royal Citadel, a powerful fortress built between 1666 and 1675, and also close to the Hoe is the Barbican area, where the old harbour was situated. The oldest part of the Barbican area, paradoxically, is New Street, a cobbled street dating back to 1581 and lined with timber-framed and jettied houses including the National-Trust-owned Elizabeth House, a Tudor house that belonged to a sea captain, and which houses many sixteenth- and seventeenth-century furnishings and textiles. In Firewell Street is Prysten House, a merchant's home and, dating back from 1498, it is the oldest dwelling in the city, built round three sides of a galleried courtyard. A few yards away is the Merchant's House, a four-storey Elizabethan building which houses a lively museum and a fully stocked apothecary's shop. Sutton Harbour, close to the Barbican area, is still used by Plymouth's trawler fleet, and also going strong is the Blackfriars Distillery, which has produced Plymouth gin since 1793. Also worth visiting in Plymouth are the superb National Marine Aquarium and the City Museum and Art Gallery, which includes works by artists of the Newlyn School whose work was inspired by the lovely landscapes of south-west Cornwall you passed all those miles back!

It may come as quite a shock to be confronted with a big city after so many days of walking through principally rural areas and small villages, but it's good to have access to such a wide range of accommodation, not to mention cash machines and laundry facilities, and excellent transport connections for those needing to break their adventure at this point. First, however, you have to get into the city proper. The ferry disembarkation point from Cremyll is Admiral's Hard in the Stonehouse district of Plymouth; walk up the road from the Hard and take the second right down Cremyll Street to the Royal William Yard, going down to meet the water again at Firestone Bay. Then at the Artillery Tower Restaurant, turn hard left away from the bay, going forward into Durnford Street, and from here you turn right onto Millbay Road and proceed along Caroline Place, heading for

Millbay Docks. You go over one roundabout, then at the next you bear right into West Hoe Road and fork right along Great Western Road; beyond the West Hoe Pier you carry on along or beside Hoe Road, from which there is easy access to the Hoe, and great views across the Sound. Keeping the Sound close to your right, go forward into Madeira Road, then follow the Waterfront Walkway to the mouth of Sutton Harbour passing the Mayflower Steps from which the *Mayflower* set sail in 1620, and the Barbican area. There are in fact a number of walking options between West Hoe Pier and the mouth of Sutton Harbour. This could include a traverse of the Hoe – I vividly recall standing on top of the Hoe admiring a vivid rainbow over Plymouth Sound when a thunderstorm broke and I was almost knocked off my feet by a fierce gust of wind. Or perhaps take a wander round the Barbican area. You would need to be in a fearful hurry just to stick to the road.

From the mouth of Sutton Harbour it's an absurdly short distance across the water to Mountbatten Point and the resumption of true coast path walking, and with the best of Plymouth now behind you, you may feel tempted to take the all-year-round ferry which avoids a fiddly 5-mile walk round Cattewater, an estuarine strip of water linking the River Plym with Plymouth Sound. If, however, you prefer to stick to shanks' pony, the walking route is as follows. You make your way across the entrance to Sutton Harbour by the swing bridge over to the National Marine Aquarium, follow the trail of silver fish in the pavement up past the aquarium and onto Teats Hill Road. Continue along Clovelly Road, then bear right to ascend Breakwater Hill, noting a huge South West Coast Path signpost, to reach a metalled cliff path. From here, walk along Cattedown Road in what is the Cattedown district of the city, bearing right into Maxwell Road, right again at the roundabout into Finnegan Road and right once more to cross the Laira Bridge, which you share with a dual carriageway. Having crossed the bridge, proceed to the roundabout and bear right here into Oreston Road, shortly bearing sharp right again and right once more into Rollis Park Road to return to the water's edge. Join Park Road and go forward along a metalled path which continues between houses and across a railway path to reach Radford Castle at the north-west edge of Radford Lake. From here follow a gravel path with Hooe Lake to your right, ascend round the district of Hooe then bear sharp right – northwards – and into Hexton Hill Road. Continue along the banks of Hooe Lake down Barton Road then follow signs through to Clovelly Bay Marina, bearing left into Undercliff Road, on into Boringdon Road, left up St John's Road, then down the steps to the marina. Follow the signs carefully between the boats and the cars, crossing the slipway of the Mountbatten Centre and then proceeding round the water's edge to the ferry landing stage from Sutton Harbour, from which it's a short way to the headland of Mountbatten Point (7). Now, are you glad you opted to walk it? This area, known as the Mountbatten area, has been extensively redeveloped in recent years and if you have walked all the way round, you could not be blamed for seeking some refreshment to celebrate.

Now you really can get back into your stride again, and enjoy what is relatively straightforward walking as far as Warren Point, the next ferry obstacle. Having rounded the headland, you proceed in a south-easterly direction away from the Mount Batten peninsula and climb back onto the cliffs, ascending gently to Jennycliff Bay. You round the bay, swinging south-westwards, and climb through woodland, in due course emerging and heading southwards to Staddon Point, enjoying some quite superb views back to Plymouth and the surrounding area as you walk. At Staddon Point you veer eastwards, joining and following a road briefly, then turn southwards again, passing Bovisand Bay and joining another road through Bovisand Park, going forward to Andurn Point. It is possible to see Rame Head from here, but Plymouth is now hidden from view, and there is no sense of having just walked through a big city. Easy coast path walking now takes you southwards then round and past Renney Rocks; you head briefly eastwards, with the village of Heybrook Bay quite close by to the left and a good view to a steep-sided pyramid-shaped islet called the Great Mew Stone to the right, then veer south-eastwards round the coastal side of the now defunct Royal Naval gunnery school of *HMS Cambridge*, to Wembury Point, the closest you get to the Great Mew Stone. A simple walk on eastwards round Wembury Bay takes you to Wembury Beach, bypassing the centre of the village of Wembury, but the village church is sited close to the sea in a truly magnificent setting.

Leave Wembury Beach by ascending towards the church. Now walk along a signed track down to the right, making for Warren Point and Ferry, proceeding very enjoyably south-eastwards, above Wembury Bay and the River Yealm estuary to a footpath crossroads at the Rocket House; here you bear right, steeply down a vehicle track, to reach Warren Point, the ferry departure point for the crossing of the Yealm to just west of Noss Mayo. To call it a ferry terminal would be a tad pretentious, as it is only really a little pier, and the method of summoning the ferry is hardly sophisticated either, consisting as it does of an arrow on the pier which shows you how to wave to attract the ferryman's attention. Once over the very pretty river Yealm (13.5), the coast path bears right along a narrow road following the south bank of the river, but you could detour left to visit the pretty fishing village of Noss Mayo and possibly the equally attractive Newton Ferrers (reachable by a separate ferry) as well. Note that the Warren Point to Noss Mayo ferry only runs from Easter to September, between about 10 a.m. and 4 p.m. If you are unfortunate enough not to catch the ferry when it is running, nor the ferryman's attention, your best bet is to backtrack to the footpath crossroads at the Rocket House, go straight over this time and continue north-westwards to the main Wembury village, and there take a taxi to Noss Mayo; from there you simply pick up a waterside road heading westwards to reach the ferry point on the south side of the Yealm. But I have to say that it is probably easiest just to make sure you do this bit when the ferry is running! On the subject of river crossings, you now need to think and plan ahead carefully, for your next river crossing (Erme) is some 9 miles ahead, and there is no ferry. You will be able to wade the river one hour, sometimes more, either side of low tide, (although note that in adverse conditions even that may not be possible) and it's essential that you study the tide tables carefully and plan your arrival at the mouth of the Erme to coincide with a time when it can be waded. This will of course depend on your own walking speed.

# Day 11
# Noss Mayo to Bigbury-on-Sea 13.5 miles (177 miles)

**Difficulty rating:** Moderate, becoming strenuous
**Terrain rating:** ▲▲▲▲
**Highlights:** St Anchorite's Rock, Beacon Point, Ayrmer Cove

Having crossed the Yealm by ferry, head westwards from the landing stage as stated along a narrow road which passes through woodland beside the Yealm Estuary and goes forward to join the Revelstoke Drive, built as a carriage drive by a local landowner, Lord Revelstoke in the 1880s. Now follow this drive initially by the estuary to Mouthstone Point where the Yealm meets the sea, and continue along it as it swings south-eastwards; the walking remains very straightforward and easy on a mixture of clear firm surfaces, and you will start to get some really good views forward to Bigbury Bay and your next major headland, Bolt Head. You proceed by Blackstone Point and Hilsea Point, veering more north-eastwards to pass Stoke Point, where it's possible to see right back to Hendersick beyond Looe, and then Stoke Beach, where you may wish to stop to inspect the partially-ruined church of St Peter the Poor Fisherman. Enjoying a splendid setting on the edge of the cliff overlooking Stoke Bay, it was abandoned after 1882 when a new church was built at Noss Mayo, but it was rescued by local effort in the 1960s and you can today view the attractively-restored tower and roofless nave. Shortly beyond the church is the hamlet of Stoke where the drive effectively ends, and you now veer eastwards along a coast path to reach Beacon Hill; tougher walking now follows, with a hefty descent and a big climb, but your reward is the remarkable tor St Anchorite's Rock to your left, and this is the prelude to some of the most beautiful walking on the entire Devon coast. From the Rock there is another big drop to the delightful inlet at Bugle Hole with a jumble of rocks set against steep gorse-clad cliffs, and then another climb takes you back onto the cliffs with superb views forward to the Erme estuary – your next river crossing. You descend to Mothecombe Beach, then after a climb through woodland on Owen's Hill you walk down to a slipway that provides the river crossing point to get over the river Erme to Wonwell Beach (9). And now comes the fun part, as you prepare to proceed, Moses-like, across the hopefully obligingly shallow waters. If you've done your homework, you can simply make your way across the Erme to Kingston Slipway at once and wonder what all the fuss was about, but if you've mis-timed, or got held up en route, or weather conditions preclude it, you've the choice between a long wait, a taxi or an extra 7-mile walk. If you decide to walk it, follow the narrow country lanes to Holbeton village, then continue on a northerly route to Ford and Hole Farm, and soon after passing Hole Farm, bear right onto a public footpath, and follow it for about three quarters of a mile to the main A379 road. Turn right to cross the A379 at Sequer's Bridge and stay on the A379 for about half a mile until you reach a right turn signposted to Orcheston. Follow this road south towards the village of Kingston but before you reach the village you'll see road signs to Wonwell Beach and make your way to the sands to resume your coastal walk. If you can't face this road detour and you've decided to wait for the next low tide, it's delve into rucksack time for your dog-eared *Harry Potter* and what's left of the pork scratchings bought in the pub last night.

If you've waded to Kingston Slipway, bear right from there and cross Wonwell Beach – it may be possible, depending on the tide, to short cut to this beach anyway from the other side – then proceed south-westwards onto a clear path that veers southwards to a mini-headland, with superb views back up the Erme as you walk. You pass Fernycombe Beach then ascend to Beacon Point, another tremendous viewpoint, before veering more south-eastwards. Really excellent walking follows, past Westcombe Beach and Ayrmer Cove with its shiny Dartmouth slate; the views both back and forward are very good indeed, and the cliff scenery is breathtaking, with sheer and monstrously high cliff faces and grotesque rock formations. The price to pay for this stunning scenery is a number of steep climbs and ascents which will really test you at the end of a long day, with no concessions for those who've been waiting half a day for the tide to recede. Slight anticlimax follows as you drop down to Challaborough Bay and its beach which, although offering some amenities, is little more than a giant caravan park, and from here it's only a short walk along the coast path to the village of Bigbury-on-Sea (13.5) with a reasonable range of amenities. The village is unremarkable but just across the water from Bigbury is Burgh Island which certainly is worth a visit. Its most dominant feature is the old hotel, built in Art Deco style and boasting a stained glass dome and sumptuous furnishings. It was built in 1929, extended in 1932 and has been carefully restored to provide what it's owners describe as a 'retreat like none other'. Also on Burgh Island are the ruins of a medieval chapel, and a pub which dates back to the early fourteenth century. At low tide the island is linked to the mainland by a sandspit, but when the sea covers the spit access is possible by means of a sea tractor. Sitting in one of Bigbury-on-Sea's pubs, you may feel you've earned a celebratory pint for negotiating the Erme, but before you get too carried away, there's another river obstruction just round the corner.

# Day 12
# Bigbury-on-Sea to Salcombe 13.5 miles (190.5 miles)

**Difficulty rating:** Moderate
**Terrain rating:** ▲▲▲
**Highlights:** Inner Hope, Bolt Head, Salcombe

Your walk from Bigbury-on-Sea towards Salcombe, your next staging post, begins in the main car park. Leave it by descending steps towards the beach which at low tide can be followed round to the left and up the banks of the river Avon all the way to the next ferry crossing at Cockleridge. At high tide you'll need to follow markers inland over Folly Hill, keeping buildings to your right, going forward to join the B3392 and follow it as far as Mount Folly Farm, then turning right as signed downhill and at the foot of the hill turning left to reach Cockleridge. The river cannot realistically be waded even at low tide, so you'll need to catch a ferry to Bantham; it runs early March to early September, 10 a.m. to 11 a.m. and 3 p.m. to 4 p.m., but may not run on Sundays and you will need to shout over to the other side at Bantham to attract the attention of the ferryman and enjoy a brief but enjoyable crossing over the delightful river. It's quite reassuring in these days of ever more sophisticated forms of communication that a full-throated roar coupled perhaps with arm-waving and jumping up and down is still regarded as an acceptable and efficacious means of securing the all-important passage, and it's a lot more invigorating than text messaging! If you arrive at a time when a ferry crossing is impossible or impracticable, you could opt for a taxi or take a 7.5 mile walking detour involving a return to the B3392 and a right turn along this road to the inland village of Bigbury, then a right turn along a tidal road beside the Avon to Aveton Gifford, another right turn along the A379 over the river, an immediate right turn onto a lane heading for Stanbury Farm, and from there a walk beside the Avon south-westwards to arrive at the Bantham ferry slipway. Now, make your way westwards along the road from the ferry slipway, and, ignoring a right fork, go forward to a car park, then down to a beach, now at the southern mouth of the Avon. The going becomes straightforward as you swing south-eastwards onto the cliffs, keeping fine views to Burgh Island to your right and Thurlestone Golf Course to the left; as not all its members are aspiring to emulate the achievements of Tiger Woods or Ernie Els, do watch for maverick golf balls.

At Warren Point you swing sharply eastwards, soon veering south-eastwards close to the golf clubhouse and southwards again past South Milton Sands and Thurlestone Rock. This is frankly a pretty uninspiring section with numerous holiday homes and hotels, but things will soon improve. You reach a car park and follow a road out of it briefly, then bear right onto a cliff path beside the Beacon Point Hotel, walking southwards once more. The path rises then drops to join a road which you follow through Outer Hope; from here you follow a metalled path, keeping the Cottage Hotel to your left, to Inner Hope (6), a particularly lovely village with a square of thatched whitewashed cottages and a backcloth of wooded hills, but there are precious few amenities. To your right, as you proceed through these twin villages, is Hope Cove, a very popular holiday beach. At the south-east tip of the cove, climb steps and go forward along a woodland path which emerges into open country, and you can now enjoy a bracing and exhilarating walk north-westwards to the headland of Bolt Tail; reaching the north-west tip of the headland, you then veer south-eastwards for a tremendous cliff-top walk to Bolt Tail's twin, Bolt Head. It's nice not to have any fiddly route-finding but simply to proceed along the obvious cliff path which climbs to the stunning viewpoint of Bolberry Down, nearly 400 feet up. The views from here are incredible, stretching on a clear day beyond Rame Head as far as Hendersick west of Looe.

Your path continues to Cathole Cliff and you descend to a footbridge above Soar Mill Cove, an exquisite narrow inlet with a golden sandy beach where you should look out for shags and cormorants, before climbing again and walking along gorse and bracken-clad hillsides to Bolt Head with its concrete shelter. The headland was an important wartime lookout and commands great views forward to Prawle Point, the southernmost point in Devon and your next major natural objective. From Bolt Head there's quite an exciting rocky scramble round Starehole Bay to Sharp Tor, swinging sharply northwards and descending, then veering right to Sharp Tor which provides another great viewpoint; the 'path' is known here as the Courtenay Way, cut in the nineteenth century to provide ease of access for visitors to Bolt Head. Then veer left again, heading northwards, initially charting a precarious course along the side of steep-faced cliffs with splendid views ahead to Salcombe and the Kingsbridge estuary onto which it looks out, then through woodland. In due course the path broadens and you bear right along a road which passes the Bolt Head Hotel and goes forward into the town of Salcombe. The highlight of the walk from Sharp Tor to Salcombe is Overbecks with its large Italianate villa and magnificent gardens boasting many subtropical plants, including the Japanese banana. Overbecks got its name from one Otto Overbeck, an eccentric inventor who lived here and believed everybody could live to the age of 350. Keeping to the road closest to or alongside the estuary, continue on into Salcombe (13.5) itself, and make for the Ferry Inn and the ferry crossing point for East Portlemouth. Yes, it's another river obstacle

– they've been coming thick and fast since Plymouth – but this one will pose no problems, as there's a daily service all the year round, so if you are lodging here you can rest easy in the knowledge that you won't have to make an uncomfortably early or late start next day to catch either the capricious tide or an almost-as-capricious ferry, and you can relax and enjoy Salcombe accordingly.

Beautifully located at the mouth of the Kingsbridge estuary, climbing picturesquely up a steep wooded hill beside the water, Salcombe was until the middle of the nineteenth century a small maritime settlement where shipbuilding flourished prior to the coming of steam power. It once boasted a castle, built in 1544 as part of the Tudor fortifications of the south coast, but it was destroyed in the Civil War. During the eighteenth century a small number of 'gentlemen's residences' were built on the cliff slopes overlooking the estuary, and then during the nineteenth century the unparalleled scenery and mild climate encouraged the growth of small villas and lodging houses. The arrival of the railway at nearby Kingsbridge in 1893 served to bolster the town's development even further, and it evolved into a popular tourist resort and sailing centre; it has held an annual yachting regatta since 1857. Among its other attractions are the maritime museum which is packed with nautical mementoes, old slate cottages in Fore Street, the mix of colour-washed houses and ships' chandlers shops, the eighteenth-century Old Watch House in Union Street, and the stone-built Custom House dating back to around 1820. It's also exactly halfway between Land's End and the finish of the South West Coast Path at the Sandbanks Ferry. The town as a whole, with its profusion of shops serving the needs of holidaying landlubbers and sailors alike, has a decidedly genteel air, attracting perhaps a higher than average proportion of well-heeled visitors, and has earned itself the soubriquet 'Kensington-on-Sea', so be sure to wipe your feet when you arrive. And be warned, your request in February for a single-night single room B & B stay in August will meet with the same reception that a potato farmer might accord to an underfed colorado beetle!

# Day 13
# Salcombe to Dartmouth 23 miles (213.5 miles)

**Difficulty rating:** Moderate
**Terrain rating:** ▲▲▲
**Highlights:** Maceley Cove, Prawle Point, Start Point

This section begins with the ferry crossing to East Portlemouth across the Kingsbridge estuary. Having disembarked, bear right along a road through the woods to reach Mill Bay, then bear right again along a footpath which passes first through woodland but emerges into more open country; initially you head south-westwards, keeping the estuary to your right, but you soon veer south-eastwards, now looking out to the open sea once more. There is a really great walk along an undulating cliff path, with dramatic drops to the sea on one side and impressive rocky outcrops on the other. You pass Gara Rock and its hotel, walk by rocks called Pig's Nose and Ham Stone, and then, continuing the porcine theme, you go on to Gammon Head, nicely described in *The Rough Guide to Devon and Cornwall* as 'craggily photogenic'. It's a short walk from there to a view of the exquisite Maceley Cove, a lovely golden carpet standing between two towering columns of rock, and it isn't far from there to Prawle Point, the southernmost point in Devon. Interestingly, looking at a map of Devon you'll see that the northernmost point in Devon is almost due north of Prawle Point, and you will travel no further south than this on your walk along the South West Coast Path, if that is any encouragement.

From Prawle Point, make for the old coastguard cottages and cross the field below them, then carry on through the fields near the coast; you go forward to a track that starts to head inland, but then bear right to resume your straightforward coast path route. Easy walking now follows, as you proceed in front of Maelcombe House and then north-eastwards, veering briefly inland and bearing right onto a track to reach the unspoilt Lannacombe Beach. You're warned by markers to keep well back from the cliff-edge as you proceed eastwards beyond Lannacombe Beach, but there's still some spectacular walking past

Limpet Cove and Great Mattiscombe Sand, with a bit of scrambling possibly needed to negotiate the headland beyond. Ahead of you now is the prominent headland of Start Point. The coast path arrives at the lighthouse access road and does in fact bear left to head away from the Point itself, but it's certainly worth going out to the lighthouse and picking up a path giving you sight of the incredible schist formations on the Point (the almost sheer south face is streaked by quartz veins), as well as tremendous views across Start Bay to the next section of coast including Slapton Sands. Now make your way back along the access road, going forward to reach an information board and car park, then bear right along quite a steep and potentially slippery path down to Hallsands. On the map this looks a modest place but there was once a more substantial village here, destroyed in 1917 by storms following a drop in the level of the nearby beach caused by excessive dredging. You've now passed the 200-mile mark!

Staying on the cliffs, continue beyond Hallsands and ascend to Tinsey Head, a nice easy walk after the tough descent from Start Point, and the walking remains straightforward and easy as you descend to Beesands, picking up a coast road that passes a pub and a church. Beyond Beesands you go forward onto a rougher road, passing to the right of a lake, then veer left, sharply uphill, to pass Beesands Quarry, and swing to the right, through pasture then trees, to arrive at Torcross (13). Here you join a promenade which you follow to the car park at the top end of the village. For much of your walking through Devon you've been on cliffs, with precious little beach walking, but from the top end of Torcross to Strete Gate picnic site you are effectively down at sea level throughout, and there's a choice. You could opt to walk all of this section along the shore-side of the main A379 main road, or, for much of the way, you could instead take a path that proceeds on the inland side of this road, alongside the waters of Slapton Ley. Either has its merits. The former route gives you the chance to walk along Slapton Sands, a very exposed and windswept section of shore which was used during World War Two by US naval and infantry divisions for rehearsing the D-Day landings. There was tragedy here on the night of 27 April 1944 when 639 US servicemen were killed, possibly by 'friendly fire' as a result of troops being given live ammunition by mistake. The latter route obviously provides a grandstand view of Slapton Ley, nurtured as a flourishing nature reserve, and abundant in aquatic flora including the rare convergent stonewort; it is notable for being home to such rarities as Cetti's warbler and many other varieties of bird including the sedge and reed warbler and the great-crested grebe as well as heron, tern and widgeon.

Whichever route you have chosen, you carry on beside the A379 – you'll have got to know this road pretty well by the time you've finished – as far as Strete Gate picnic site, where the road bends sharply inland. However, you are able to continue close to the shore on a metalled path which runs uphill then goes forward to an access road bringing you back to the main road again; turn right and follow the road through the village of Strete, picking up a path running parallel with and to the right of the road. Watch for and take a metalled road bearing right off the main road, then shortly turn left to leave it and go over a footbridge and proceed over fields below Landcombe House. Soon you're back at the main road, onto which you turn right and follow to Blackpool Sands; note that the South West Coast Path signposts a more intricate route on the inland side of the main road, which you can take if you wish but it may add a few extra minutes to your walk. Keeping to the main road, pass Blackpool Sands – no Tower or Golden Mile, thankfully, just an unspoilt cove flanked by steep wooded cliffs – then proceed uphill on a wooded path that runs parallel with the main road, and shortly bear left onto a minor road which brings you straight to the church at Stoke Fleming (20). The fourteenth-century church has a tall tower which has traditionally been a most useful landmark for shipping.

Turn right just beyond the church to reach the main road again, then bear left to follow the main road through the village. As the road veers a little left, fork right onto a very undulating minor road which you follow to a car park just before Little Dartmouth, then bear right and proceed through fields to arrive back at the coast again. Pause to enjoy the lovely view, then veer left and proceed along a good coast path initially through open country – a very pleasant change after the rather messy walking you've had since leaving Torcross – and then into woodland. You go forward onto an access road to Wavenden, bearing right and then right again down a wooded hillside, and right once more down a zigzag path; steps down and up then follow, leading to a metalled path and then a road. You bear right and descend steps to Dartmouth Castle, now looking out onto the estuary of the River Dart, and from here you'll be walking inland, away from the sea towards Dartmouth. However, any withdrawal symptoms at leaving the sea are more than relieved by the quite breathtakingly beautiful views up the estuary – the castle, with its polygonal lookout tower rising above the battlements, could not make a more impressive gateway. It was built between 1481 and 1494 and was the first in England to be constructed specifically to withstand artillery, although its defences were never to be tested. You pass the attractively sited church of St Petroc and proceed along a metalled path to a road. Continue beside Castle Road, keeping the estuary to your right, and on through the village of Warfleet, then bear right down steps, passing Bayards Cove Fort and along cobbles to the ferry crossing to continue your journey along the Devon coast. (If you were the least bit tempted to walk round to the other side, you may want to think again when I warn you it'll take you a 30-mile walk to do it!) However, before making the crossing you will surely want to explore Dartmouth, the centre of which lies just beyond.

Dartmouth (23) is one of Devon's most ancient ports, its sheltered position on the River Dart making it a favoured harbour from the early Middle Ages. It was the assembly point for fleets which left for the Second and Third Crusades, but its principal trade during medieval times was in wine shipped from Bordeaux. During the sixteenth century, trade was dominated by the export of cloth and tin to France in return for linen and manufactured goods. Although it declined as a merchant shipping port in the eighteenth century, its fortunes revived in the nineteenth century as it became a base for fast steamships bound for Australia and South Africa, and it was to become famous and arguably best known for its Britannia Royal Naval College which was built here between 1899 and 1905. Fishing has also been popular here, but like Salcombe, 20 or so miles back, the prevalent industries in the town are now sailing and tourism, with so many points of interest for the visitor. These include the timber-framed Butterwalk, a four-storey seventeenth-century arcaded building overhanging the street on granite columns and richly decorated with woodcarvings; the Dartmouth Museum, mainly given over to maritime curios; St Saviour's Church, rebuilt in the 1630s and containing timberwork captured from the flagship of the Spanish Armada; Agincourt House, built after the battle of that name and restored in the seventeenth century; the well-restored eighteenth century waterfront houses of Bayards Cove, looking out onto a cobbled quay, and nearby the grand Custom House, dating back to 1739; the town quay, created in 1584; Fairfax Place, a row of shops with pargetting and slate-hanging in two colours; the five-bay, three-storey brick-fronted Mansion House, dating back to the eighteenth century; and a charming river harbour called Boatfloat. Lest it be thought that Dartmouth is a museum piece or, like Charlestown many miles back, not much more than a good setting for a BBC period nautical drama, Brewers point out that Joyce Molyneux at the waterfront Carved Angel restaurant has 'put the town in the vanguard of the renaissance of British cuisine'. Don't worry, there's also a takeaway.

# Day 14
# Dartmouth to Paignton 17 miles (230.5 miles)

**Difficulty rating:** Strenuous
**Terrain rating:** ▲▲▲
**Highlights:** Coleton Fishacre, Berry Head, Brixham

Your boat journey onwards, like the last, won't give you any problems, as the ferry across the Dart to Kingswear runs daily throughout the year; moreover, you'll find the boat somewhat more spacious and sturdy than most of those you'll have used on your south coast pilgrimage thus far, so on this occasion you can dispense with the shipping forecast and the sea-sickness pills. Having left the ferry at Kingswear, walk through an arch by the post office then left up the Alma Steps, bearing right at the top and exiting from the village by a narrow road, going forward towards Kingswear Court by means of a private road. Fork left and walk inland along the road, then bear right down steps into Warren Woods and carry on along a zigzag path downhill; cross a stream then walk briefly up an access road before bearing left up steps and going forward to another zigzag path through trees. Continue along a wide path, enjoying excellent views across the Dart Estuary to Dartmouth Castle. In due course the path narrows but the scenery remains superb as you look out to Inner Froward Point which marks the eastern mouth of the Dart and the site of a World War Two gun battery; it is perhaps with some reluctance that you now veer away from the Dart, this being one of the lovelier inland interludes on your route, but it's good to have the open sea for company again and relatively uncomplicated coast path walking as far as Sharkham Point. You descend a zigzag path towards the sea then veer left and swing uphill again and onto Outer Froward Point where you turn more resolutely north-eastwards. Excellent walking now follows as you round Pudcombe Cove, through very attractive woodland, and the fine terraced gardens of Coleton Fishacre, which contains trees, ferns, bamboos and other plants from South America and China. For a while the walking becomes easier, but then follows one of the most demanding pieces of walking on the whole journey, with some very tough up-and-down work as you negotiate Ivy Cove and drop down steeply, along paths which could be very difficult to negotiate during or after wet weather, to within shouting distance of Scabbacombe Sands. There's a brief climb and drop, then a positively back-breaking ascent above Long Sands; you then enjoy a more humane descent to Man Sands, but another massive climb ensues, up onto Southdown Cliff, followed by an easier descent along a zigzag path and then a straightforward walk across grass to Sharkham Point. You'll probably arrive here with mixed feelings: relief that some of the hardest walking on the Devon coast has been completed, but sadness that ahead of you is some of the messiest and fiddliest, with not a great deal of good scenery in return for your efforts.

There's no difficulty in negotiating your way round Sharkham Point, beyond which you begin your walk round St Mary's Bay en route for Berry Head. Initially things are straightforward but you're then forced inland around St Mary's Holiday Village to avoid a landslip, turning right into Douglas Avenue to return to the coast. It's then a straightforward walk out to Berry Head which gives an excellent view ahead to Torbay and its towns of Brixham, Paignton and Torquay, and the agenda is set, as it were; gone are the remote cliffs and cosy coves, to be replaced by a much more populous and bustling part of the Devon coast. It's worth following the road all the way to the fort on the end of the headland, as this is steeped in history. It's the site of an Iron Age cliff castle, and it was extensively and impressively fortified between 1794 and 1804 when French invasion was perceived as a very real threat. The headland and the country park created on it is a paradise for birdwatchers; there is a large breeding colony of guillemots here, and skuas and shearwaters can be seen offshore. From here you make your way fractionally south of west away from the headland, following a road to a set of gates, then bear left down a gravel path, descend steps to the right and then bear right down a road which passes the Berry Head Hotel and goes forward to Shoalstone car park. From here it's straightforward waterfront walking alongside the road to reach Brixham (11), arguably the most attractive of the towns around Torbay, with fine old buildings around the pretty harbour. Brixham has always been first and foremost a fishing community, and in the nineteenth century it had one of the largest fisheries in England; although this was subsequently to decline, it still supplies fish to restaurants as far afield as London. Arguably its most impressive sight is the full-size reconstruction of Sir Francis Drake's vessel the *Golden Hind* which stands in the harbour. The town has two other famous associations besides Drake; it was the landing place of William of Orange in 1688 on his way to taking the English throne, and the first incumbent of the church of All Saints was one Henry Francis Lyte who wrote one of the most famous hymns in the English language, 'Abide With Me'. Proceed to the head of Brixham Harbour, passing the *Golden Hind* reconstruction and walking round the harbourside. Keep along the signed route between the harbour office and the seamen's mission, then after passing the AstraZeneca building you climb steps into the Battery Gardens, heading inland to the Battery Heritage Centre.

From the Heritage Centre you bear right along a metalled path to reach an area of woodland called The Grove, then descend along a woodland path to Churston Cove, crossing it and then climbing steps to follow a further woodland path. You emerge from the woods to pass along the shingle at Elberry Cove, then follow initially through woodland and then open grassland to the rather larger cove at Broadsands which is unfortunately spoilt by a profusion of beach huts. Work your way past the huts, then just beyond the final one join a metalled path that rises up beneath a railway viaduct, bearing right to ascend steps and passing between houses or mobile homes and the railway. This is a rather long and tiresome stretch which if you've been walking all day having started from Kingswear you could do without. At length, following a climb and then a descent, you cross back to the seaward side of the railway and with some relief forge on along the promenade at Goodrington Sands. Beyond the sands – there's a South Sands and a North Sands – you veer sharp right, eastwards, and make your way up onto Roundham Head with a number of options as far as negotiating the headland; if in doubt, simply stick to the path running closest to the bay and all being well, you will arrive at Cliff Road, turning right onto it and following it to the harbour at Paignton (17). At first sight Paignton is an unremarkable suburb of Torquay, much of it developed in the late nineteenth century on salt marshes and sand dunes that separated an earlier settlement from the sea, but there are one or two gems to be found if you have the time and inclination to detour into the town from the seafront. These include the town zoo, St John's Church with some magnificent monuments to the Kirkham family, and the Oldway Mansion, built by the sewing machine tycoon Isaac Singer; blessed with what *The Rough Guide* describes as a 'gaudily neo-classical' appearance, it has a particularly impressive marble stairway. Gilbert & Sullivan enthusiasts in the party may be interested to note that the English version of *The Pirates Of Penzance* was premiered in Paignton, and tennis fans may be interested to know that the town was tennis player Sue Barker's birthplace.

# Day 15
# Paignton to Teignmouth 13 miles (243.5 miles)

**Difficulty rating:** Easy at first, becoming strenuous
**Terrain rating:** ▲▲▲
**Highlights:** Torquay, Oddicombe Beach, The Ness

To continue from Paignton, you proceed through a covered gap in the Harbour Light Restaurant to reach the Esplanade and you now have the choice between following that or the beach. In due course you reach the beach huts of Preston Sands, then go forward to a metalled path over a small headland and bear left to cross a bridge over the railway, back onto the inland side of the railway once more. Having crossed the bridge you bear right into Hollicombe Park, proceeding to the main gate and turning right to follow the main road which soon crosses to the seaward side of the railway, and you then have a choice between walking along the roadside or the sea wall. You might even go to the inland side of the road to visit Torre Abbey and pass through the grassy open spaces around the abbey as an attractive alternative to the tarmac; Torre Abbey dates back to the end of the twelfth century and although the original abbey buildings are ruined the site has been built on and it now holds an art gallery with a fine collection of silver, glass and sculpture. But whatever you decide, you will shortly reach the harbour at Torquay (1.5).

Like many large resorts on the south coast, Torquay was once a quiet fishing village, although during the Napoleonic Wars there was an important naval base here. Its development as a seaside resort began at the end of the eighteenth century when the south coast of Devon was caught up in the new fashion for sea-bathing, the mild climate proving a particular asset. Princess Victoria visited the developing town in 1833, the aristocracy followed in due course, and by 1850 it was proclaiming itself as 'queen of the watering holes', attractive not only to prospective bathers but also to invalids to whom it became what *The Rough Guide* describes as a 'fashionable haven'. The earliest of the new buildings were terraces in Georgian town-house tradition, but particularly popular in Torquay were stuccoed Italian villas in their own grounds. It was consequently to acquire an ambience that Brewers describes as 'both Mediterranean and quintessentially English, the Mediterranean influence apparent not only in the villas but the rich variety of vegetation including palms and pines'. The town was the birthplace of Richard Burton and Agatha Christie, and there is a room devoted to Agatha Christie's life and work in the Torre Abbey gallery. In 1996 it was proclaimed the country's second most popular resort, beaten to the top spot only by Blackpool. Besides Torre Abbey there are a number attractions to entice the visitor including Kent's Caverns, tracing a mere two million years of history; Bygones, with its life-sized recreation of a Victorian street; the town museum with exhibitions of a Devon farmhouse, World War Two life and Agatha Christie gallery; the old harbour with quayside shops and cafes; and Living Coasts with a huge aviary containing avocets, redshanks, puffins, terns and seals. For many, the one person who comes to mind when Torquay is mentioned is Basil Fawlty, whose fictional hotel was of course situated in the town, and if you do decide to stay here, it's best to avoid sidling up to reception and asking the proprietor not to mention the war. You should also bear in mind, if lodging in the resort, that it attracts a fair multitude of what *The Rough Guide* describes as 'drink-sodden revellers'; indeed, your muddy gaiters and stripey bobble hat, while wholly acceptable on the windswept heights of Bolt Head, may look somewhat out of place in the kebab queue among the boob tubes, thigh-length boots and six-inch heels. And some of the women's clothing is a bit radical too!

The negotiation of the hugely sprawling town of Torquay is not one of the highlights of your south coast pilgrimage but it has to be done. Carry on walking from the harbour up Beacon Hill to the Imperial Hotel then bear right along a metalled path and left up steps to a viewpoint. A descent and shortly a climb up further steps brings you to the so-called Rock End Walk, which you follow beneath a castellated summerhouse, beyond which you climb to an open area and car park. From here, keeping close to the edge overlooking the bay, you descend steps and follow a metalled path to a road, then bear right down more steps passing to the seaward side of the Osborne Hotel. Beyond the hotel you walk along a coast road beside Meadfoot Beach, then on reaching a car park follow a signed path uphill to a road onto which you turn right, heading uphill. Landslip activity has meant that in order to make progress you need to keep to the road as it heads eastwards then veers north-westwards past the Hope's Nose headland. However, you should certainly detour along a path to reach Hope's Nose, as you will get your last view back across Torbay; you will also be able to see out to Ore Stone, just offshore, as it hosts Devon's largest breeding colony of kittiwakes. Rejoin the road now, leaving Torbay behind, and having proceeded shortly north-westwards, bear right onto a signed path for Anstey's Cove along what is known as the Bishops Walk. At a junction fork left and go forward to a car park, then turn right along the Palace Hotel road, and from this road bear right onto a signed path which climbs steps then bears right onto the cliffs. Proceed along the grassy cliff-top then descend into a wood; you zigzag down steps to reach a road bend then bear right through further woods to another road bend, descending to a beach. Using walkways provided over the rocks, you then climb steps and bear right to follow the wooded edge above Oddicombe Beach, looking out here for the splendid cliff railway. Follow the beach access road away from the sea, then bear right to follow a path uphill beside the cliff railway, then under it. Continue along the path downhill then back up to a road at Babbacombe, turning right and then right once more to follow Petitor Road, then bear left to follow a coast path through woods towards Watcombe. Now, at long last, you're beginning to pull away from the suburbs of Torquay and can enjoy true coast path walking again.

There's a descent to the access road to Watcombe Beach, then undulating walking follows as you pass Watcombe Head and head on to Maidencombe through a mixture of fields and woodland. Notice the rich reddish-brown sandstone of the cliffs, which will be a feature of much of the coastal walking through the rest of Devon, and which contrasts vividly with the granite of west Cornwall. You arrive at a beach access road which you follow to the left, aiming for a tempting pub, but before the pub you bear right to return to proper coast path walking. On paper the going is quite straightforward with no route-finding difficulties, but this is in fact a very tough section of walking indeed, with a succession of huge climbs and descents; frustratingly many of the hilltop views are partially obstructed by trees, but the last rise yields a tremendous view towards your next two coastal towns, Teignmouth and Dawlish, and beyond. You skirt your old friend the A379 then bear right again and make a steep descent, passing a golf course, then climb yet again into Ness Woodland and enjoy a super view from The Ness, a prominent tree-clad headland of rich brown sandstone. From here you descend along a narrow road to arrive at Shaldon (12.5). At Shaldon, with its pleasant cluster of small streets containing attractive thatched cottages, you can choose between a ferry crossing of the Teign from the Ferryboat Inn to Teignmouth, or, if you prefer, a walk round to a road crossing of the river and then a fair road walk to reach the waterfront at Teignmouth (13). The birthplace of Charles Babbage, reckoned by some to be the 'father of the computer', Teignmouth was famous as a port and shipbuilding centre long before acquiring fame as a resort. It prospered as a port in the eighteenth century, becoming particularly important for the export of Dartmoor granite and local clay, and indeed in 1821 it sent to London a quantity of Dartmoor granite that was used to build London Bridge. It has continued to serve as a port in modern times, importing animal feed and fertilisers and exporting clay. It was at the start of the nineteenth century that the resort began to develop; it was one of the first seaside resorts to be developed in Devon, benefiting hugely from the arrival of the railway in 1846, and it had a number of distinguished visitors including Jane Austen, Fanny Burney and John Keats. Although there are some splendid Georgian and Victorian buildings in the town, including some elegant villas, Pevsner is a lot less happy with later additions, referring to 'a deplorable assortment of twentieth century clutter'!

# Day 16
# Teignmouth to Exmouth via Topsham 19 miles*
# (262.5 miles)

**Difficulty rating:** Easy
**Terrain rating:** ▲▲
**Highlights:** Dawlish, Starcross, Lympstone
*Please note that this mileage presupposes that the longer route via Topsham is used, this being my preferred option. If you choose to catch the ferry from Starcross to Exmouth the length of this section is reduced to 9 miles.

Whichever way you've chosen to get to Teignmouth from Shaldon, make for the pier on the promenade – the pier once segregated male and female bathers – and keep along the promenade to the yacht club. Outside of high water, there's no problem in continuing along the sea wall, keeping the railway immediately to your left, as far as Smugglers Lane at the south end of Holcombe where you bear left to go up to the A379. At high water, however, you're forced to follow a road from the yacht club over the railway and then along a track beside a park, going towards the A379 and bearing right along that road to be reunited with the low-water route at the junction of the A379 and Smugglers Lane. Follow the A379 through Holcombe then bear right into Windward Lane and left to follow a coast path, an undulating path with the railway close by to your right. You're then forced back to the road again but soon you're able to join a minor road to the right; this returns to the main road but shortly you can bear right again onto a footpath which climbs to a red sandstone cliff-edge and then zigzags down to the front at Dawlish (5). The town, perched behind bright red cliffs, prospered as a resort from the end of the eighteenth century, and although it is described by *The Rough Guide* as a 'modest resort with low key appeal', it boasts some fine architecture including the Strand with its spacious feel and Regency and early Victorian buildings; Baron Terrace with its villas in a pleasant variety of early nineteenth-century styles including Grecian, Gothic and Doric; and Haldon Terrace with its three-storey stuccoed houses. The town, which is mentioned in the work of Jane Austen and Charles Dickens, also has beautiful ornamental gardens called The Lawn in its centre, and the cove is the starting point for mackerel fishing trips.

Follow the sea wall away from the station at Dawlish until you reach a footbridge over the railway at the point where the A379 strikes out away from the sea. Again there may be a problem with flooding at high tide and if the sea wall is inaccessible you may be forced to follow the A379 from the station to the point where it strikes away from the sea, and here bear right onto a path to be reunited with the sea wall route. Your coast route now proceeds through a park and then parallel with and to the inland side of the railway, going forward via woodland onto a wide track that takes you to Dawlish Warren. The track arrives at a junction with a road and, continuing in the same direction, you join the road, almost immediately passing Dawlish Warren station. East of the railway is a nature reserve of national importance; it attracts a large number of wildfowl including dunlins, black-tailed godwits and brent geese, and there is a multitude of flowering plants including some flowers that cannot be seen anywhere else in mainland Britain. Sadly there is no through route on from the reserve, so if you want to make a detour to visit it you'll have to return to pick up the route. Follow beside the road which veers north-west then north-east to stay close to the railway which is to your right; the road passes the little village of Eastdon and soon arrives at Cockwood, reaching a T-junction with a main road, and you turn right to follow this road into the village of Starcross (10). The village, itself unremarkable, acquired fame in the mid-nineteenth century for being the location for a relic of an ill-fated experiment in rail transport, namely the Atmospheric Railway. Motive power was derived from the pressure of the atmosphere; there was a cylinder between the lines and ten pumping stations along its course, one of which still survives at Starcross. Air was pumped out of the cylinder, creating a vacuum, which acted on a piston which pulled the train. The problem was rats, who took a liking to the grease that was used on the mechanism, and also the fact that horses had to be used to pull the train in the first place!

You have now reached the estuary of the River Exe, the very last river obstruction you will have to negotiate in Devon and in fact the last until the Sandbanks ferry right at the end of the South West Coast Path, but, as if to test your resolve for one last time, the crossing of it is not entirely straightforward. Between April and September you should have no problem in crossing by ferry from Starcross to Exmouth where the coast path resumes, but outside that period, the ferry doesn't run and you then have a choice. The first and perhaps more appealing option, if you want an excuse for a couple of hours off, is to use public transport from Starcross to Exeter, with train and bus services available from Starcross to Exeter and then from Exeter to Exmouth. A more virtuous option, which my edition of the South West Way Association guide suggests should be regarded as the official route, is to continue on foot up to the Topsham ferry, which does operate on winter weekends. To do this, continue by road from Starcross to Powderham Church, keeping the railway to your right and the lovely Powderham Park on your left, boasting a heronry and castle that's been the home of the Earls of Devon since 1390. Having passed the church, the road swings sharply left, but you go straight on ahead on a track, cross the railway and strike out on a path which continues beside the river and then beside the Exeter Canal; these waterways attract a tremendous variety of bird life including grey heron, kestrel, golden plover, pintail, mallard, kingfisher and avocet. Soon you reach the ferry and use it to cross to Topsham. Within easy reach of the cathedral city of Exeter, and linked to it by train, Topsham was once Exeter's main port, prospering on shipbuilding and the wool trade; it boasts many historic buildings including some fine old merchant's houses dating back to the seventeenth century. From Topsham there are regular trains and buses to Exmouth, but if you want to walk it, join the road which runs eastwards from Topsham to Marsh Barton, joining a footpath and then a lane to bring you to the A376 at Ebford. Turn right onto this road and follow it through Exton, then beyond the Royal Marines Barracks turn right down a minor road to Lympstone, a pretty village of thatched cottages and Regency villas and once a fishing port from which boats sailed as far as Greenland. At Lympstone you can join the East Devon Way which hugs the railway on one side and the estuary sands on the other, providing tremendous views back across to Dawlish Warren nature reserve, and soon bringing you into Exmouth (19). Here you will be reunited with the indolent couch potatoes who've got the ferry from Starcross or trained or bussed it all the way, and you can smugly polish your halo, or seek out the nearest cafe for a slab of triple-decker cream sponge that your extra efforts have undoubtedly earned you!

# Day 17
# Exmouth to Sidmouth 15 miles (277.5 miles)

**Difficulty rating:** Moderate, strenuous in places
**Terrain rating:** ▲▲▲
**Highlight:** River Otter, Ladram Bay, Peak Hill

Exmouth, once a fishing port, began to develop as a resort during the eighteenth century, its excellent beaches making it a very popular base for sea-bathing, and in fact it claims to be the oldest seaside resort in Devon. The first houses overlooking the sea were built in 1792, and during the nineteenth century there was a surge in building followed by sprawling suburban development in the twentieth century. The old port, meanwhile, has now been developed as a marina, although there are still some working fishing boats. The wives of both Lord Nelson and Lord Byron lived in the town, but despite these famous associations, it does lack the charisma of Torquay or the architectural richness of Dawlish. Indeed, rather than linger here you'll probably be anxious to get going on what's known as the 'Jurassic Coast'. In 2001 a 95-mile stretch of coastline of East Devon and Dorset between Exmouth and Studland Bay was declared England's first natural World Heritage Site and was named the 'Jurassic Coast' for its 185 million year history. It provides a remarkable diversity of cliffs, from the red sandstone sea stacks (try saying that quickly a few times) of Ladram Bay to the white chalk of Beer Head, and are the richest mid-Triassic reptile sites in Britain. So, relaxed in the knowledge that there are no more ferries to rush to catch before the season ends, follow the town's waterfront to get level with the very distinctive Maer Rocks out to sea; here you need to look out for a car park by Foxholes Hill to your left where you pick up a signed path heading for Budleigh Salterton, ascending along a metalled path to the High Land of Orcombe, an area of grass above the beach. Avoiding a descent to the beach, you proceed eastwards along the coast path, ascending then dropping to Sandy Bay with its beautiful golden beach and its massive, and rather less beautiful, holiday park. You pass through a car park then swing sharp left, north-eastwards, and rise steeply, cutting round the Straight Point headland which is used as a military firing range. With the holiday park to your left and the range to your right, it's not ideal walking, but soon you rise above Littleham Cove and can now enjoy fine views to Budleigh Salterton, your next objective. Now at last you can shake off the holiday park and proceed along field paths, interrupted by a wooded valley, then climb up to the trig point on Beacon Hill; from here you descend past the golf course and through woodland to reach a metalled path which in turn takes you to Budleigh Salterton (7). The town's name is derived from the salt pans situated here, in which seawater was evaporated to manufacture salt. The industry is long defunct, and the town is now a sedate resort, described in *The Rough Guide* as the 'apotheosis of Devon respectability'. Having developed as a resort in the early nineteenth century, in the wake of Royal visits to nearby Sidmouth, it has attracted a number of famous visitors including P. G. Wodehouse and Noel Coward, who gave the town a mention in his famous play *Blithe Spirit*. There are some attractive houses in the town, most notably Fairlynch on South Parade; now a museum, it's a delightful early nineteenth-century cottage with a tiny thatched belvedere rising above the roof. The town's sea wall featured in John Everett Millais' celebrated 1870 painting *The Boyhood Of Raleigh*.

You proceed along the sea front as far as a car park, to arrive at the River Otter, but this time there's no need for a ferry as your walk to the nearest bridge isn't too long; simply bear left, inland, from the car park and follow the riverside path to the road bridge crossing, cross the bridge and then bear right as marked to follow a path along the east bank of the Otter to return to the coast. Although it's always a shame to leave the coast, the walk around the Otter is a very pleasant one indeed, with a wildlife reserve on its bank. Now turn sharp left, north-eastwards, to climb up onto the cliffs of red sandstone, passing the mini-headlands of Black Head and Brandy Head. The walking is reasonably easy along gentle cliffs and very enjoyable. Just beyond a slightly more prominent headland, Smallstones Point, you come to Ladram Bay with its grotesquely formed red sandstone stacks that make an often photographed scene, and you should look out for fulmars and cormorants on or around the stacks. It's a pity that the effect is spoiled somewhat by another holiday park which you have to walk through, but having crossed the beach access road and ascended once more, you again find yourself in unspoilt and spectacular scenery. A stiff ascent through trees brings you close to the summit of High Peak, which is over 500 feet above the sea and boasts an Iron Age hill fort; although the Coast Path leaves it out, you may decide to go for it anyway, but if you do, you'll then need to get back onto the course of the national trail which joins a wide path on the far side of High Peak. From here, you descend and bear right, ascending again onto the slopes of Peak Hill, its highest point only a fraction less high than High Peak, and another quite magnificent viewpoint. You descend along a path through woodland, arriving at a road, then bear right between a road and cliffs to descend into Sidmouth (15).

Described by *The Rough Guide* as the region's 'architectural aristocrat', Sidmouth was previously a small fishing town, but it was 'discovered', so to speak, by Jewish businessman Emmanuel Lousada who in the late eighteenth century decided to turn it into the most elegant and genteel holiday resort in England. Its cause was helped by the fact that the well-to-do were unable to travel abroad due to the French Revolution and its aftermath. The aristocracy flocked here and it soon became a fashionable resort, developing fast during the first half of the nineteenth century; its popularity was certainly enhanced by a visit in 1819 from the Duke of Kent and his baby daughter, the future Queen Victoria. Another famous visitor to Sidmouth was Elizabeth Barrett Browning who lived here between 1832 and 1836. The late Georgian and early Victorian architecture of Sidmouth is particularly interesting, including what Pevsner calls 'solid capacious pattern-book villas'. As you wander through the streets you will find terraces with castellated parapets, Gothic windows, elegant wrought-iron balconies, white painted facades, enhanced by fine floral displays and colourful gardens. One particular gem is the three-storeyed Beach House with its giant Ionic corner pilasters and charming Gothic windows. There are also some older buildings of interest, with an old town around Old Fore Street and the High Street, the oldest building in the town being Tudor Cottage, formerly a late medieval hall house.

# Day 18
# Sidmouth to Lyme Regis 17 miles (294.5 miles)

**Difficulty rating:** Strenuous
**Terrain rating:** ▲▲▲▲
**Highlight:** Salcombe Hill, Weston Cliff, Axmouth–Lyme Regis Undercliff Path

The walk from Sidmouth to Seaton provides some of the finest and most enjoyable walking on the whole of the Devon coast. To exit Sidmouth, follow the esplanade and go over the river Sid by crossing Alma Bridge, then follow a metalled path up a wooded slope, heading inland; walk along Cliff Road and then Laskeys Lane, returning to the cliffs and now climbing through woods onto Salcombe Hill. In due course you emerge from the woods to enjoy really splendid views over 500 feet above the sea. You proceed along field paths then drop steeply down towards Salcombe Mouth; you are forced a little inland to cross a stream in woodland, then climb back, again very steeply, up onto the cliffs, using a zigzag path to reach Higher Dunscombe Cliff. Again, after a fine high level walk, you turn inland round the head of a valley then swing seawards again, heading downhill through woodland to reach the beach at Weston Mouth. Then there's yet another massive climb, this time onto Weston Cliff from which there are absolutely fantastic views which extend back to Sidmouth, Budleigh Salterton, Dawlish and even some of the tors of Dartmoor. Now things get easier for a while as you walk along the cliff-top, then go forward to Coxe's Cliff, veering briefly away from the cliffs to cross a valley, continuing from here along the cliffs. Once again you veer inland, losing height, to join a track, and now head downhill along what is a mostly wooded track, getting views to your left to the stunningly beautiful village of Branscombe, but losing sight of the sea for a while. You then emerge from the woodland and walk through fields to reach Branscombe Mouth. In summer and on fine weekends this gets very full of day-trippers, a rather rude shock after the wonderfully unspoilt walking you've enjoyed from Sidmouth, but it provides the opportunity for a detour to Branscombe village itself if you have the time. The village boasts a number of picture book thatched cottages strung along a meandering valley and has a beautiful old church, St Winifred's; a visit to an old church may not be everyone's idea of an entertaining diversion, but this is one of the best country churches in Devon, with a late Norman tower incorporating a priest's room, one of only two triple-decker pulpits in Devon, and fragments of medieval wall paintings. And you'll enjoy your drink back at the Branscombe Mouth pub all the more for having detoured to see it all.

Back at Branscombe Mouth you cross a river by way of a footbridge then bear right to make the ascent of East Cliff. You have a choice here between proceeding to Beer Head via the tops of Hooken Cliffs, or via an undercliff path. The cliff-top route is straightforward enough, and on a clear day you will enjoy views that extend as far eastwards as Golden Cap and Portland Bill in Dorset. The undercliff route does not start too propitiously, passing first into a caravan park, but after bearing left and then right you reach the Hooken Undercliff itself; this is a 10-acre landscape which broke away from the cliff in 1790 and is now what the *AA Devon Guide* describes as a 'wilderness of rocks and pinnacles' as well as supporting a wide variety of insect and bird life. Moreover, it is certainly dramatic and although the views aren't perhaps necessarily as good as on the cliff-top, it's that bit nearer to the sea and thereby that bit more coastal, and also it's a bit different! In due course the undercliff path rises to the cliff-top and you bear right to be reunited with the cliff-top route, going forward to Beer Head; notice how the red sandstone which so characterised the cliff scenery around Budleigh Salterton and Sidmouth has now given way to chalk, and in fact Beer Head is the most westerly chalk cliff on the south coast. Having reached the headland, swing left, just east of north, and proceed along field paths and past a caravan site, then bear right along Little Lane and right again into Common Lane to reach the centre of the village of Beer (7). Once a magnet for smugglers, it previously had a renowned lace-making industry established by Dutch refugees, Beer lace being used to decorate Queen Victoria's wedding dress. Another once thriving industry here has been quarrying: Cretaceous limestone which is quarried hereabouts is much prized and was used in the construction of the Tower of London and Cathedrals in Winchester and Exeter. The village's refreshingly alcoholic name – perhaps itself a reason why it's something of a magnet for tourists – is actually derived from the word 'bearu' meaning grove or small wood which in turn is derived from its location, huddled in a narrow cove between gleaming white headlands. And nothing to do with the quality of the local brew.

Above the beach and across from the Anchor Inn, follow the path which begins on a reasonably level course then rises past gardens to the cliff-top. Go up a set of steps and continue along the cliff path for about a quarter of a mile. The path goes forward into a narrow lane; turn sharp right down this lane to Seaton Hole, and for the shortish walk between here and your next port of call, the town of Seaton, you have a choice. You could simply follow alongside the cliff road east for about 600 yards to the far end of a large terrace of houses to the right, then follow a signed path to proceed to the seafront at Seaton. But if the tide permits, it's perfectly possible to proceed to the beach from Seaton Hole and continue to Seaton that way. Seaton (9) was strategically important as far back as Roman times but its importance declined with the accumulation of pebbles across the mouth of the nearby River Axe and until the mid-nineteenth century it was just a fishing village. A modest resort then slowly developed here, helped as so many south coast resorts were by the advent of the railway, and the town still boasts some Victorian and Edwardian architecture among the sprawl of modern buildings. However, it is perhaps the least appealing of the south-east Devon coastal resorts with a really rather tacky feel to it, its only redeeming feature being the open-topped Seaton Tramway which follows a pleasant course through the Axe valley to Colyton, and may provide a welcome change from walking. Follow the promenade to emerge from Seaton, bearing left, away from the sea, alongside a boatyard to a T-junction with the B3172, and turn right to follow this road over a bridge across the River Axe; the bridge was built in 1877 to replace a ferry and was one of the first in Britain to be made of concrete. You probably won't be too concerned what it was made of, simply glad it's there at all and you're not having to wait till next Easter for the next ferry crossing.

Having crossed the bridge, don't take the first footpath turning on the right but continue a little further along the main road and then bear right up the access road for Axe Cliff Golf Club. However, if you've time, it's worth detouring up the road to visit the village of Axmouth, once an important port and a centre for the export of wool and iron. The port ceased to thrive as a result of the silting of the Axe estuary which restricted access to the estuary to yachts and pleasure craft, and visitors to the estuary are now more likely to be tourists and birdwatchers with binoculars trained for sightings of curlews, redshanks and sandpipers. Axmouth is a delightful village, with a mix of colour-washed and thatched cottages with natural stone walls and tiled roofs grouped round the church of St Michael which itself boasts a handsome Norman doorway and medieval wall paintings. Back on the route, having walked up the golf club access road to the club house you carry straight on across the golf course, then having continued away from the golf course along a track still heading in a roughly easterly direction, you are directed right, just east of south. You walk through fields then turn easterly along the top of some wooded landslip slopes, before entering a thick wooded area and following the famous Undercliff Path that will take you all the way to Underhill Farm just west of Lyme Regis. The Undercliff landscape itself is the result of a massive cliff slip that occurred in 1839 when 800 million tons of earth and rock crumbled away from the cliff leaving a gash 6 miles long between just east of Axmouth and Lyme Regis. Far from being an ecological disaster, it now supports thick woodland rich in wildlife and plant life, with deer and badgers roaming and some 120 species of bird having been recorded in the Undercliff. For you, the walker, it will prove a mixed blessing. The path is very easy to follow; although there are twists and turns and changes in surface, you will not get lost, and on a hot day the woodland will prove cooler and more refreshing. That's the good news, the bad news being there is no possibility of escape, nor are there any amenities, and you will feel quite cut off both from the sea to your right and the open countryside to your left, with no sea views to speak of and none of the broad, open panoramas that you will have enjoyed between Sidmouth and Branscombe. The walking can be quite strenuous in places, especially if there are obstructions on the path; I walked this section after a period of very stormy activity while the path was officially closed, and although it was passable there were many twigs and branches littering the route which made progress difficult. Assuming I haven't put you off, you will knuckle down, get on with it, and then heave a sigh of relief when you reach Underhill Farm and go forward on to the access road beyond which you emerge from the woods. It's great to have this challenging section behind you, and to bear in mind that in completing it, you have also effectively completed your walk through Devon. Your entry into Lyme Regis from here takes you over the border into Dorset, less than 100 miles now separating you from the end of the South West Coast Path section of your south coast walk. Land's End might as well be on another continent!

Leaving the woodland behind, you bear right onto a path over Ware Cliffs, then right again down an area of grassland flanked by woods; you go over a stream and bear right once more, entering a wood and dropping down to the Cobb, arriving now in the heart of Lyme Regis (17). The town was a port of great strategic importance, being raided regularly by the French and in turn supplying Sir Francis Drake's fleet with ships to face the Armada, and in 1685 the Duke of Monmouth landed here prior to the Battle of Sedgmoor. As late as 1780 it was larger than the port of Liverpool and between 1500 and 1700 trade flourished with the Mediterranean, West Indies and the Americas, while smuggling also thrived. By late Georgian times the fashion for sea-bathing had turned it into a popular resort, and despite a serious fire in 1844, the prevailing character even today is of a late Georgian resort, with some elegant Georgian and Victorian buildings dotted around its streets. It features not only in the work of John Fowles but also Jane Austen who loved the town; she wrote *Persuasion* in the town in 1818 and set part of the novel here. The cliffs around Lyme have always been fragile – you will see further evidence of this as you proceed eastwards from here – but the Norman church of St Michael enjoys a superb position on the Lias cliffs. The Cobb is perhaps the biggest draw for visitors; this solidly built semi-circular stone breakwater provides shelter for the harbour, which Edward I used during his wars against the French, rewarding the town by conferring its royal title upon it. If you're brave enough to attempt it, it is a spectacular place to stand on a stormy day with the waves smashing into its sides. If you've seen the film *The French Lieutenant's Woman*, based on John Fowles' novel, you can almost expect to see Meryl Streep standing there, gazing mysteriously seawards. And if you've had a few pints too many in celebration of completing the Undercliff path and the Devon coast, then perhaps you will!

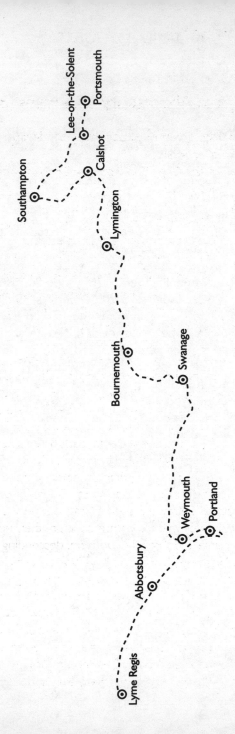

**DORSET/HAMPSHIRE**

Lyme Regis

Abbotsbury

Weymouth

Portland

Swanage

Bournemouth

Lymington

Southampton

Calshot

Lee-on-the-Solent

Portsmouth

# Day 19
# Lyme Regis to Abbotsbury 18.5 miles (313 miles)

**Difficulty rating:** Strenuous, becoming moderate
**Terrain rating:** ▲▲▲
**Highlights:** Golden Cap, Thorncombe Beacon, Abbotsbury

Having found your way to the Cobb at Lyme Regis, proceed to the promenade and follow it all the way to the Rock Point Inn, then shortly beyond the inn the promenade peters out and there is now another choice to be made. At low tide you can simply walk along the shore to Charmouth, the next settlement on the Dorset coast, but if you're unlucky with the tides – it should go without saying that you ought to check tide tables before setting out – you have a long inland detour. This is because of massive cliff erosion between Lyme and Charmouth, and in fact it's interesting to look at older maps and see how the route of the South West Coast Path has been forced further inland between the two towns. By the time of the first reprint of this book, I confidently expect to be diverting you via Birmingham! For now though, walk by a zigzag path along steps and ramps from the end of the sea wall, going forward through a churchyard to reach the main A3052; walk uphill beside the road, but just beyond a car park bear right onto a signed path that runs north-eastwards and swings shortly northwards through fields to enter woodland, rising then dropping to a minor road. Turn right onto the road and follow it to arrive at a T-junction with the A3052. Bear right again to follow this road briefly, but very soon turn right again to follow a well-marked path eastwards, then north-eastwards across a golf course and through woodland, descending back onto the A3052. Thus far the path planners have bravely avoided succumbing to lengthy road walking on this inland slog, but now have to bow to the inevitable; bear right to follow the roadside to a roundabout and then right again to follow the road to Charmouth, reaching the shore via either Higher Sea Lane or Lower Sea Lane. Both shore and inland routes now unite by the beach cafe and shop by the shore and take you forward to the river mouth. Charmouth (3) is world famous for its abundance of fossils, and it was here that in 1810 the discovery was made of the first complete fossil of an Icthyosaurus, a meat-eating reptile resembling a giant porpoise. Catherine of Aragon, the first wife of Henry VIII, stayed here when she arrived in England, and Charles II turned up here in disguise following his defeat at Worcester, looking for a boat to France. He failed and ended up traipsing all the way to Shoreham in West Sussex, the route he took now forming the basis of the Monarch's Way, a gentle stroll of just 600 miles or so.

At the river mouth, bear left and follow alongside the river, then cross the river by the footbridge, follow a path straight uphill from here, go over Stonebarrow Hill then descend into a valley and over a footbridge across a stream south of Westhay Farm. Ascend from here, veering north-eastwards away from the sea, descend once more to cross a further stream, then climb again and descend again via fields to go over a stream just north of St Gabriel's Mouth. Now comes the most significant climb of your entire south coast walk, as you proceed just south of east up steps, zigzag up a gravel path with more steps, and continue to the trig point on the summit of Golden Cap which at 627 feet is the highest cliff-top on the south coast. Golden Cap, the site of a lookout station established during the Napoleonic Wars, gets its name from the golden-tinged sandstone on the summit of what is a cliff of blue lias clay. The effect is perhaps slightly dulled by the amount of intervening land between the top and the sea itself – it perhaps lacks the stark drama of Beachy Head or the Needles – but the views are truly magnificent. It would be nice to believe that having reached the summit of the south coast the hard work had been done and it was now downhill all the way to Dover, but sadly that is wishful thinking. From the summit you proceed briefly even further inland, entering a patch of woodland, but then veer south-eastwards through fields interspersed with more woodland and descend to a road, turning right onto it and following it to arrive at the modest coastal settlement of Seatown. This is an unremarkable place but features in Hardy's novel *The Mayor Of Casterbridge*, it being here in the novel that Henchard came to the fair with his wife and sold her while the worse for drink. You have now passed the 300-mile mark!

Cross over a footbridge and pass through a car park, then leave Seatown by climbing on to Ridge Cliff; some tough hilly terrain follows, culminating in another big summit, that of Thorncombe Beacon which is just over 500 feet above the sea and offers superb views back to Golden Cap and Lyme Regis. Not surprisingly there's a steep descent from here, followed ironically by a small climb, then it's downhill all the way to Eype's Mouth just below the village of Lower Eype. There's a footbridge crossing over a stream by the beach, then another climb, this time on to West Cliff; you are now getting your first views of Chesil Beach, which will be a major feature on your south coast walk for much of the next 20 miles or so. You pass a campsite then drop down to the sprawling and rather unlovely village of West Bay (10), arriving at the west end of the village via the promenade. Until the coming of the railway, West Bay was known as Bridport Harbour, and from the harbour, constructed in the middle of the eighteenth century, Bridport rope was transported to naval shipyards elsewhere on the coast. Later, the harbour was to become a base for the export of fish, shingle and sand and the unloading of timber from the Baltic. It's now a bit of a mish-mash of fish stores, industrial buildings and holiday accommodation. On reaching the harbour mouth, turn briefly inland up the road to a roundabout, bearing right to round the harbour, with the River Brit to your left; you then follow the road beyond the harbour just south of east as far as the West Bay pub, where the main road goes off left to the attractive town of Bridport. If you've time, it's worth a detour to this town, which contains many fine Georgian houses along its wide streets, the pavements of which were originally 'ropewalks' for twisting and drying the cord and twine which were made here. The town offers a wide range of amenities including bus links to railheads at Axminster and Dorchester, if just over 300 miles in one hit has proved enough for you. But if your plan is to press on along the coast path from the West Bay pub you need, assuming you detoured from it, to make your way back there and bear right, south-eastwards, from the pub, pass through a car park and begin the ascent of the orange stone East Cliff.

The ascent of East Cliff is the last significant cliff climb till you reach Portland nearly 20 miles further on (or, if you omit Portland, the other side of Weymouth well over 25 miles further on), but the bad news is that it's a very tough climb indeed. Once you've reached the top of the cliff, picturesquely described in the *Readers Digest Illustrated Guide to Britain's Coast* as 'soaring (and) wind-sculpted', things are easy enough for a while, but then comes a short steep descent and climb, and a further descent to a holiday park. Now you have to negotiate another river crossing, that of the River Bride. You could risk wading it, but if you don't fancy it, the South West Coast Path bears left, along the left bank of the river then over the footbridge and back seawards again; whether you've waded it and lived to tell the tale, or used the approved route, you now proceed resolutely along the coast once more, passing over Burton Cliff and dropping to the beach at Burton Hive. At Burton Hive there's a possibility of a detour to Burton Bradstock which, like Branscombe and Axmouth, is an example of a lovely village just off the coast path. It's largely made up of stone or rubble-walled houses and cottages with thatched, stone or slate-tiled roofs, mostly some 300 years old; there is also a fourteenth-century church with handsome medieval panelling and a triangular green bordered by the White House which dates back to 1635. Back on the coast route from Burton Hive there's a climb beside Bind Barrow, a Bronze Age burial mound, then you pass a further holiday park and on to Cogden Beach. Having made your way to the beach, you have quite a tough piece of shingle walking but things get easier as you join a track at the back of what is the beginning of the famous Chesil Beach, also known as Chesil Bank. This is an extraordinary phenomenon, consisting of a long bank of pebbles among which are to be found plants including thrift, sea-kale, sea-spinach and sea-beet. The bank was formed 10,000 years ago at the end of the last glacial period, when the rise in sea level and large waves from the south-west pushed huge quantities of rock debris and sediments inshore. It extends from here all the way down to the Isle of Portland, the pebbles gradually increasing in size from west to east, from the size of peas at the western end to 3 inches in diameter at Portland. It is theoretically possible to follow Chesil Beach all the way to Portland, but 17 miles of shingle tramping is a very tall order indeed, particularly in bad weather, and I would not recommend it other than as penance for sins, particularly as once you reach The Fleet there's no possibility of escape. Both the South West Coast Path planners and my suggested route opt for an easier passage. However, having passed inland of Burton Mere, you've really no option but to follow Chesil Beach for the moment, maintaining a staunch south-easterly course; this isn't easy walking and it may seem a bit of an anticlimax after the splendid walking between Charmouth and West Bay, but it will give you a taste of what a walk along the complete bank might be like.

At length you reach the beach car park at West Bexington (15), a popular location for sea anglers, and the point at which the South West Coast Path divides into two with both a coastal and inland alternative route offered between here and Osmington Mills, well beyond Weymouth. South coast walkers of course will stick to the former, but be careful not to be lured by signposts taking you to such delights as the Hardy Monument, Limekiln Hill and Bronkham Hill and the wealth of prehistoric remains; those will have to wait till you've made it to Dover. Beyond West Bexington there's more shingle tramping as you continue south-eastwards. In due course, however, you will have the luxury of a coastal road for a while, then, beyond a car park from which there's access to Abbotsbury Subtropical Gardens, you veer away from the sea towards the village of Abbotsbury itself. Leaving the shingle, the last significant stretch of shingle you'll have to cope with this side of Bournemouth, you join a track and head north-eastwards, bound for Abbotsbury, then swing sharp right to cross over Chapel Hill. To the north, not on the course of your coastal route, is the fourteenth-century St Catherine's Chapel whose internal length is less than 45 feet but is perched magnificently on a hill some 250 feet above the sea. You descend to a track which provides the possibility of a detour north to Abbotsbury village and south to the famous Abbotsbury Swannery, a wetland reserve for a breeding herd of mute swans, which dates back to the fourteenth century. Abbotsbury (18.5), with its barns, thatched cottages and orange stone houses, is the undoubted gem of what is essentially an unexciting section of the walk, its principal glory being the Abbey barn which at 272 feet by 31 feet is the largest barn of its kind in Britain, dating from about 1400. The Abbey itself, of Benedictine origin, goes back to the middle of the eleventh century, but very little of it remains today.

# Day 20
# Abbotsbury to Fortuneswell (Cove House Inn)
# 13 miles (326 miles)

**Difficulty rating:** Easy
**Terrain rating:** ▲▲
**Highlights:** The Fleet, Moonfleet Hotel, Chesil Beach

Having reached the track which as stated in the above paragraph gave the opportunity for detours to Abbotsbury or its swannery, you go straight ahead following a lane heading eastwards, then as this lane swings to the right you leave it and continue just south of east through open fields past Clayhanger Farm. Just short of a trig point on Merry Hill turn sharp right, heading just east of south, passing the eastern edge of a strip of woodland. Beyond the trees you bear left, heading eastwards across a footbridge and another lane, then swing right, southwards past the eastern edge of Wyke Wood and drop downhill to arrive back at the water's edge. This is not the sea but The Fleet, a lagoon which is separated from the sea by Chesil Beach. It began just a little south-east of the point where you headed away from the sea towards Abbotsbury, and ends at Ferry Bridge, the link between the mainland and the Isle of Portland; it is a very attractive stretch of water and attracts a number of wading birds including the curlew and dunlin.

Having reached the banks of The Fleet at Rodden Hive, you'll find the going gets extremely easy all the way to Ferry Bridge some 7 miles away, with a good path almost all the way. For virtually all of it the path hugs the water's edge, faithfully following its numerous mini-peninsulas and mini-inlets, so you do not progress south-eastwards anything like as quickly as the proverbial airborne crow; that said, it's certainly quicker going than the shingle, and in its own way, is just as captivating and satisfying as the cliff walking. You pass close to, but out of sight of, the village of Langton Herring, then cut across the mini-peninsula at Herbury and, returning to the water's edge go on beside the Moonfleet Hotel which may remind you of J. Meade-Faulkner's splendid novel *Moonfleet* and its story of the smugglers' battles with excise men on this section of the Dorset coast. Continue past the hamlet of East Fleet and close to the village of Charlestown, not to be confused with its much more memorable namesake that you passed though in Cornwall more than 200 miles back! You arrive at the Tidmoor Army Rifle Ranges where, if no firing is taking place, you can simply stick to the shore, but if there is firing, you're signposted round the inland side; for a while there's more shore-side walking, then having been forced round the inland side of the Wyke Regis Training Area Headquarters, you can enjoy a straightforward march down to the Ferry Bridge with surroundings that are now noticeably more built-up. In due course, you arrive at the busy A354 at the Ferry Bridge (11), this road providing access to the Isle of Portland, and thus the question arises whether or not to include Portland on your travels. Strictly it isn't an island, as it is joined to the mainland by Chesil Bank, and it is now officially incorporated into the South West Coast Path. Therefore I assume you will do it. If you decide not to, choosing rather to cross the A354 onto the signed South West Coast Path direct route to Weymouth, I don't suppose those who've sponsored you to walk the south coast will say you've cheated, but you'll certainly have missed out on a great experience. And it may be an unwelcome nag on your conscience.

Portland is an extraordinary place: the coastal paths, with cliffs rising to nearly 500 feet, provide many moments of quite majestic beauty, but it has a real workaday feel with its many quarries which have provided stone for St Paul's Cathedral, the external surface of the UN building in New York, and two large penal institutions. If you're going to give it a go, turn right alongside the A354 and walk along the right-hand pavement across the bridge, then once across it you'll soon reach the

Chesil Visitor Centre which is to your right. There's a useful cafe here, and the visitor centre keeps a regular log of both bird sightings and hauls from the nearby waters which might include shrimp, grey mullet, bass, shore crab and goby. Whether or not you patronise the centre, you'll also need to decide how to progress from here, and you have two options. One option is to stick to the footway which proceeds beside the busy A354, passing an oil storage depot which is to your left, going over a couple of roundabouts, and reaching the outskirts of Fortuneswell (13). Keep to the right-hand pavement as you enter the built-up area, and immediately beyond the Little Ship pub turn right onto Pebble Lane and follow it gently uphill to the Cove House Inn, here joining a wide promenade. The alternative option from the Chesil Visitor Centre is to climb on to the top of Chesil Bank and follow it all the way to the Cove House Inn, going forward onto the wide promenade, remembering that there's always the possibility of escape back to the road if it all gets too much. Whichever option you choose you get a fine view of Fortuneswell and the hills towering above it, and the sight of Chesil Bank ending abruptly at the base of the limestone cliffs. The first option is certainly more tame but makes for good quick walking, while in direct contrast, the shingle bank provides much better views, and as previously explained, is pretty tough. Even just the stretch from the visitor centre to Fortuneswell may seem akin to that time you made love on top of a tumble drier – good to have experienced it, fun to pretend you've really enjoyed it, but something you're unlikely to want to do again.

# Day 21
# Fortuneswell to Weymouth 15 miles (341 miles)

**Difficulty rating:** Moderate
**Terrain rating:** ▲▲▲
**Highlights:** Portland Bill, Cheyne Weares, Church Ope Cove

The promenade beyond the Cove House Inn provides pleasant walking, with good views ahead to tall cliffs, the tallest you'll have seen since West Bay, with sheds perched precariously on the hillside.

Don't go right to the end of the promenade beyond the Cove House, instead bear left close to the end onto a signed tarmac path which climbs reasonably gently at first, but once the tarmac stops and is replaced by grass, the going gets a great deal tougher and steps aid the last bit of the climb. Pause here to enjoy superb views back to Chesil Bank, The Fleet, Weymouth and across to the spectacular chalk cliffs between Weymouth and Lulworth and beyond. Bear right at the top and now enjoy a quite fantastic walk, some of the best walking of the entire journey, along a clear green path high above the sea with great stacks of limestone to the left, and the cliff-edge to the right. Keep to the obvious cliff-edge path, passing a former quarry and walking underneath a rock arch, enjoying fantastic views back to Chesil Bank all the while. There's another climb, but something of an anticlimax follows at the crest of the hill as you suddenly find yourself confronted by very ugly housing developments that are to your left; despite this, the walking remains airy and enjoyable, and rather easier as you proceed along a grassy path close to the cliff-edge. Moreover, you can continue to admire the amazing sheer cliff faces, the views out to sea, and the exciting prospect of Portland Bill getting closer with each step. You pass a business park which is to your left, then walk by the inland side of a coastguard station; beyond the coastguard station you can veer right to follow a good path along the cliff-edge, noting the old lighthouse to your left. You're forced away from the cliff-edge by fencing and development immediately behind, but then resume a southerly course to reach Portland Bill (4.5), the southernmost point in Dorset, and proceed to the areas of quarried stone immediately before reaching the sea. The South West Coast Path is signposted left, round the headland, but you should detour, weather permitting, for a scramble through the rocks to a flat stone platform and the very distinctive Pulpit Rock. There are warnings about climbing onto the rock, and if in doubt you shouldn't attempt it, but the views from here are potentially among the best you will meet anywhere on the south coast; on a clear day you may be able to see Start Point which you will recall was one of the most southerly points in Devon! Having enjoyed a rock scramble, you may also wish to visit the lighthouse and enjoy a cuppa at the handy cafe.

Begin working your way up the east-facing coast of Portland, along a clear path proceeding north-eastwards from the cafe, passing some beach huts and then along low cliffs; look out for a hand crane – a stone crane now used to lower boats into the water – on the right, and close to it, the impressive Cave Hole; a low but quite broad cave furnished with little columns of rock. In due course, at Cheyne Weares, you're forced up to the road; bear right to follow alongside it and you will soon reach a turn off to a car park on the right. It's worth detouring to the car park to enjoy a very fine high level viewpoint; a noticeboard tells you which birds to look out for here – these may include black redstart, whinchat, fulmar, kittiwake, skylark and swift. Return to the road and continue along it briefly, then turn right onto a signed path that takes you to Church Ope Cove. This is quite an exciting path with some downhill zigzagging and then a twisting, undulating, under-cliff walk brings you to within a whisker of the cove itself; with its stark shingle beach it lacks the charm and charisma of some of the golden Cornish coves but is still a delightful spot. Follow the coast path as marked, now climbing very steeply (there's a signed detour to the thirteenth-century ruins of St Andrew's Church if you fancy a bit of extra climbing), and continue past the fine fifteenth-century Rufus Castle, also known as the Bow and Arrow Castle. Now comes the most exhilarating piece of walking on the east side of the island, as you bear right as signposted and right again on a clear track, shortly forking left to proceed along the high cliff-tops. The views from here to the Dorset coastline east of Weymouth are tremendous, on a good day extending as far as Durlston Head and the Purbeck Hills, and far down below you will see a fascinating under-cliff landscape.

Now an anticlimax follows; you pass a quarry which is to your left, and then continue past the Grove Young Offender Institution (YOI) also to your left. The views to the right are still superb, but the walls of the YOI certainly detract from the majesty of the scene. Carry on beside the YOI, going forward onto a metalled track; despite the 'private' sign this is the correct route. Then follow the coast path signposts very carefully as, having at last left the YOI behind, you veer away from the cliff-tops across rough grass in a north-westerly direction, and aim for the inland side of the very prominent mast you can see ahead of you. Still observing the very good signposting, go forward to a tarmac road which takes you to the entrance to the Verne Prison, formerly a fortress. Just behind the prison entrance sign is a tunnel mouth leading into the prison, the access road going across an extraordinarily deep moat, so vertigo sufferers beware! You might expect the coast path to forge a route round to the right (east) side of the Verne, but the MOD installations and other development between the Verne and the east-facing coast, including what is the largest artificial harbour in Britain, renders that impracticable. Accordingly, the coast path chooses to turn hard left onto a road that leads past a turning to the High Angle Battery, a late nineteenth-century fortification cut into the rough grassy hilltop, and goes forward along a grassy strip to the right side of the road, providing pleasanter walking than the tarmac. Soon you reach a magnificently sited war memorial, the view from which provides a splendid climax to your Portland walk, with excellent views to the coastlines to both east and west of Weymouth. From the war memorial go on to a road marked 'NO THROUGH ROAD' leading steeply downhill to the right; turn right to follow it briefly then shortly left onto a path that takes you to a main road. Turn right onto the main road and soon cross it to gain access to a green area including the *Spirit of Portland* sculpture depicting a quarryman and fisherman. Continue briefly westwards from the green up the slope and you'll find yourself at the point which you'll recognise as the top of the very steep path from the Cove House. Retrace your steps to the Cove House to be faced with another choice to make. The easier option begins with a walk down Pebble Lane to the A354 by the Little Ship Inn; follow the A354 past the first roundabout – where you could detour eastwards to Castletown to visit Henry VIII's castle on the north shore – and go on to the second roundabout beyond the oil storage depot. Now follow a green path along the right (east) side of the road, with the waves gently lapping the shore immediately to your right. The path is actually the course of an old railway and there are fine views, even from this low level, to the coastline east of Weymouth. The path brings you to the Ferry Bridge (12) which you simply cross to return to the mainland and resume your walk on to the centre of Weymouth. The alternative option from the Cove House is a tramp along Chesil Bank, but remember to leave it to drop down to the visitor centre on the south side of Ferry Bridge to gain access to said bridge. Otherwise you'll be stuck on the bank all the way back to Abbotsbury, an awfully long way back.

Now on the signed path heading eastwards from the A354 towards Weymouth, you initially follow a metalled footpath, quickly veering north-eastwards; for a while you're on the Rodwell Trail, the course of an old railway, but shortly you bear right onto a parallel coast path. As you approach the ruins of Sandsfoot Castle, you need to bear left onto a road which initially follows parallel with the Rodwell Trail and passes a park giving access to the castle ruins. You are now tramping through the suburbs of Weymouth, the biggest town you've met since you pulled away from Torquay. Shortly before the road reaches the main Weymouth–Portland road you bear right onto a road and go forward to another right turn onto a road that brings you back to the coast again. Follow a footpath over cliffs into Nothe Gardens, looking ahead to Nothe Fort; you could detour to the end of the point to visit the fort, but to progress you need to veer sharply westwards and make your way to the Town Bridge to cross the River Wey, then once over the bridge, bear right to access the waterfront and then left to follow the front overlooking Weymouth Bay. Weymouth (15) has been described as the 'Georgian seaside resort par excellence,' and unless you are in a great hurry, you are sure to want to take some time out of your walking schedule to explore what it has to offer. There has been a settlement here from the tenth century, and it is infamous for being the first place in England to suffer from the Black Death in 1348. It became a seaport with industries including not only fishing but sailmaking and brewing, and ferry links developed from here to France and the Channel Islands. Its potential as a watering place was commended to the Duke of Gloucester who wintered here in 1780; George III first visited here nine years later and regularly stayed at the Gloucester Hotel. There is some splendid Georgian architecture including the Royal Crescent, built around 1807, and Royal Terrace, dating back to 1816, and there are a number of pleasant groups of Georgian and early Victorian houses, some with fine ironwork balconies, some bow-windowed, stretching in a line from the harbour to the end of the promenade. The focal point of the town is the statue of a fully-robed George III carrying a sceptre before an outsized stool with a crown on it, erected on the Esplanade in 1809. The town, regularly visited by Thomas Hardy, was the birthplace of the writer Thomas Love Peacock, and John Endicott sailed from here in the 1620s, not far behind the Pilgrim Fathers, on his way to establishing a settlement at Salem, on the Atlantic coast, in what is now Massachusetts. It has an excellent range of amenities including a railway terminal with direct trains to London (the first station on the south coast since Exmouth) and, just over the road from the station, an outdoor store where you can replenish your supplies of socks, boot leather treatment and Kendal mint cake. But don't ask about buses; on enquiring about buses to Portland, I was told by the lady working there that she didn't use the buses. So green campaigners of Weymouth still have some work to do!

# Day 22
# Weymouth to Lulworth 12 miles (353 miles)

**Difficulty rating:** Easy at first, becoming moderate then strenuous
**Terrain rating:** ▲▲▲▲
**Highlights:** Swyre Head, Hambury Tout, Lulworth Cove

You leave Weymouth by proceeding along the waterfront Esplanade, then carry on along the sea wall keeping Lodmoor Country Park to your left, separated from it by the A353. From the sea wall you go forward to a road passing the Spyglass Inn, then bear right onto a grassy slope above Furzy Cliff, ascend and then drop down to Bowleaze Cove. Here you have to negotiate a holiday park then, having passed to the right of the Riviera Hotel, follow the coast path past Redcliff Point, landslip activity having forced the coast path to be routed some way back from the sea at this point. There's another climb and a drift further inland to pass Black Head, beyond which you head initially seawards again but are then directed away from the sea once more, downhill to an area of woodland. Reaching a road, you bear right, your South West Coast Path route now incidentally reunited with the inland alternative from West Bexington, and walk down to Osmington Mills (4.5); proceed past the Smugglers Inn, keeping it to your right, and then veer left to ascend back onto the cliff-tops which here are clad with quite thick vegetation. You then descend through trees to Ringstead, arriving at and following a track which veers away from the sea towards a car park and useful cafe, but just prior to these amenities the coast path bears right. Follow the track uphill, passing through more woodland, then emerge onto Burning Cliff above Ringstead Bay; from here, go forward onto a narrow road to pass another St Catherine's Chapel, albeit not such an interesting landmark as its namesake at Abbotsbury. Above the chapel you bear right along a path through woods, heading resolutely south-eastwards and rising to the cliff-top.

Now, after rather bitty and not very rewarding travelling from Weymouth, the walking gets really very good indeed, but you should prepare yourself for some hard work! Keep to the cliff-top round the headland of White Nothe, passing just to the right of the old coastguard cottages, then descend to a green hollow known as the Warren, the calm before an onslaught of three huge climbs and descents separating you from Lulworth. You begin with a climb above a sheer but crumbling chalk cliff, then drop down past Bat's Head before another big climb to Swyre Head; you descend from there and climb once more, getting tremendous views to the limestone arch Durdle Door, one of the most famous sights on the entire coastline of Great Britain. The coast path itself doesn't provide the best views to it, but a detour is available for you to inspect it more closely. Keep on uphill to Hambury Tout above St Oswald's Bay and from here enjoy magnificent views ahead to Lulworth Cove, a bay about 1,500 feet across almost enclosed by cliffs, with high cliffs of crumbling chalk forming a natural amphitheatre around the oyster-shaped bay. It's now downhill all the way to the cove itself; you walk along an excellent stone path to the Heritage Centre, turning right here and on to the village green, although as you walk from the Heritage Centre towards the green you could detour to Stair Hole immediately below you, with its caves pierced through the mass of limestone. Beyond the green, you arrive at the village of Lulworth Cove (12) which with its neighbour West Lulworth a little to the north provide a very reasonable range of amenities.

# Day 23
## Lulworth to Swanage 19 miles* (372 miles)

**Difficulty rating:** Strenuous
**Terrain rating:** ▲▲▲▲
**Highlight:** Worbarrow Tout, Tyneham Cap, St Aldhelm's Head
* This presupposes the coastal path from Lulworth to Gaulter Gap is open

The next 7 miles to Gaulter Gap provide some of the best and most memorable walking on the whole of the south coast, but there is a nasty catch; the walk passes through army firing ranges, known as the Lulworth Ranges, and this stretch is normally closed to walkers on weekdays. However, it is usually open throughout the school holidays as well as most weekends, and I really urge you to plan your itinerary carefully to ensure you can do this walk, checking ahead to ensure the range walk is open on the day in question. Otherwise you will not only miss out on what could be one of the highlights of the complete walk, but you will be faced with a painfully lengthy inland detour which could add up to 12 extra miles to your itinerary. At best this will require you to follow the B3070 from Lulworth Cove and north-eastwards via West Lulworth, Lulworth Camp and East Lulworth to West Holme. Bear right to follow a minor road eastwards via East Holme to Stoborough, right again to proceed via Creech to Steeple, and on from Steeple to Kimmeridge village, continuing along a lane beyond the road end to arrive back at the coast beyond the ranges at Gaulter Gap. At worst, if the B3070 is shut beyond Lulworth Camp, you'll need to follow the B3071 up to Wool, bearing right just before the railway station onto a minor road via East Stoke to West Holme, then simply stay on that road eastwards to East Holme and on to Kimmeridge. If you're a day or more out of kilter in your schedule, you may just prefer to cut your losses and take a taxi, and calm your conscience by saying you'll return some other day to do the Lulworth Ranges walk. And rue the day lost by staying an extra day in Budleigh Salterton to be first in the queue for the chemist's weekly delivery of fresh blister pads!

Assuming all is well, you proceed along the road to just short of Lulworth Cove, then bear left up steps by the beach cafe; continue uphill then bear right to follow a fence round the top of the cove, before bearing right again and descending steps, then veering left at the foot of these steps. Go forward to Pepler's Point with good views back to Lulworth Cove, then proceed eastwards to enter the Lulworth Ranges at Fossil Forest, which consists of rock that once contained tree stumps from a forest that existed well over 100 million years ago. As you proceed through the Ranges it is impossible to go wrong as the path is marked by yellow posts. The coastline itself provides the most spectacular scenery but it is worth looking inland too as you continue, for the absence of farming in the surrounding countryside owing to Army activity has produced a kind of green wilderness that is almost unique so close to the coastline of southern England. Next, swing north-eastwards to walk round Mupe Bay, climbing very steeply over Bindon Hill with its awesome sheer chalk cliffs, then drop equally steeply to the tiny cove at Arish Mell; further steep chalk cliffs zealously guard its entrance. The next back-breaking climb takes you round Worbarrow Bay past the Iron Age fort at Flower's Barrow, and then there's another big descent to the south-east corner of the bay; it's worth detouring to the Worbarrow Tout viewpoint, giving a glorious view of Worbarrow Bay, Mupe Bay and Bindon Hill, as well as back to Hambury Tout and forward to St Aldhelm's Head. From here you swing from south-eastwards to eastwards to begin the assault on Gad Cliff, still following the yellow markers. Having reached this cliff-top, you can detour left to visit the deserted village of Tyneham; this village was evacuated in late 1943 in order that the Army could use it as part of the D-Day preparations, but the villagers were fated never to return and it is now, literally, a museum piece. Of particular interest is the lovingly maintained church and the school, furnished to look just as it did before the evacuation. Having returned to the main coast path through the Ranges, you proceed just north of eastwards on Gad Cliff, but should detour again to your left to climb onto Tyneham Cap, just under 550 feet above the sea, and enjoy what on a clear day will be a quite tremendous view. Back on the marked route, you now swing south-eastwards and descend past Horbarrow Bay; you pass the modest headland of Broad Bench and veer north-eastwards to follow round Kimmeridge Bay along a clear track, passing a 'nodding donkey' oil pump which marks the end of the Lulworth Ranges walk. Veering south-eastwards again, keeping Kimmeridge Bay to your right, you pass the cottages at Gaulter Gap (7) where if you need some refreshment you can join a track leading north-eastwards to the grey limestone village of Kimmeridge. It's this track that the poor unfortunates who've had to miss out on the walk through the Lulworth Ranges will use to rejoin the coast.

At Gaulter Gap you climb some steps to reach a car park, then go round to a further car park and join a road briefly, turn left and proceed along the cliffs once more. There's a steep climb to reach the original site of Clavell Tower, a circular three-storey folly, later used as a coastguard lookout, built by a vicar named John Richards around 1830, and boasting what Pevsner describes as a 'scholarly mixture of motifs (including a) colonnade of Tuscan columns of primitive type favoured by French painters'. At the time of writing it has been dismantled and there are plans to relocate it slightly further away from the cliff-edge to safeguard it for future generations. There's then some quite strenuous up-and-down work, including a number of footbridge crossings over streams, as you proceed in a direction that's generally just south of east past Rope Lake Head, Egmont Point and Egmont Bight with its delightful waterfall and woodland. The cliffs along this section are known as the Kimmeridge Ledges and the path, high above the sea, is often perilously close to sheer drops. This splendid section culminates in a big climb onto the limestone peak of Houns-tout Cliff; you descend sharply from the summit, then owing to cliff slips are forced to swing inland, bearing left across a field and embankment to reach a road. Bear right onto the road heading initially back towards the sea, but then bear left onto a track heading to the hamlet of Hillbottom. This marks the halfway point of the entire south coast walk. Congratulations on making it this far, keep hanging in there, and remind yourself that once beyond this point, it's less far to keep on to the end than it is to turn back!

On reaching the hamlet you bear right onto an unmade road, right once more onto a track, then shortly left and then right again onto a path that crosses West Hill and returns to the cliffs, with the inlet of Chapman's Pool to your right. Heading in a predominantly southerly direction, you now proceed via Emmets Hill towards St Aldhelm's or St Alban's Head. There's a huge descent and climb as you near the headland, some 354 feet above the sea with views on a clear day to Portland and the Isle of Wight, and a good place to view guillemots and razorbills which nest hereabouts. You should detour to the left to visit St Aldhelm's Chapel, a solid, perfectly square construction built in the latter half of the twelfth century, possibly as a marker for Channel sailors. Now veering north-eastwards, you stay close to the sea as you proceed to Winspit, where you're forced a little away from the sea and down into a valley to get round some quarries; Purbeck stone quarries will feature quite largely in the landscape all the way from here to Swanage. On reaching the lane in the valley, the coast path turns right onto it but it's worth detouring left onto the lane in order to visit Worth Matravers (14), a very pretty village with a pond and cottages of Purbeck stone. For centuries Worth Matravers was one of the main centres for the quarrying of Purbeck marble; used in the construction of the tower and spire of Salisbury Cathedral. The church of St Nicholas boasts Norman windows, nave and chancel, and in the churchyard is the grave of Benjamin Jesty, a Dorset yeoman, said to be the first person to inoculate a patient with cowpox to immunise against smallpox.

Back on the coast path, follow the lane at Winspit briefly back towards the sea, then go left to regain the coast. Not for long, though, as after proceeding north-eastwards you're forced left, inland, to negotiate the quarries at Seacombe, then swing hard right to return to the coast. Now the going becomes very straightforward as you head due east for nearly 3 miles, keeping the limestone cliff-edges close to your right. You pass Dancing Ledge, where a swimming pool was cut by quarrymen at the beginning of the last century, then go into Durlston Country Park, passing Anvil Point and lighthouse and veer north-eastwards past the Tilly Whim Caves. These large black holes in the steep limestone cliff face opened as a visitor attraction in 1887 but closed in 1976. From here you carry on to Durlston Head; once again there are excellent views from this headland, but what makes it particularly interesting is its globe, which was made out of Portland stone and completed in 1887, one assumes to coincide with the opening of the nearby caves. Pass close to a visitor centre and also Durlston Castle, built around 1890 not as a defensive fortification but as a restaurant, and indeed it still boasts a bar and restaurant today. Beyond the castle you follow a wide track, bearing left to reach a road. Turn right onto this road, then right into Belle Vue Road, but as this road bends left, bear right onto grass and proceed beside Durlston Bay to Peveril Point and its coastguard station. Depending on the tide, either a footway by the shore or a road can be used to head westwards from Peveril Point to join the promenade taking you into Swanage (19), the last town on the South West Coast Path. Swanage was a port in Anglo-Saxon times and King Alfred's defeat of the Danes in Swanage Bay north of the town in 877 is commemorated here by a column topped with cannonballs. It became a trading centre for Purbeck marble but in the early nineteenth century began to develop as a resort; baths, with billiard and coffee rooms, were erected close to the shore in 1825 and Princess Victoria visited here in 1835. The railway arrived around 1880, and with a boom in the building of boarding-houses about that time, the town blossomed as a holiday resort. Architecturally there's little to see, but there are a couple of curiosities. The town's clock tower stood at the southern end of London Bridge until 1867 and, providing another capital connection, the facade of the Town Hall was a re-erection of the Portland stone facade of the Mercers' Hall in the City of London, designed by Sir Christopher Wren. It's an unremarkable and unpretentious place; my brother's greatest memory of it was, and I guess always will be, his excitement at seeing the BBC film crew present just outside the town to record what has proved to be one of the classic moments in TV sitcom; Michael Crawford alias Frank Spencer dangling from a cliff-edge holding on to the back bumper of his car!

# Day 24
# Swanage to Bournemouth 14 miles (386 miles)

**Difficulty rating:** Moderate
**Terrain rating:** ▲▲▲
**Highlights:** Ballard Point, Old Harry, Studland Heath

Follow the promenade out of Swanage, leaving it by proceeding north-westwards, away from the sea along Ulwell Road, passing All Saints Church. At the next big road junction bear right into Ballard Way, going into a private estate, then veer left as signposted, and north-eastwards, to a cliff-top green. Bear left on the green to return to true coastal walking, going down steps and over a footbridge then up further steps to arrive on Ballard Down. Bearing right, through a gateway, you veer more eastwards to pass a trig point and reach Ballard Point, then veer north-east again along the cliff-tops to reach The Foreland, the last headland of any significance on the Dorset coast and indeed on the South West Coast Path. Looking to your right you will see the Old Harry rock stacks, one of the most memorable sights off the Dorset coast, and you will get plenty more views of them as you proceed eastwards from Bournemouth. It's amazing to think that these rock stacks were once part of a continuous chalk ridge linking up with the Isle of Wight! The sheer cliffs are particularly impressive here, providing a grandstand finish to your long acquaintance with the South West Coast Path, and although there's still plenty more cliff walking to come, there is arguably little or nothing better, on the mainland at any rate, until you reach the Seven Sisters in East Sussex. At the headland you swing south of west to continue along the cliffs, an easy walk descending throughout, then bear right and go down to South Beach just east of the village of Studland. Proceed along the beach then ascend steps to walk along a wooded platform and arrive at a beach access road. You could choose, rather than going down to

South Beach, to walk straight on to the middle of Studland instead, then having passed through the village (4.5) with its attractive Norman village church, follow signs to the Middle Beach car park and meet up with the main route. From Studland it is beach walking all the way to South Haven Point, heading north-eastwards alongside Studland Bay with Studland Heath Nature Reserve to your left; the reserve is an area of heath, woodland and mudflats, providing a haven for lizards, snakes and roe deer. There's a somewhat bizarre aspect to the walk beside Studland Bay from Studland, in the form of a nudist beach, and however blasé you feel about the dishevelled state you're in after the best part of 400 miles' walking since Land's End, you're likely to feel somewhat overdressed as well as self-conscious as you go by! Finally, you swing north-westwards to arrive at South Haven Point (8) and the Sandbanks Ferry, with Poole Harbour, the largest natural harbour on the south coast, suddenly opening out impressively to your left; the chain ferry, which saves you what would be a 36-mile walk round the harbour, runs all day every day and is very popular with motorists as well as cyclists and walkers.

As you smugly hop onto the ferry having walked past what could be quite a long queue of motorists wondering how long they'll have to wait to get across the water, you can reflect with huge satisfaction on what you've achieved – the completion of the South West Coast Path section of the south coast walk.

There's no room for complacency, and once your short ferry journey has been completed you'll no doubt be anxious to get going again with still five counties, including the Isle of Wight, to cover. As you walk up the slipway, your way forward appears to be straight ahead, but by turning hard right in front of the Haven Hotel, you will be able, by means of a metal ladder, to access the rocks. A sign indicates that this path is shut on 2 January. You have to endure a brief scramble over the rocks but very shortly you find yourself on the sands, and it is now an easy walk along the beach with the houses of Sandbanks to your left. There are excellent views to the Old Harry Rocks across the entrance to Poole Harbour, and in fact the headland guarded by the rocks will remain in sight for most of the next 25 miles. Poole Harbour is one of Europe's most extensive natural harbours, with more than 90 miles of coastline (now do you still feel a pang of conscience about taking the ferry?) and 10 square miles of tidal waters. If you want another piece of trivia, it was the third largest embarkation point for US troops for the D-Day landings. In a few hundred yards you find yourself effectively on a causeway between the sea to your right and a large swathe of Poole Harbour to your left; there's fairly easy access to shops and cafes here, but especially if you've had a long wait for the Sandbanks ferry, you will probably want to press on.

Ahead of you is the great sprawl of Bournemouth, one of the largest settlements you will meet on your walk. Just past the Sandbanks brasserie and bar, you are able to access the metalled promenade and indeed it is possible for you to stick to this for the next 7 miles or so. It is assuredly good for your morale and confidence to reel off so many miles so quickly, and although Bournemouth pier is always that little bit further than you think, it is superbly fast walking with the added bonus of great views out to the Isle of Wight, and, to your left, the constant fascination of the cliffs. There are occasional steps or pathways up to the cliff-tops, but it is impossible to construct a satisfying coastal route using the tops of the cliffs because those tops are broken up by steep wooded pine-clad valleys, or chines as they are known, once favoured by smugglers seeking an easy passage away from the shore. Simply continue along the promenade, ticking off the chines as you go – Alum, Branksome, Durley among them – and enjoying the variety of colour on the cliff faces, from the light brown of the rock to the vivid purple of the heather and the occasional profusion of brightly coloured flowers. There are plenty of pine trees about too, serving as a reminder that Bournemouth was built around profusions of pines. In due course you will reach the town pier (14), which is as close as you get to the centre of Bournemouth, and if you've been longing for some good old retail therapy, or, more prosaically, a train or bus home, this is a good place to leave the seafront. At the start of the nineteenth century, Bournemouth as such did not exist at all. In 1812, Lewis Tregonwell built himself a holiday home here and many others followed suit, including local landowner George Jervis who laid out a marine village in the neighbourhood of Tregonwell's house. Following a recommendation by the eminent physician Dr Granville that climate was an aid to recuperation, the second half of the nineteenth century saw Bournemouth expand into one of the leading English seaside resorts and acquire the soubriquet 'Queen of the South Coast'. There are spacious promenades, parks and gardens cover 2,000 acres or one sixth of Bournemouth's total town area, as well as long sandy beaches and cliff-top hotels. The association between the town and genteel leisure is highlighted in the fact that it has its own Symphony Orchestra traditionally based at the Winter Gardens concert hall which dates back to 1875. The town enjoys a mild climate, beautiful golden sands and promenades and garden walks given natural shelter by the 100-foot cliffs. This is all beginning to sound like a holiday brochure, so it perhaps should be remembered that it has its social problems and is not loved by everybody. *Brewer's* refers a little euphemistically, one suspects, to its 'lively club and drug scene' and the authors of *Crap Towns II* highlight its 'very ordinary shopping precinct, very hostile clubs, love of traffic and depressing labyrinthine suburbs', expressing the hope that 'the sea level will rise and wash it all away'.

# Day 25
# Bournemouth to Barton-on-Sea 18 miles* (404 miles)

**Difficulty rating:** Easy at first, becoming moderate
**Terrain rating:** ▲▲▲
**Highlights:** Warren Hill, Christchurch, Steamer Point
*This mileage presupposes that the Mudeford ferry is NOT used

Immediately beyond Bournemouth pier, it is worth leaving the promenade to join the cliff-top route. This is accessed not hugely promisingly by a climb up a road flanked on one side by KFC and on the other by Harry Ramsden's, but once up on the cliff-top the walking is easy and enjoyable, with very good views out to sea. In particular, you should look out on the left for an Italianate villa which houses the excellent Russell-Cotes Art Gallery and Museum. You pass one particularly tall block of quite vivid white-coloured flats, and these will feature in almost every view back towards Bournemouth until the other side of Hurst Castle spit, as well as from the Needles Battery on the Isle of Wight. As the cliff-top road bends away left, your metalled path drops down to another pier, that of Boscombe (2); you could opt to join the seaside promenade again here, but there is easy and obvious access back up onto the cliff-tops beyond Boscombe Pier and it is a greatly superior route. You pass through some fine and beautifully kept gardens then through a gate with the local Rotary Club motif inscribed on it and out along a cliff-top path that provides absolutely superb views forward to Hengistbury Head and the Isle of Wight. It's good, easy walking with a mixture of metalled and grassy surfaces, and it is disappointing to have to leave the cliff-top, but leave it you must; the houses of Southbourne are interposed between the coast road and the sea and there's no cliff-top route past them. Accordingly, when you reach the signboard marked 'Gordon's ZigZag' and a bench dedicated to Kathleen Lawrence, use the steps to drop down to the seaside promenade and plough on eastwards. You pass a rather ugly cafe complex and not far beyond it the reassuring metalled promenade ends; however, an obvious and clearly marked grassy path takes you on beside the dunes, and you now head resolutely for the stark green lump of Warren Hill. Occupied many times since the early hunter-gatherers of the Stone Age and used as a cemetery in the Bronze Age, it has an astonishing variety of wildlife including 300 species of bird and, wait for it, 600 species of moth!

There's a choice of routes to the top of Warren Hill, you could even use a metalled road if you fancied it, but whichever way you choose, you'll be rewarded with a quite magnificent view in all directions, including Durlston Head, Swanage, the Isle of Wight, and ahead of you Christchurch Harbour with the town of Christchurch and its Priory clearly visible. It may not have the drama of certain views on the South West Coast Path, but for variety it's one of the best views on the whole of the south coast. Now continue eastwards from Warren

Hill along a clear path which takes you past Hengistbury Head; this is really splendid walking, and in due course you could opt to leave the main wide path and follow one that stays closer to the cliff-top before returning to the main path again. Aim for the long spit immediately ahead that you'll see is lined with beach huts, use the main path to drop down to sea level, and here you need to make a choice. If you are to miss out Christchurch and are going to cross to Mudeford Quay by ferry, saving yourself roughly 6 miles of walking, you are advised to follow the spit to its very end, passing to the right of the line of huts. It seems a long way to the end of the spit, but you are saving yourself up to two hours or so by missing Christchurch, so you shouldn't feel too hard done by. Pause at the end of the spit, effectively the gateway to Christchurch Harbour and another wildlife and plant life haven – a signboard invites you to look out for such intriguingly named plants as the sea rocket and cat's ear – then walk round to the other side of the huts to arrive at the landing stage from which ferries run to Mudeford Quay across the harbour mouth every day in summer but only at weekends in winter. If the ferry is unavailable or you fancy a trip to Christchurch (such a lovely town that I recommend you do in fact walk via Christchurch rather than take the ferry, despite the extra walking involved), bear left, away from the spit, along a path that hugs the water but eventually comes up to join a metalled road; a signed path, indicating you are now on the Stour Valley Way, leads off the road to the right and it is now a very straightforward walk, initially along a footpath then along a pleasant riverside greensward. Passing level with Christchurch Priory (the clock on the tower tells you how much later you are than expected) and it is no doubt to your consternation that you realise you have to walk quite a bit further upstream to reach the bridge crossing. Cross the bridge, bear first right into Willow Drive and then turn right again along St Margaret's Avenue, which you follow to the centre of Christchurch (8) and its priory. The priory church, which dates from 1094 and thankfully survived the dissolution, is England's longest parish church, around 300 feet if you have the energy to tramp it, and its tower contains the two oldest bells in the county, dating back to 1370. The church's structure is a blend of styles from Saxon times to the Renaissance; there is a splendid Norman nave with massive pillars, a fourteenth-century reredos which portrays the Christmas story in carved stone, choir stalls which are older than those in Westminster Abbey, and a monument to the poet Shelley. The town itself, which has Saxon origins, has an excellent range of amenities and many fine old buildings including the remains of a Norman house and castle, and is certainly pleasanter to potter in than Bournemouth. From Christchurch to Emsworth, at the border between Hampshire and West Sussex, much of the journey described below will coincide with the Solent Way which is a waymarked route linking these two towns; you may also see 'E9' waymarks, 'E9' being a European coastal route containing large sections of the south coast of England.

Exit Christchurch along Castle Street to begin what is now a rather messy walk back to Mudeford Quay, and I suspect that if the Mudeford ferry were available, you will feel excessively virtuous as you walk this section. Castle Street becomes Bridge Street; you cross two river bridges and after the second bear right into a car park, passing along the right side of the council offices and through the car park behind, bearing left past the entrance to the leisure centre. Go straight on through yet another car park which leads directly to a cycle/footpath, that in turn takes you eastwards to Stanpit, the road leading to Mudeford Quay. A footpath sign to the right gives the option of a walk along a parallel path by the quayside and good views to Stanpit Marsh Nature Reserve, but at Argyle Road you are forced back to the road. Follow it on, crossing a bridge over the river Mude then turning first right along a narrow road taking you to the attractive buildings and pub of Mudeford Quay (12). Whether you have used foot power or boat power, it is certainly good to get to Mudeford Quay and to look back across to the sand spit, the line of beach huts and Hengistbury Head behind. On a fine summer day the place will be packed, and you are unlikely to be on your own as you head eastwards from Mudeford Quay, passing two long lines of beach huts, those of Avon Beach and Friars Cliff. Immediately beyond the second line of huts there is again a choice. You could simply press on along the shore, but I recommend you bear left along a path running parallel with the shore and going uphill to reach the woodlands of Steamer Point Nature Reserve, which belonged to the Ministry of Defence until

1983 but is now a most attractive mixture of fauna and flora including birch, willow, oak and bluebell in season. From here a path drops via steps to the beach again but very soon you can climb a further flight of steps to detour to the magnificent Highcliffe Castle, which was built in the 1830s with gardens designed by Capability Brown; there is no cliff-top option immediately beyond Highcliffe Castle so use the steep steps to return to the shore. It's a bit of a trudge initially from here, but before long you find yourself on a wonderful wide path that proceeds resolutely alongside the sea. This is tremendous walking, with the Isle of Wight and particularly the Needles now seemingly very close, and the waves from the incoming tides crashing against the rocks nearby. In due course there are possibilities of gaining the cliff-top but in a sense this is a disappointment, for although the views are good you find yourself in a semi-urban environment with the houses and flats of Highcliffe just behind. It's more fun to be down below where you can at least pretend you are miles from civilisation! There's good news as you walk this bit: you've passed the 400-mile mark.

Almost too soon you reach a bridge crossing over a fast-flowing stream. You will see a small cove and note that there's no way forward beyond it, meaning that you are forced inland. This break in the cliffs, a sort of mini-chine, is Chewton Bunny, which sounds like a hot cheesy snack on offer in one of the posher cafes in Christchurch; sorry to disappoint, but a 'bunny' in this context is no more and no less than a natural glen and in fact this deep, tight valley was a well-known smuggling route 200 years ago. Cross the bridge over the stream and turn left, inland, over the grass and then up an obvious path, ignoring a tempting looking path leading to the right. A signed path leads off slightly to the left over a footbridge and you now follow this path uphill, not too steeply, to arrive at the busy New Milton to Christchurch road. Turn right, entering Hampshire here, and walk along this road for a few hundred yards, then right again down Western Avenue and you find yourself back on the cliff-top. It's lovely being back on the cliffs and the going will now be fast and easy all the way to Milford-on-Sea. Turn eastwards and enjoy a bracing walk along the greensward to Barton-on-Sea (18). I may be prejudiced by the fact that when I arrived there on a sunny July Saturday evening nothing was open except a restaurant selling overpriced omelettes, but Barton-on-Sea is not in my opinion a place to linger, its only real claim to fame being that it's the most south-westerly town in Hampshire, although it's just a few minutes on foot from here to New Milton with its shops and railway station.

# Day 26
# Barton-on-Sea to Lymington via Hurst Castle
# 14 miles (418 miles)

**Difficulty rating:** Easy
**Terrain rating:** ▲▲▲
**Highlights:** Hurst Castle, Keyhaven, Lymington

Unless you're hoping to find some more of the fossils that have been discovered hereabouts, some revealed to be the remains of sea creatures including crocodiles and sharks and dating back a mere 45 million years, don't allow yourself to be sucked down onto the under-cliff path once you reach Barton-on-Sea. It arrives at a spectacular dead end but waits for about a mile before deciding to do so with no escape route up the cliffs, and you would be crazy to try and forge a passage up the soft clay (I know I was, and I did.) Instead, go round the landside of the modest parade of shops and Beachcomber Café, and then walk along the cliff-top.

Once clear of the urban sprawl of Barton, New Milton and Old Milton, there is some lovely open cliff-top walking, with great views back past Bournemouth to the mouth of Poole Harbour and beyond, and the Isle of Wight to your right keeps getting closer and closer. There's a slight dip to cross another bunny, Beckton Bunny to be precise, and yes, you may see a few real bunnies as well among the wild grassy cliff-tops. Having negotiated Beckton Bunny, there's a slightly longer descent to reach Taddiford Gap with a path coming in from the nearby road. Climbing from Taddiford Gap, it's then easy cliff-top walking to reach Milford-on-Sea (4). At first sight this really does look most unattractive, with blocks of flats that look like little more than insensitive lumps of concrete blighting an otherwise beautiful and memorable landscape. If you're prepared to delve deeper, however, you may be in for a surprise or two, as it has an interesting history. It could have become another Bournemouth or Brighton if a local landlord Colonel William Cornwallis-West had had his way, but despite his attempts in the 1880s to turn it into a grand resort, its centre, away from the seafront, retains a certain dignity and charm; set back from the ugly concrete you will find Victorian and Edwardian villas, a narrow shopping street, a small green and a thirteenth-century church. This is a reconstruction of a previous Norman church, the rebuilding taking place at a time when Milford flourished with the sea salt industry that operated along this section of coastline. The seafront looks out directly towards the Needles, and at the time of my visit there was a most appropriately named cafe, Needles Eye. With the Isle of Wight now directly in front of you, you have reached the Solent, the stretch of sea separating the island from the mainland.

Beyond Milford-on-Sea it's decision time again. The promenade leads directly to a shingle bank. Proceed along the bank, looking down to your left for two foot-bridges over a channel running parallel with the bank; descend to cross the second footbridge towards Lymington. The recommended route continues along the shingle bank, the result of tidal shifts of huge quantities of shingle up the English Channel, as far as Hurst Castle and the adjacent lighthouse. Shingle tramping is never the easiest kind of walking, and although the top of the bank is reasonably firm and the going isn't too arduous, it will seem a bit of a slog. Moreover, when you arrive at Hurst Castle, you will need to remember to go round to the left of the fortifications, because if you follow your instincts and go to the right, you will hit a spectacular dead end. The earliest parts of the castle date back to around 1540, this being one of many defensive fortifications built by Henry VIII, and Charles I was held prisoner here for a short time before his trial and execution. The fortification was added to and greatly strengthened during the Napoleonic times, and it remains a most impressive construction today with its twelve-sided tower and two 38-ton guns on display. It is not, however, particularly attractive to look at, and if you want to pause for a breather before exploring the fortification, or indeed instead of doing so, you should progress via stone steps past the splendid bright white lighthouse, to the very end of the spit, which is as close you can get to the Isle of Wight while still on the mainland. This is a great spot; there are tremendous views to the island, back to the Keyhaven Nature Reserve. A seasonal ferry runs to the Keyhaven landing stage a little further up the direct route, and also all the way round to Durlston Head. Enjoy the views to this headland as you return along the shingle bank (assuming you're not using the ferry) to the second footbridge above, for once you descend to the bridge you will lose this wonderful view, only seeing it again when you reach the western end of the Isle of Wight. Now back on the direct route to Lymington, head resolutely by the side of the metalled Saltgrass Lane away from the footbridge heading north-eastwards then, as the road bends left, continue on the path, passing a little landing stage offering a ferry service to Hurst Castle and other boat trips including full-day fishing excursions.

From here it's a short walk to Keyhaven (8.5), surely one of the loveliest and most unspoilt of Hampshire coastal villages, although until the 1840s there was a flourishing industry here in the form of salt production from the nearby waters of the Solent. You pass close by the village with its profusion of boats, then swing right to briefly join a road to cross another channel before bearing right again along a clearly signed path promising Lymington ahead. What follows is a naturalist's and birdwatcher's paradise as the clearly marked path continues resolutely along the shoreline past the Keyhaven Nature Reserve with its profusion of marshes, inlets and lakes, its array of salt-resistant plants, and its huge variety of bird life at any time of year. As well as twitching for terns, for which the reserve is an important breeding site, you should look out for the curlew, dunlin, redshank and oystercatcher, and even if you are too busy striding ahead to consult your bird book, you can't fail to enjoy the sight of waders proceeding gingerly through the nearby waters. The course of the path is often sinuous and at times you won't feel as though you're making much progress towards the cluster of yachts of the Lymington marina, but will you mind? Perhaps you will if it's pouring with rain or you are disappointed by the lack of cliff scenery, of which there will be no more on the mainland at any rate until you get well past Southampton. But if the sun is shining, waters and lagoons are sparkling, and the only sounds you hear are the songs of the mass profusion of birds, this walk won't seem an inch too long. One word of warning; bear in mind that this path is very popular with cyclists and you may need to keep a wary eye out for them and give way to them if necessary.

Continuing along the shoreline and virtuously avoiding any shortcuts, you finally reach the mouth of Lymington Harbour, some entertainment value being provided in the form of the large and frequent Lymington–Yarmouth ferries negotiating their way in and out of the harbour. A slight anticlimax follows as a well-marked path – watch for and follow the Solent Way markers – directs you round the edge of the marina and through a large car park. Keep the harbour and marina to your right, and pass an attractive (and in the summer possibly very tempting) swimming pool which is to your left. Continue until you reach an uncompromising locked iron gate into what is another part of the marina. Once here you are forced left to reach a road which you follow to arrive in the centre of Lymington (14). Founded in 1200 as a harbour, and attractive to Isle of Wight travellers as providing the shortest feasible crossing to the island (as it still does today), it flourished on the salt industry from the Middle Ages right through to the mid-nineteenth century. When salt production declined, it became first and foremost a place associated with boats and boat-building, and it is now a major yachting centre. It has always been an affluent place, and you can see that in its fine old houses and shops. It has a particularly fine church with plasterwork ceilings and galleries, Tuscan columns and a white cupola on an old stone tower. The broad High Street boasts a variety of attractive houses and shops, many of the buildings dating back to the eighteenth century, while Quay Hill, with houses containing portholes, is described in *George Philip's County Guide to Hampshire* as '(exemplifying) the town's maritime atmosphere'.

# Day 27
# Lymington to Beaulieu 11 miles (429 miles)

**Difficulty rating:** Easy
**Terrain rating:** ▲▲
**Highlights:** St Leonards, Bucklers Hard, Beaulieu

You could choose any number of routes through Lymington but to leave it you need to get yourself to the main road bridge crossing over the harbour just above the town station, then, having crossed the bridge, bear right along Undershore Road, and follow it past the entrance to the ferry terminal and car park. Beyond the terminal the road swings from south-east to north-east and becomes South Baddesley Road; it's all a little tedious, and it's a relief to turn right off the main road... to join another road. This one, Lisle Court Road, just a few hundred yards beyond the terminal to the right, is at least much quieter and you have the luxury of some good views to the right to the coastline. At a sharp left bend in the road, turn right onto a footpath which drops gently down to the shore, then on reaching the shore bear left and walk eastwards along it. The going at first is rather rough, with no path to speak of, but shortly a stile gives access to a permissive path which follows a parallel course through woodland before emerging on to the shore again. This is actually very agreeable walking; it's much less walked than the path alongside Keyhaven Nature Reserve, and although one hesitates to say it's undiscovered, it's certainly easier to feel the silence and the solitude, with lovely views to your right across the Solent to the Isle of Wight and a bewitching mixture of woodland and water to your left. All too soon you reach a parking area and a house, at the bottom end of Tanners Lane, and you are forced inland now up this lane. You could go a little further along the shore, but very soon you reach an area of thick glutinous mud washed in by the constantly incoming tides, and I cannot rule out the possibility of your getting into serious difficulties. There is no right of way along here in any event, and no further access roads down to the shore this side of Beaulieu River which is the next major obstacle for coastal walkers. You can take consolation from the fact that even if you were able to continue beside the shore you would have to walk well away from the coastline to cross the Beaulieu River. It's a pity to have to leave the coast behind particularly as you won't be seeing it again for the next 10 miles. With a heavy heart, make your way up Tanners Lane away from the sea to begin a lengthy road walk to your next significant objective, Bucklers Hard. You bear right at the next road junction, signposted Bucklers Hard, which indicates that this village is 4.5 miles away, but it somehow seems more. You can at least put the map away as the road signposting is perfectly adequate to get you there, and there are some consolations; gaps in the hedgerows to your right reveal lovely views to the Solent and the Isle of Wight beyond, you may see the occasional New Forest pony (you are now on the fringes of the New Forest itself) and there are two interesting little settlements. Firstly there's Sowley with its pond which was created to satisfy the need of the monks from Beaulieu Abbey for fish, and then St Leonards, the one outstanding feature of which is the ruin of what was an enormous grange barn, which when complete was 216 feet long and 60 feet high. There is also the ruin of a chapel which dates back to about 1300.

At length, and about a mile beyond St Leonards, you reach a T-junction with a wider metalled road and straight over the road is Bucklers Hard (9). Use the kissing gate to access the swathe of green that separates two immaculate rows of Georgian redbrick cottages, built in the 1740s and 1750s which leads down to the river. It is almost too perfect. Originally intended as a new port town by the second Duke of Montagu, the village's heyday was in the latter half of the eighteenth century when it became an important shipbuilding centre. Many vessels for Lord Nelson's fleet were constructed here, including the *Agamemnon* which saw action at Trafalgar. These heady days, which effectively ended when the shipyard folded in 1811, are recalled in the village's excellent maritime museum. Descend to the water's edge alongside the left row of cottages, one of which houses the village pub, which, in keeping with the timeless atmosphere of the place, does not advertise its presence with garish signs or A-boards outside it, so you may be forgiven for missing it at first. When you reach the water's edge bear left along a very well signed path which will take you the couple of miles to Beaulieu. Two of Hampshire's gems and so close to each other. There is early on the option between a 'direct' and 'waterside' route, the latter certainly to be recommended even though it's a bit muddy on the ground and takes a bit longer; the views to the river Beaulieu through the trees are lovely, there is an air of exclusivity about the surroundings, and you almost feel as though you are trespassing in a huge private estate! Before long the two routes merge and it is then an easy walk, albeit sadly some way back from the river, to Beaulieu village itself (11). Turn right onto the main road past the abbey church to continue, but however much in a hurry you are, it's almost obligatory to stop awhile in the village, best known historically for its Cistercian abbey, founded by King John in 1204. Its refectory was to become the abbey church after the dissolution in 1538, and this church, with its fine stone pulpit reached by a vaulted staircase, is a very popular concert venue. Most people of course now associate Beaulieu with its motor museum in the grounds of Palace House, the home of Lord Montagu. The Tudor house was adapted from the original fourteenth-century abbey gatehouse, and was rebuilt in the nineteenth century to become the Palace House as it appears today. The motor museum, now one of the principal tourist attractions in Hampshire, was founded in 1952. The village, with its pretty street of eighteenth- and nineteenth-century houses, has numerous places for refreshments and is an ideal place to recharge the batteries before heading back to the coast again.

# Day 28
# Beaulieu to Hythe for Southampton 15 miles (444 miles)

**Difficulty rating:** Easy
**Terrain rating:** ▲▲
**Highlights:** Exbury Gardens, Lepe Country Park, Hythe

Leave Beaulieu, as stated, by following the road past the abbey church, heading north-eastwards towards Hythe. You now have an unavoidable 5 miles of tarmac crunching, and the first part of your road walk, after a very pleasant stroll along a green by the water's edge with the abbey church on the other side of the road, is hardly inspiring; there are some unpaved stretches, there is some uphill work, and there is a lot of traffic. You emerge from the shade of trees to find yourself in a much pleasanter landscape, with Beaulieu Heath, part of the New Forest, ahead of you, and you shortly arrive at a road junction. Turn hard right along the road signposted to Exbury, avoiding the right-angled turn signposted Holbury; the Exbury road is rather nicer than the latter, being narrower with much less traffic, but it is still a long road march, much of it in woodland with neither the coast nor Beaulieu River in sight. Exbury (4) is best known for its beautiful gardens, landscaped on what prior to World War One was an area of fine natural woodland with great cedars as well as mature oak and beech. It was here in the 1920s that Lionel de Rothschild established an important collection of rhododendrons, regarded as one of the greatest in the world. Exbury Gardens contains a fantastic array of trees and shrubs, with a huge variety of colours in a breathtaking setting with ponds and waterfalls on the River Beaulieu. You may feel you've earned a couple of hours off to enjoy them after all the tarmac tramping. Beyond the gardens, continue past the church and on reaching a sharp bend to the left, follow the minor road. As you follow it, give three cheers as you see the coast and the Isle of Wight ahead of you! The road heads initially south-east, bends south-west then at another, sharper bend, turns south-east again, heading in a dead straight line before swinging sharply eastwards and then south-eastwards to arrive at the shore again. As the road reaches the shore, look out for and join a signed shore-side public footpath going off to the right.

It's certainly nice to be off the road and on a proper path again, but the going can be rough, with a number of felled trees creating a succession of natural obstructions; moreover, it may be flooded at very high tide, in which case you may have to stick to the parallel road or wait till the waters recede, which shouldn't take too long. The views from the path are absolutely beautiful, with the Isle of Wight clearly visible across the Solent, and looking back you can see the Beaulieu River flowing into the Solent. It is all very pleasant and unspoilt. As you proceed eastwards along the shore-side path, you soon come to the visitor centre, with an excellent cafe, marking the entrance to Lepe Country Park. This is a hugely popular spot in the summer, as no doubt you will see from the number of vehicles in the adjacent car park. There used to be a shipbuilding centre hereabouts, with the 50-ton vessel *Greenwich* launched from here in 1784. The area of beach combined with the grasses and vegetation on the adjoining land is known for its variety of habitats with reed beds, marsh and brackish ponds supporting extensive marine and bird life. Birds to be seen on the shore include brent geese, oystercatchers, dunlins and grey plovers; the ponds attract the shelduck, redshank, moorhen, heron and kingfisher, and the sea may wash up bladderwrack, cockleshells, whelks, limpets and periwinkles. Unfortunately, there is no through route from here to Calshot, the next settlement along the coast, and it's necessary to follow Lepe Road inland just before the visitor centre. You can continue for roughly half a mile beyond the visitor centre beside the beach, going on to Stansore Point and beyond until a fence obstructs further progress, ironically within sight of the beach huts of Calshot. It is worth making this detour as around Stansore Point there are really good views to the Isle of Wight – indeed this is the site of gas mains to the island – and concrete platforms stand where sections of Mulberry Harbour were made before being taken to Normandy for the D-Day invasions. Then, sadly, it's back to Lepe Road inland from the visitor centre, although you could proceed through the country park on your return run for a bit of variety. Follow Lepe Road for half a mile or so, then turn right onto Stanswood Road which you follow for nearly 2.5 miles, doubtless cursing your inability to forge a through coastal route to Calshot. It's not unpleasant and has a nice rural feel, but you won't be sorry when it's over.

On reaching a T-junction with the B3053 Holbury to Calshot road, note the very conspicuous tower of Fawley Power Station straight ahead of you and bear right along it to reach Calshot (8). The village itself is uninteresting so pass through it quickly, reaching a point where the road forks right and left, creating a mini one-way system. Fork right here – as a walker it feels quite liberating to disobey a 'NO ENTRY' sign – and walk down to arrive at the shore once more. Cowes is now directly ahead of you across the Solent on the Isle of Wight. Bear left to continue along the back of the beach past a long line of beach huts; although you could walk along the beach itself, progress is quickest by walking immediately in front of the beach huts, but bear in mind that beach hut owners may claim the area in front of their hut for their own sunbathing and relaxation, forcing you either on to the beach or round the back of the hut beside the road. On reaching the last of the beach huts, follow the beach right round to the north tip known as Calshot Spit. You have reached Southampton Water, the widest strip of water separating two sections of coastline on the south coast, and from here you can enjoy great views towards Southampton, across to Netley, Hamble, Lee-on-the-Solent, the Spinnaker Tower at Portsmouth and beyond. It's also fascinating to watch the variety of craft on the water, from speedboats to huge passenger ferries. Now make your way round the spit, passing Calshot Castle which, sadly, is rather dwarfed by the huge and rather unsightly activities centre immediately opposite, but it is certainly worthy of exploration. The castle was built during Henry VIII's reign as a defence against the French, and has quite a stark feel with a stone keep and sheer walls punctuated by a few arrow-slit windows. The castle surrounds were used in the first half of the last century as a base for the RAF Flying Boat Squadron.

Continue round the west side of the spit and make your way back past the car park warden's kiosk to the neck of the spit, then bear right onto an obvious path which proceeds along the western shore of Southampton Water towards the massive Fawley Power Station complex. As you become level with the first of the two huge power station buildings, over to your left, you have to cross a swing bridge over a channel of water linking the power station with Southampton Water. Continue along the path, keeping the second power station building to your left. Having left the power station behind, you continue in a north-westerly direction, with extensive marshes, tidal saltings and mudflats to your right. You now approach the lovely Ashlett Quay area with pub and sailing club; your path makes a beeline away from the shore towards the pub, but you can carry on along the shore-side for a bit longer along a subsidiary path before being forced away from the shore to Ashlett (11). This village boasts a very pretty little green, a popular pub, The Jolly Sailor, and a large tide mill with millpond. On a fine day the allure of this pub, with beautiful views to the shores, will be irresistible, and indeed you should make the most of it as you are now forced inland to get round the massive Fawley Oil Refinery complex. Follow the road going inland from the pub, ignoring the left fork and going uphill to a T-junction; bear left at this junction and walk along the road to another T-junction where you turn right to reach the centre of the village of Fawley. Very shortly turn left into School Road, signposted Holbury, and follow this road through Fawley, then as the road swings sharp left, go straight ahead onto what is effectively a short cut to reach Fawley Road, the B3053 Holbury–Calshot road.

Turn right and follow this road – there is a pavement initially and then a parallel footpath so it's not as bad as it could be. On reaching a notice restricting access to allotment holders only, you will need to join the roadside for the short walk on to the junction with the A326. Turn right to follow this road through Holbury, using the cycle path/footway running alongside it on the left, until you come within sight of a sign indicating a roundabout junction. Cross the road and continue beside the A326 but on the right-hand side of it, passing Main Road; you then take the next turning on the right, a lane which heads just west of north away from the A326, and follow the lane past a little church. You arrive at a T-junction with Cadland Road, ignoring what looks like an old road coming in from the left just before the junction, turning right at this junction and then shortly left up New Road which looks as though it's heading straight into a works area. However, in a couple of hundred yards look out on your left for a Solent Way footpath sign, and take the signed path leading away from the road to the left, a wide and well-defined path which runs just west of north. Ignore a wide track, Hardley Lane, coming in from the left, and shortly after that, ignore also a tempting path going off to the right, but rather keep straight on, proceeding through woodland and predominantly downhill.

In due course you pass the houses of the hamlet of Frostlane, now on Hart Hill, and then arrive at a T-junction with a proper metalled road onto which you turn right. Follow this road into Hythe, initially heading north-east and crossing the industrial railway then swinging north-west, at last beside Southampton Water once more. Separated from the water by industrial buildings, you proceed on to the centre of Hythe, turn right into the High Street, an attractive pedestrian precinct, and follow it round to arrive at the station. Hythe (15) was once a fishing hamlet from which cargo and passengers were ferried to Southampton; the earliest reference to the Hythe Ferry was on a map of 1575, ancient custom requiring the ferrymen to deposit one boatload of stones against Southampton's walls every six months. At one time it was the point of departure for Imperial Airways' Flying Boat services to the Empire. It is now a most attractive town with buildings dating back to the 1600s as well as a waterside promenade and marina village. It was once the home of Lawrence of Arabia and Sir Christopher Cockerell who invented the hovercraft. Arguably its most interesting and endearing feature is its Victorian pier housing the world's oldest continuously working pier train which, as well as being a popular tourist attraction, provides access to the Hythe Ferry which you need to use to continue your coastal pilgrimage. (A foot journey to Southampton, crossing the first bridge over the water at Totton, is not recommended.) Notwithstanding the easy availability of the pier train, you could, and perhaps if you are a purist should, make the journey along the pier on foot. Providing the weather is kind, the pier walk is exceedingly enjoyable, and there are great views up and down Southampton Water with massive ocean superliners likely to be moored along its banks. Ferries from the pier head to Southampton Town Quay, where the walk resumes, are frequent and the journey is quick, but if you are unfortunate enough to miss the last one (on Sundays there is no service after about 6 p.m.) there is a regular bus service from Hythe into Southampton via Totton, and free buses then link the Central Station with the Town Quay. The route continues by making your way from the Town Quay to the crossroads, controlled by traffic lights, then proceeding eastwards from here alongside the A33 road – marked on maps as Platform Road – but you will surely wish to detour north from the crossroads to access the centre of the bustling city of Southampton.

# Day 29
# Southampton to Lee-on-the-Solent 17 miles (461 miles)

**Difficulty rating:** Easy
**Terrain rating:** ▲▲
**Hihglights:** Southampton, Netley, Hamble

Southampton is one of the great maritime cities in the country, having been a major port since the eleventh century and by the fourteenth century was one of England's most important ports. A large part of England's trade with the Mediterranean during the Middle Ages was carried through Southampton, and it became a key passenger port for France, with Winchester, England's ancient capital, only a short distance away. During the seventeenth and eighteenth centuries it lost much of its business to London. But in the 1840s it recovered its prestige with new docks, and a direct rail link to London. In 1911 the White Star Line moved its base to Southampton from Liverpool, and Southampton thus became the principal port for transatlantic passenger traffic; infamously it was the departure city for the *Titanic* in April 1912. New docks were completed in 1934, accommodating exceptionally large liners which were able to take advantage of the Solent's double tides (four per day) and it went on to become the UK's principal passenger port for ocean liners. The old town was virtually wiped out by bombing raids in World War Two, but miraculously much of its twelfth-century town wall, built all the way round the town as a defence against the French, survives to this day. Also preserved was the fine medieval church of St Michael, the Tudor House museum, the medieval Merchant's House, God's House Tower with its display of archaeological work, and the Dolphin Hotel which was once frequented by Jane Austen. Alongside the preserved buildings there are many fine modern structures, including the huge civic centre, university and aviation museum which is right on your route. The city remains a very busy passenger and container port, and is now dominated by the massive West Quay shopping centre, which at busy times can get excessively noisy and crowded. Town Quay, however, where you disembark the ferry, still has a pleasant ambience and with its cafe and views up and down Southampton Water is a good place to pause and collect your thoughts before pressing on.

Back on the route now, follow beside the A33 Platform Road, then walk straight on into Canute Road (B3029), going over the level crossing with an industrial railway and arriving at a crossroads with Royal Crescent going off to the left and Ocean Way to the right. The Solent Way, and perhaps the safer option for you, goes left into Royal Crescent then very shortly right into Albert Road South, past the Aviation Museum, then shortly beyond the museum look out for and follow a flight of steps on the left taking you up to the Itchen Bridge. A more adventurous option is to turn right into Ocean Way, and shortly left across the parking area to join a concrete waterside walkway beside the smart new Ocean Village marina. After a few hundred yards you're forced briefly away from the waterside, but on reaching a T-junction, turn right as this then provides access to a further section of the marina-side path, with new houses and apartments to your left and luxury boats to your right. You round a corner and find yourself walking right beside the River Itchen, which incidentally unites with the River Test a short way south of here to become Southampton Water, with the Itchen Bridge ahead of you. Continue along a clear waterside path until you reach the Itchen Rowing Club shed, and just beyond this bear left through a parking area to access and follow Crosshouse Road. Go straight over the crossroads and follow Crosshouse Road on, shortly reaching a flight of steps taking you to Itchen Bridge where you rejoin the Solent Way and the safer route described above. The reason for describing this route as adventurous is that there's no public right of way along the waterside path past and beyond the marina; signs make it clear that access is only with residents' consent, so you may be challenged if you opt for it. Your decision!

Cross the Itchen Bridge, using the pavement on the south side, then take the flight of steps off the bridge to the right, arriving at Victoria Road in the Woolston district of Southampton. Turn right and follow this road south-westwards away from the bridge. It is a depressing walk, with rows of rundown houses and shops, and the area is clearly overdue for redevelopment. You arrive at a car park to the left, and jetty to the right; the road swings left here, but you go straight on to reach Weston Point and join a footpath beside Southampton Water. The surroundings aren't hugely promising at this early stage, with grim rows of tower blocks to the left, but you then enter a wooded area and the walking soon becomes pleasant and enjoyable. The views across Southampton Water to Fawley Oil Refinery are fascinating, as is the huge variety of craft on the water from huge container vessels to ocean liners, from Red Funnel ferries bound for the Isle of Wight to yachts and other pleasure craft. The bird life is very diverse, and on a walk from Weston Point into the woodland you may be fortunate enough to sight a great-crested grebe, little egret, curlew, oystercatcher or dunlin. The path is initially metalled, and the going continues to be very easy with a clear path running parallel with the shoreline. Look out in just over a mile for the austere grey building of Netley Castle to your left, in the shade of the trees, then shortly beyond this point the path gives out and you have a choice. Providing the tide isn't too high you can simply continue along the beach, but if the tide is right up and/or you wish to visit Netley Abbey you should bear left over the recreation ground to the road. From here head south-eastwards through the village of Netley (5) along the road past the entrance to the ruins of the abbey, founded in 1239 by Cistercian monks from Beaulieu and all but destroyed in the Dissolution. The road and shore routes are reunited at Netley Hard at the south-east end of the village where the shore-side path resumes and there ensues a lovely walk beside the Royal Victoria Country Park past the chapel. It's hard to believe that there was once a massive hospital here, known as the Royal Victoria Military Hospital; it was built in the mid-nineteenth century to treat soldiers wounded in the Crimean War, it was able to accommodate 1,400 patients in 138 wards, and it even had its own pier, to facilitate the landing of casualties by ship.

It was shut in 1955 and demolished in 1966 following a fire, and the domed hospital chapel, known as the Royal Chapel, is the only surviving part of the original complex. The country park was opened in 1980 and consists of more than 100 acres of grassy open spaces and terraces with cedars and other exotic trees.

A little beyond the chapel, the Solent Way is signposted left, away from the shore, but it would seem that at low tide you could simply continue along the beach. The Solent Way passes by the chapel then, clearly signposted, bears right; shortly a cliff path is signposted and you join this path, snaking through pleasant woodland on low cliffs and passing Hamble Cliff House. Again the two routes reunite for what is initially a bit of a slog on the shingle, but shortly a concrete path becomes available, passing underneath the jetty leading out from the BP terminal. In due course you reach a car park and from here you can see a tempting looking path ahead, but this is a dead end; you will need to go slightly back on yourself, along the road – don't take the driveway leading into Hamble Marina – then very soon bear right onto a path. There is a lack of Solent Way signage here, but you should follow the Hamble Circular Path arrow signs for a delightful walk through woodland and round the edge of a charming inlet. This area is known as Hamble Common with a rich mixture of heath, saltmarsh and woodland, and a variety of wildlife including mallard ducks, redshanks, nesting stonechats and linnets. You reach a T-junction with an imposing brown wooden signpost pointing the way to Hamble to the right; now follow the path to Hamble (8) as signed, soon emerging in this delightful and very exclusive village on the west shore of the River Hamble. The full name of the village is Hamble-le-Rice, the 'le Rice' bit meaning 'in the brushwood'. Although, to quote *Philip's County Guide*, it 'undoubtedly embraces some of the glamour of very rich people and their floating gin palaces' – TV connoisseurs may recall it as the setting for the 1980s drama *Howard's Way*. Hamble has traditionally been a busy workaday place with many ships having been built in dockyards along the river banks down the centuries. It was once the site of an Iron Age fort, has seen landings by Saxon, Danish and French invaders, and was a favoured place of embarkation for forces engaging in the Napoleonic Wars. Now it is predominantly a yachting centre and the cobbled streets ooze prosperity with exclusive shops and restaurants.

With no bridge crossing over the Hamble available, you need to proceed by ferry to Warsash. The Warsash ferry is well signed, and the crossing is inexpensive, quick and very enjoyable; the surroundings are absolutely delightful, with its combination of rippling waters, variety of river craft and beautiful countryside on both banks. To request the ferry, it's necessary just to stand at the landing stage and the ferryman, if on the other side, will come over for you. Note, however, that the ferry does not run before 9 a.m. nor after 5 p.m. on weekdays or 6 p.m. at weekends, and is subject to weather conditions. Warsash is today best known as the location of the College of Maritime Studies, probably Britain's most advanced nautical school; like Hamble, Warsash has an important industrial past, with a factory here until the 1880s dedicated to the manufacture of alkali, and it still boasts a small fishing community today, with crabs and lobsters among the catch. Turn right away from the ferry terminal and proceed via Shore Road to the quay and splendid D-Day memorial, then following the Solent Way signs, begin a splendid very straightforward march beside the Southampton Water, passing but not walking along a spit which is known as the Hook because of its distinctive shape. Much of the surrounding area is a nature reserve, visited by oystercatchers, shelducks, linnets, kingfishers, warblers and meadow pipits, and the views from here are breathtaking, with huge sections of the Isle of Wight on view and, nearer at hand, Calshot Spit and its sixteenth-century castle. The going is very easy until you reach Workmans Lane at the western end of the Solent Breezes Holiday Park; the lane's name calling to mind the alkali factory mentioned above which once stood nearby. Progress from the lane will depend on the state of the tide. At low tide you can easily follow the beach past the park then scramble onto the cliff path on the east side of the park, or you could in theory climb steps from the beach into the park then head south-eastwards through the park to join the cliff path, aided navigationally by excellent plans of the site on signboards around the park. At high tide it may be necessary to head inland along Workmans Lane and then access the cliff path by taking the first right turn off this lane then bearing right as signposted beyond the park.

Once on the cliff path beyond the park the going is easy and hugely enjoyable, with fantastic views to the Isle of Wight; you drop down to the lovely secluded lagoons of Brownwich then rise again, continuing along the cliff-tops before descending to a line of beach huts. Walk along the inland side of the beach huts to arrive at a road, turning right onto the road and following it, passing Titchfield Haven Nature Reserve which is to your left, and the harbour at Hill Head (14), once a smugglers' haunt, to your right. The nature reserve, effectively the mouth of the River Meon, is a fascinating area with its marshes and extensive waters hosting a huge diversity of bird life including Cetti's warbler, reed warbler, common tern, Sandwich tern, coot and heron. Easy walking on a good path ensues beyond the reserve and harbour, but in due course this gives out and you are directed left by a Solent Way signpost to Hill Head Road. Turn right onto this road and follow it past the Osborne View pub, a very apposite name because looking across to the Isle of Wight you can indeed see Queen Victoria's beloved Osborne House in the woods just to the left (east) of Cowes. Look out shortly on the left for Cottes Way – just beyond on the right is a narrow footpath which you follow back down to the shore; on arrival at the shore bear left and walk along the shingle to a car park at an open space called the Salterns. There's excellent fast walking now along a concrete promenade, with just one break to pass round a hovercraft slipway serving HMS Daedalus, the training establishment of the Fleet Air Arm. A mile or so from the Salterns you arrive at the seafront at Lee-on-the-Solent (17); not to be called Lee-on-Solent unless you want to upset the locals. It was a property developer, John Robinson, who sought to develop what had been a modest village into a seaside resort in the late 1880s, and a 750-foot-long pier was built as well as viewing tower. Despite boasting a pleasant seafront and a cheerful row of shops and cafes overlooking the Solent, it has never become a major holiday centre and both the pier and tower have long since been demolished.

# Day 30
# Lee-on-the-Solent to Portsmouth 6 miles (467 miles)

**Difficulty rating:** Easy
**Terrain rating:** ▲▲
**Highlights:** Gilkicker Point, Gosport, Portsmouth

Beyond Lee-on-the-Solent the going continues to be very easy initially, but as the road to your left (B3333) swings inland you reach the western end of the Browndown military training camp. If no red flags are flying you can continue along the shore, but there's no path and you'll have to tramp over the shingle until you emerge from the danger area at the first Stokes Bay car park. If red flags are flying you may have to continue along the B3333 road to access the car park. You can do this by turning right along Browndown Road and then right at the roundabout, but as Browndown Road is in the danger area it may be necessary to continue along the B3333, across one roundabout then right at the next one along Gomer Lane, and straight over another roundabout to reach the car park. The moral is to avoid firing times; information about these should be available either on the Internet or from local tourist information offices. From the car park on the east side of the danger area it's now easy walking along a concrete promenade with Stokes Bay to the right, and Gilkicker Point, the southernmost point between Southampton and Portsmouth and effectively the eastern mouth of Southampton Water, clearly visible ahead. As you approach the Point with Fort Gilkicker, you once more find yourself on shingle, but by keeping a course a little further from the water and closer to the fort you should be able to pick up a firmer path. You can in fact climb onto the fort itself, and as you make your way round the top of it the buildings of Portsmouth suddenly appear in front of you; this is a superb spot, with views to Portsmouth, the Solent and the Isle of Wight coast between Seaview and Ryde, and on a fine day it's a great place to linger. The fort was built in the 1860s as one of the so-called Palmerston's Follies, a series of defensive fortifications built at the behest of Lord Palmerston all around Portsmouth and Gosport to counter the perceived threat of Napoleon III. The vegetation hereabouts is particularly rich and includes tufted vetch, sea kale and bird's foot trefoil.

Descend to the water's edge and enjoy a good walk along a firm path on the shoreline, now heading north-east, away from the Point, with two lagoons to your left. Unfortunately, you can't progress further along the shore, so you need to follow the Solent Way inland along the west side of the lagoons then beside a golf course to reach a T-junction with Fort Road. Turn right into Fort Road and follow it for roughly half a mile to a junction with Clayhall Road going off to the left and Haslar Road going off to the right. Turn right and follow Haslar Road, passing a large hospital and the Royal Submarine Museum where the Royal Navy's first ever submarine, launched in 1901, can be seen, then cross a bridge over an extensive inlet. Immediately after crossing the bridge, bear right onto a footpath which proceeds past Haslar Marina to the Gosport-Portsmouth ferry terminal; you need to turn left to buy your ferry ticket and also access the shops and other attractions of Gosport. Gosport began as a small fishing hamlet but developed into an important victualling station and principal armaments depot for the Royal Navy. At the beginning of the twentieth century it became a submarine base, its massive fortifications played an important part in the defence of the fleet, and it was also a major embarkation point for D-Day landings. The name Gosport is said to be derived from 'God's Port', a name supposedly given to it by the Bishop of Winchester who landed here in the twelfth century after a stormy crossing from Normandy. Among the more interesting buildings in Gosport is Holy Trinity Church which was built as a garrison church in 1696; its nave boasts two rows of huge columns made from the trunk of a single oak tree, and its organ is thought to have been used by Handel to compose some of his music. Arguably the town's greatest popular visitor attraction is Explosion, a museum of naval firepower using multimedia and interactive displays. Ferry crossings from Gosport to Portsmouth are very frequent and the brief journey is most enjoyable, with superb views to *HMS Warrior* and *HMS Victory* as well as the Spinnaker Tower. You emerge from the ferry in the heart of Portsmouth (6), just outside Portsmouth Harbour railway station.

Portsmouth, built on what is effectively a large peninsula known as Portsea Island, may not be the most beautiful settlement on your coastal walk, but it is certainly one of the most absorbing and, especially if the weather is good, you may find yourself lingering here longer than you expected. Even in the days of Alfred the Great there was a port here, and in 1194 King Richard recognised its strategic importance by creating a settlement on Portsea Island. It quickly became a significant naval station and it was here in 1496 Henry VII established a Royal dockyard and constructed what was then the world's first dry dock. It expanded further at the end of the seventeenth century and became the UK's main naval base. In its harbour you will see Nelson's flagship *HMS Victory*, *HMS Warrior*; the Navy's first iron-clad battleship, and the *Mary Rose* which capsized in 1545 and was famously raised in 1982. It was very badly bombed during World War Two and suffered from some horribly insensitive rebuilding, notably the 1966 Tricorn centre which was generally acknowledged as an eyesore and there were few regrets when it was demolished. However, some of Old Portsmouth remains with some very attractive streets of old houses and there is a cathedral which began as a chapel in the twelfth century and has only been completed comparatively recently. At the top end of the old town is the area known as the Point, or Spice Island because it was here that exotic cargoes were landed in former times. The most exciting part of Portsmouth is the Gunwharf Quays area, an excellent pedestrian complex of fashionable shops and restaurants, and it is a very short walk from the complex to Spinnaker Tower. Completed in 2005 and now the most distinctive feature of the city's skyline, it is a real triumph of modern architecture and symbolic of the extensive rejuvenation of Portsmouth in the new millennium. If you have time (and funds) it really is worth taking a lift up the tower for superb views of the surrounding area. For the less adventurous, there are several museums including one devoted to Charles Dickens, who was born in the city in 1812.

You must now decide whether you are going to walk round the Isle of Wight. If you wish to do so, there are a number of ferry options but you may feel the most convenient is the FastCat, which runs from the terminal immediately beside Portsmouth Harbour station to Ryde. The description of the circular walk round the Isle of Wight now follows.

The first and most obvious question is do you walk the Isle of Wight or not? It is not part of the south coast of England as such, but an island off its shores, so there is justification for omitting it; however, unlike virtually the entire Hampshire coastline, which looks out onto the Solent and the Isle of Wight beyond, the south-facing coast of the Isle of Wight looks out onto open sea, and much of it is stunningly beautiful. It is included here for completeness, and to encourage you to consider it either as part of your south coast adventure or indeed as a separate expedition. It does, however, have to be said that because large parts of the coastline are in private ownership or inaccessible for geographical reasons, there is quite a bit of inland walking, some of which is candidly rather tedious, none more so than the first 8 miles from Ryde to Cowes when your view of the sea is restricted to the first 50 yards of walking. If you're pushed for time, you could restrict your walking to the stretch of coastline between Yarmouth and Ventnor; the southern and western coastal areas of the island are very much more interesting and provide better walking than the northern and eastern sections. But it's your decision.

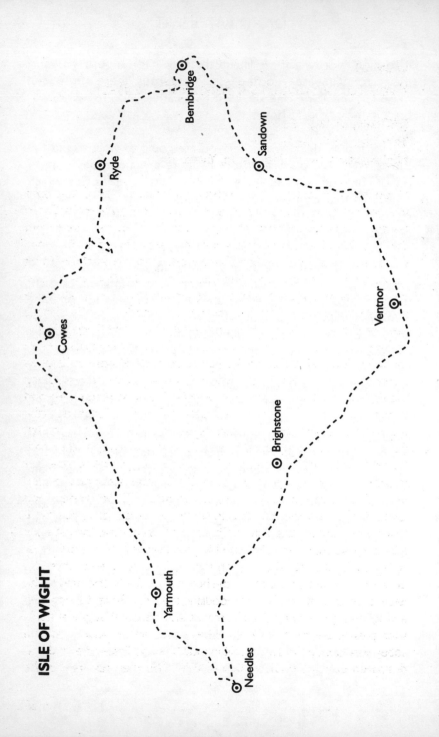

# ISLE OF WIGHT

Bembridge

Sandown

Ryde

Ventnor

Cowes

Brighstone

Yarmouth

Needles

# Day 31
## Ryde to Yarmouth 24 miles (491 miles)

**Difficulty rating:** Easy
**Terrain rating:** ▲▲
**Highlights:** Cowes, Newtown, Yarmouth

If you've come straight from Portsmouth, perhaps having just used the Gosport ferry, the chances are you'll use the Wightlink FastCat to transport you across the Solent, and it is recommended you walk from the Ryde Pier Head ferry terminal along the pier to its entrance. A train will do the same job, but that's hardly starting your coastal travels on a conscientious footing, is it? Well, you can always walk along the pier when the time comes to take the ferry home. Ryde is an attractive resort, developed in the late eighteenth and nineteenth centuries; its pier dates back to 1813 and is one of the oldest and longest in the country, and while architecturally there is nothing of special note in the town, it has all the amenities you could possibly want in its often steeply sloping streets. From Ryde pier entrance, head west along the Esplanade – there, that was your coastal walk between Ryde and Cowes – then bear away from the sea into St Thomas' Street, and take the first right turn into Buckingham Road. You veer round to the left past Buckingham Close, uphill to reach a junction with Spencer Road, then turn right into this road and follow it for roughly half a mile till it becomes a gravel track ending at gates. Beyond the gates you cross the entrance to Ryde House on the right to footpath R48 to Binstead and Quarr, then follow this tarmac path which descends past a golf course to a bridge and rises to Binstead Church. Follow round to the left away from the church, which has some Norman features, then shortly bear right into Church Road and soon right again onto a level driveway, avoiding the R46 beach path. At the house gates follow the path to the left and proceed through level woodland to Quarr Road, turning right and following the lane which descends and becomes a gravel track, soon passing the ruins of Quarr Abbey which are on your right. The abbey was founded in 1311, built in local Binstead limestone, and was destroyed during the Dissolution in 1537. You then continue in the same direction past the new Quarr Abbey built in the early twentieth century, also to your right, arriving at a T-junction with Fishbourne Lane. Turn left onto the lane, passing the car ferry terminal which is to your right, then beyond the terminal look out for a phone box to the right, turning right here onto footpath R1 signed to Kite Hill and follow the path between houses to a barrier. Turn left into Ashlake Copse Road, then when this road bends left, you carry on ahead on a path into woodland, descending to a footbridge then rising to reach the A3054. Turn right and follow the road downhill to Wootton (4.5) and its bridge.

Cross the bridge, using the pavement on the south side, then cross to the north side of the road and pass immediately in front of the Sloop Inn just beyond, going forward to a short gravel lane at the top of which an alley runs up between houses to New Road. Turn right into New Road then after about 100 yards turn left onto an unmade road adjacent to the Wootton Youth Club. At the end of the unmade road carry on in the same direction along a rising alley between the rear gardens of houses and exit next to lock-up garages; follow the access road on to St Edmunds Walk then turn left, passing Whitehead Crescent which is to your right, and turn left again into a short alley past houses and more lock-up garages. Continue ahead on steps up a small bank to another short alley between houses to reach Church Road. Cross over into Footways and carry on to the end to turn left into Palmers Road, then take the first turning right into Brocks Copse Road, your long and rather tedious walk through suburbia now finally completed. Now simply follow this road which descends steadily to a brook then rises steadily, merging with Alverstone Road that comes in from the left. Continue along the road to Whippingham, passing a post office and reaching a T-junction with a main road. Turn right onto the main road, following it all the way down to East Cowes past the entrance to Osborne House, and in fact you may wish to enliven the otherwise rather dull road walk by detouring to visit it. Designed largely by Prince Albert in the style of an Italian villa, it became Queen Victoria's favourite retreat, and has been left almost unchanged since she died; one of the most endearing features of the grounds of Osborne House is the Swiss Cottage, a life-size Wendy house for the royal children. Continuing beyond the entrance road you walk on downhill, then shortly after passing the Town Hall on the left, bear left into Ferry Road and continue to the chain ferry which, free of charge, will take you across the River Medina to Cowes (8).

Having left the chain ferry, walk along Medina Road away from the ferry and turn right at the police station into Birmingham Road. Continue via Shooters Hill into the High Street and follow it through the centre of the town, with charming old houses and shops lining the narrow thoroughfare. Cowes is first and foremost a yachting town, and is the home of the National Sailing Centre and Royal Yacht Squadron. Cowes Week, held during early August, is the best-known yachting regatta in the world, the first regatta dating back to 1776 and a yacht club having been established here in 1815. Shortly after passing the Island Sailing Club turn right down Watch House Lane to reach Victoria Parade, and turn left to walk along the promenade. At last you have some proper waterside walking on the Isle of Wight, and it's now a lovely easy walk along the front all the way past Egypt Point, the most northerly point on the island, to Gurnard and another sailing club. Here the promenade gives out, but don't take the narrow path ahead, rather follow the road, Shore Road, round to the left; proceed up Shore Road then shortly take a signed tarmac path leading off to the right taking you to Worsley Road. Turn right into Worsley Road then take the first right turn into Solent View Road and descend, the road becoming Marsh Road. Cross a little bridge then immediately beyond it turn right along a path beside the stream, before very shortly turning left in front of Marsh Cottage onto a signed path. At the time of writing the stile here had broken but the route is clear and the path, although starting unpromisingly, soon improves hugely, proceeding resolutely on to the cliffs. This is lovely easy walking, although it is sad to see how erosion has taken its toll on the cliff faces.

Eventually you drop down to Thorness Bay and follow the path at the back of the beach. Unfortunately, you are now again forced away from the coast in order to negotiate Newtown Estuary; look for the holiday park up to your left, and when you are level with it follow the path leading to the complex, passing right through the middle of it. Keep to the main road through the complex, observing the coast path signposts, and follow it all the way out of the complex (briefly leaving the route of the coast path) reaching a T-junction with a narrow lane. Turn right onto the lane and proceed briefly along it, keeping your eyes peeled for a coast path sign pointing off the lane to the left, then, rejoining the coast path, take the signed path with farm buildings to your right. The correct route goes forward along this path to reach a field very shortly, and your route bears sharp left to follow the left-hand field edge, but when I walked this section, not only was there no signpost for this left turn but the path was also obstructed and the guidebook I was using gave an inaccurate description of the surroundings; I trust that all these defects will have been remedied by the time you come to walk this section! Having entered the field, follow the left-hand field edge downhill, then continue through three more fields with the hedge to your left, emerging thankfully by the side of woodland onto a road. The messiest part of the day is over. Turn right and follow the road into the village of Porchfield, then continue along the road signposted Shalfleet and Yarmouth, eventually reaching another road junction at Locksgreen, bearing right at the wooded triangular island at the intersection. You shortly cross Clamerkin Bridge then at the next junction take the road signposted for Newtown on your right; I suggest that although the coast path goes off to the left shortly, you stay on this road, which gives better views to the Newtown Estuary, noteworthy for its huge variety of bird life. In due course you arrive at Newtown, an extraordinary place which dates back to the twelfth century and which was once an important port with two members to Parliament, but declined in importance as a result of silting in the estuary. Turn left at the road junction and pass the Town Hall, now restored and open to visitors as a museum piece, then proceed along the road to a T-junction. Turn right here, walk to Corf Farm where you bear right along a narrow lane to Shalfleet Mill, then pass over a footbridge and bear left along Mill Road to reach the main road through Shalfleet (18) by the New Inn. The pub is acknowledged to be one of the finest on the island, and the food is excellent if rather pricey.

Turn right onto the main road and follow it. As it descends in just over a quarter of a mile, take the signed path going off to the right, informing you that Yarmouth is just over 6 miles away. Pass along the right-hand field edge then make for the far corner of the field aiming for a footbridge crossing of an inlet, then having crossed the bridge turn right and follow the path bearing left through the wood to reach a gravel forest track. You have now clocked up 500 miles! Turn right onto the track and follow it over Ningwood Lake Bridge, then beyond Pigeon Coo Farm which is to the left, take the next right turn and follow a clear track via Creek Farm and Lower Hamstead farm to just short of Hamstead Quay; this is a particularly attractive spot, with beautiful views to the marshes and creeks around Newtown Estuary whose tributary courses have forced you so far inland. Here turn left as signposted onto a path which follows a right-hand field edge then at a belt of trees bears left to follow an embankment along the edge of a river inlet. The obvious path then bears round to the right, using boardwalks across the marshes, to reach a field, and although its course on the ground is rather faint you continue along the path through the field in roughly the same direction, following the left-hand field edge and rising a little. Look out for a stile in the hedge as you begin to lose height, and cross it; beyond the stile there is a clear path running diagonally through the next field to reach another boardwalk, beyond which you follow the right-hand edge of the next field, then descend a bank to arrive back on the shore. It really is nice to be back by the Solent for the first time since Thorness, and there's the bonus of being able to look across the water to a section of coastline on the mainland that was unavailable for walking, between Lymington and the mouth of the Beaulieu River.

You turn left and follow a rough path along the shore, but unfortunately almost at once you're forced away from it again, following the path as it leaves the shore and proceeds uphill to Hamstead Farm gate. Keep the same direction with the farm on the left and just after a second, sharp left-hand bend take the stile on your right and cross to a stile roughly halfway along the right-hand boundary of a small field. Aim for the left corner of the next field then make for West Hamstead Farm to the right ahead. Keeping the farmhouse on your right, carry on past the greenhouses and orchard to another stile, passing Cliff Cottage, and carry on along the access road; turn left on reaching a gravelled track and then after about 270 yards turn right along another access road for just over 150 yards. At the Greenacres entrance turn left as signposted then right to cross a small field close to the right-hand edge to enter Bouldnor Copse, then follow the track through the copse. After the appallingly fiddly walking you've had to endure, this is a real treat; the thick forest to the left makes a dramatic and appealing inland vista, and the views to the right across the Solent include sight of Lymington and its plethora of yachts. It's a pity when you are forced down to the beach which you follow to gain, very shortly, a path through the woods on the other side running parallel to the cliff-edge. The wood soon ends and you are now directed left along a track to reach a gravel access road on to which you turn right and which you follow to the main road, then turn right to follow the main road towards Yarmouth. Just past the Thorley Road (B3401) look for steps leading down to the sea wall, and follow the sea wall into Yarmouth (24) itself. In the Middle Ages, this was one of the most important towns on the island, and Henry VIII had a castle built here in 1547 as a defence against the French; it now enjoys prosperity not only as a very pretty little town, with many visitors being attracted by its quaint streets of old shops and restaurants, but as a car ferry port for Lymington. It also boasts a 700 ft long pier which dates back to 1876.

# Day 32
# Yarmouth to Brighstone 14 miles (505 miles)

**Difficulty rating:** Moderate
**Terrain rating:** ▲▲▲▲
**Highlights:** Headon Warren, Needles, Tennyson Down

Leave Yarmouth by passing the car ferry terminal and then joining the main road to cross the bridge over the River Yar. Continue alongside the main road beyond the bridge then as the road bends left, you turn right to follow the sea wall; towards the end of the

*The Lizard in Cornwall – the most southerly point of your walk.*

*The choppy waters of the Helford River in Cornwall.*

*Lulworth Cove in Dorset, a geologist's paradise.*

*The marked path through the army ranges between Lulworth and Kimmeridge.*

*The distinctive chalk coastline at Swanage in Dorset.*

*The coastal footpath at Chewton Bunny in Dorset.*

*Lymington, one of the prettiest coastal towns in Hampshire.*

*Buckler's Hard in Hampshire.*

*The sixteenth-century Calshot Castle at Southampton Water in Hampshire.*

*The quay at Ashlett in Hampshire.*

*The Spinnaker Tower at Portsmouth Harbour, Hampshire.*

*The cliffs at Alum Bay on the Isle of Wight.*

*The pretty village of Bosham in West Sussex.*

*The Palace Pier in Brighton.*

*The Seven Sisters cliffs near Eastbourne, Sussex.*

*Looking towards Folkestone in Kent from the Leas Promenade.*

sea wall, look for steps leading off to the left into the woods, and use these steps to access a short woodland path leading to Westhill Lane. You're now embarking on another section that enjoys precious little in the way of coastal views, but it's thankfully relatively brief and the first part of it, at least, is very agreeable. Turn right along the lane then very shortly left on to a signed and very beautiful woodland path that proceeds through Fort Victoria Country Park along an old military road. The Fort itself was in fact a nineteenth century defensive measure against the French and there is within the park a big exhibition centre and amusement park, although your route does not pass them! The coast path emerges from the woods and continues between fences to Monks Lane where you turn left and follow the lane, bearing right on reaching the access road to Brambles Chine holiday camp. Follow the road into and through the complex, then on the far side you take the signed path to the left through the chalets, the path continuing on past a farm which is to your right and arriving at a junction with a main road. Turn right on to this road and follow it for just over a quarter of a mile all the way to the Colwell Bay Inn, then opposite the inn turn right on to Colwell Chine Road, following it down to the beach at Colwell (4). The reward for your arrival is three-fold. Firstly, it's very nice to be back by the sea again, and indeed it will hardly be out of your sight from now all the way round to well beyond Sandown, over 30 miles distant. Secondly, there is the immediate prospect of the best walking of the whole Isle of Wight coastal path, as you begin your journey towards and away from the Needles. Thirdly there is a great view from the beach to Hurst Castle, which you will recall from your Hampshire coast labours between Milford-on-Sea and Keyhaven, that is assuming you made the detour. This is the nearest point the mainland gets to the island, and it does look extraordinarily close, almost swimmable, from here.

The signpost for your next path is oddly placed at the beach. You need to go all the way down to the water's edge, only then seeing the sea wall going away to the left, and having turned left on to the sea wall you can enjoy a really lovely walk to Totland Pier, using the sea wall throughout. Pass the pier, restaurant and lifeboat station then shortly before the end of the sea wall turn left to climb up the steep steps through Widdick Chine; when you reach the road you turn right to follow it past the Hermitage Hotel then take the signed path to Alum Bay shortly beyond the hotel on your right. Follow the path which climbs on to the magnificent heather clad slopes of Headon Hill and Headon Warren, and make for the summit from which there are magnificent views across the island and over the Solent to the mainland. There is evidence of settlers having used this area for grazing their livestock in Neolithic times, and on the summit is a Bronze Age burial mound; now not only does it provide superb walking but it also attracts a wide variety of bird and insect life including the tiger beetle, digger wasp and Dartford warbler. Although there are numerous paths to and round the summit, which is fenced off, there is a clear path proceeding south-westwards, but it is important to come off the hilltop as signed in order to join a track that leads down towards the main road in the valley to the left. Keeping the little golf course immediately to your right, walk down the obvious track which eventually arrives at the B3322 road, then turn right onto the road and follow it past the phone box to the bus stops by the entrance to the Needles Park. If any of the philosophical musings of Alfred Wainwright have rubbed off on you, you will recoil with horror from the unashamedly hedonistic variety of amusements that line the concrete thoroughfare leading away from the bus turning area, but the scenic beauty of the Needles (7) and their immediate surrounds hasn't been compromised at all... and you may actually welcome the chance to grab a choc-ice and/ or a bowl of chips before pressing on. Well, AW will never know, will he?

At the bus stops bear left (southwards) along the roadside past the glass factory and car and coach park, going slightly uphill, then swing round to the right to follow the roadside as it climbs towards the Needles; looking down to your right, you get a grandstand view of Alum Bay with its famous cliff of vertical sandstone strata in twelve different and vibrant colours. In due course a coast path sign points you left, away from the road and up a rough hill-side path past the coastguard cottages which eventually takes you onto the cliff-top. Just ahead of you is the Needles Battery, a nineteenth-century defensive fort which has been restored and is open to visitors, and out to sea just beyond are the Needles themselves, one of the most famous examples of chalk sea stacks in the country. The three 100-foot pinnacles, with a lighthouse sited on the one furthest out to sea, are among the remains of a chalk ridge that once joined the Isle of Wight to the mainland, and if you have faithfully walked all the way from Cornwall you may recall Old Harry just east of Swanage in Dorset which formed the other end of the ridge. If the weather is good, you really will find it very difficult to pull yourself away from the area round the Battery. You may decide to explore the Battery itself, passing through a 200-foot tunnel carved into the rock taking you to the very outer edge of the island itself, and inspecting the original gun barrel mounted in a carriage in the parade ground. You may on a clear day enjoy the extraordinary view to the mainland, which runs all the way from Durlston Head beyond Swanage in Dorset, as far as the Fawley Oil Refinery and possibly even beyond. Or you may simply stand on the edge of the sheer chalk cliffs looking down the terrifyingly long distance to the sea, doing your best to suppress any feelings of vertigo that may well up inside you. And only if your booted feet are covered in blisters will you ask yourself if it's worth detouring back to the Needles Park to see if any of the shops have had the prescience to stock souvenir trainers.

Having enjoyed your Needles experience, you now need to walk back away from the Needles, but this time on the cliff-top, keeping the coastguard cottages to the left (north) of you. It was in this vicinity during the 1950s that there was a rocket testing site from where a rocket launched the satellite Prospero into space, although it wasn't till 1972 that the site was abandoned. You now begin a quite fantastic walk on the ridge-top, maintaining height as you cross over West High Down, then staying on the cliff-top you ascend onto Tennyson Down to reach the Tennyson Monument. Named after the poet Alfred Lord Tennyson who lived in the area between

1853 and 1869, the monument is quite magnificently sited, and the views you will get from it on a decent day will undoubtedly provide one of the highlights of your coastal walk. You descend off Tennyson Down, keeping to the cliff-top path, and drop steeply down to a lane, turning left onto the lane and following it to the inlet and village of Freshwater Bay (9). During the 1860s this was the home of Julia Cameron, a pioneer portrait photographer; Lord Tennyson sat for her, as did Charles Darwin and Robert Browning, and her work is exhibited in the Dimbola Lodge Museum in the village. Bear right at the end of the lane to arrive immediately at the little bay itself and proceed around it to the wooden steps at the far end which take you back to the cliff-top, and you now enjoy a superb cliff-top walk past Compton Chine and on to Shippards Chine, going forward to Brook Chine. A chine is derived from the word 'cinan' meaning 'yawn' or 'gap' and in geological parlance is a deep ravine cutting into a cliff-edge; you will encounter a fair number between here and Chale, and although they might be regarded as rather annoying interruptions to the rhythm of your cliff-edge walk, they are fascinating features in their own right. Note that east of Freshwater the chalk of the Needles and the cliffs below Tennyson Down is replaced by a darker rock, another sedimentary product known as Wealden marl. For virtually all the way to Brook Chine the going is really straightforward with an obvious and magnificent cliff-top path throughout, the reassurance of the road – an old military road – to the left, and the satisfaction, along this stretch, of passing the halfway mark on your walk round the island. At Brook Chine, the site of a now ruined lifeboat station which was operational for 76 years, it's necessary to go a little way from the cliff-edge to negotiate the ravine, but the way round is obvious and it's a short walk back to the cliff-edge on the other side. Look inland and you will enjoy beautiful views to the hill on which the upper part of Brook is built, including what must be one of the most superbly sited churches on the island. Another foray away from the cliff-edge is necessary to pass Chilton Chine and the nearby Isle of Wight Pearl, but you may wish to stop off to visit the centre and its welcome cafe, the only refreshment opportunity on the route between Freshwater Bay and Chale. Then it's back to the cliff-edge before a further slight interruption to negotiate the caravans of the Grange Farm Camping Park, beyond which you're shortly forced down into the next chine, Grange Chine, with a long climb back up the other side. It's a little reminiscent of some of the steep drops and ascents you had to cope with in Cornwall, although the ruggedness is somewhat compromised by the presence of holiday homes you pass as you make your descent! Just to the north of Grange Chine, where this section ends (14), is the village of Brighstone, reachable by bearing left to the military road immediately before the descent into the chine, but it's a fair old detour and you may prefer to press on.

# Day 33
# Brighstone to Sandown 15 miles (520 miles)

**Difficulty rating:** Moderate
**Terrain rating:** ▲▲▲
**Highlights:** Chale, Blackgang Chine, Ventnor

Emerging from the chine, the going is straightforward initially as you continue along the cliffs, and indeed the cliff scenery along this stretch is particularly fine, with one splendid ascent to reach a yellow sandstone cliff-top affording tremendous views in all directions. You are forced away from the cliff-edge to negotiate Cowleaze Chine, and then at the next chine, Shepherds Chine, you actually walk some way down into the cleft, heading away from the sea, before passing a dam and pumphouse and climbing back onto the cliff-top. The piece of coastline, while innocuous and picturesque on a good day, has been notoriously bad for shipping, with many vessels having foundered on the reef at Atherfield Point hereabouts. The going is then relatively level and straightforward again, passing coastguard cottages, before you reach your next obstacle, Whale Chine; this is extraordinary, a very deep, narrow cleft in the cliff with surreal formations of rock on the face of the almost sheer slopes of the chine, and deriving its name from an incident in 1758 when a 63-foot whale found itself stranded here. Veterans of the Pembrokeshire Coast Path may be reminded of Huntsman's Leap near Bosherston, to which Whale Chine bears more than a passing similarity. Again you're forced round the back of it and then through a car park before a signpost shows the path back to the cliff-edge. Then you pass the much more modest Walpen Chine, with no foray away from the cliff necessary, then soon afterwards find your path turning inland from the cliff-top, heading straight for a village dominated by its church. This is the village of Chale, perched on a hillside with St Catherine's Hill towering above it. The hill is off the route, but contains two distinctive and clearly visible features, the 'salt pot' and 'pepper (or mustard) pot', which are in fact the remains of two long obsolete lighthouses dating back to medieval times. You'll probably approach Chale with mixed feelings. Doubtless you'll be disappointed not to be able to continue along the coast past the chine at Blackgang, its name derived, incidentally, from a gang of ruthless smugglers, and which has comparatively recently fallen victim to terrible erosion rendering the inland detour necessary; however, your more earthy instincts may be delighted by the prospect of a pub only a stone's throw from the route! Walk along the path to reach Chale (4) and on arrival at the road turn right, continuing up the road past the church. Although it looks an idyllic place of worship, there are reminders here of the darker side of life, its graveyard outside filled with bodies that have been pulled from the sea, and its tombs were once used as a hiding place for smugglers' contraband. On a less sombre note, there is a lovely pub, the Wight Mouse, reached by turning left off this road just beyond the church; a short way beyond this turning you continue your coastal pilgrimage by bearing right along the Terrace then left along bridleway C15, which shortly brings you back to the road again.

You now have to follow the main Niton to Freshwater road, which can be busy. Walk uphill beside it, passing the roundabout with an exit to the Blackgang Chine amusement park, but ignore this exit and continue along the main road for about a hundred yards until you reach footpath C10 leading off to the right. Follow this path uphill to a car park, then turn right across the car park to take the obvious path heading seawards and begin what is the best section of the Isle of Wight coastal path. Just a short distance beyond the car park you will get a fantastic view of the cliff-tops you have covered since Freshwater, with views extending right back to the Needles; indeed it is suggested you might on a clear day be able to see Portland Bill, miles beyond the Needles to the west. Looking ahead, you can now see St Catherine's Point, the most southerly point on the island, and you will be struck by how much under-cliff there is between you and that point, the result of an erosion landslip caused by layers of rock and earth lying on a bed of soft clay sliding off due to rain or seepage of spring water. However, your walk still feels like a coastal route as you now swing from south-east to north-eastwards, on a clear and glorious path, where you really will feel on top of the world in every sense. The seas at St Catherine's Point, while magnificent to look at, have been described as a 'swirling maelstrom' caused by a variety of tidal flows, and there have been numerous shipwrecks here with an average of ten per year between 1748 and 1808. The salt and pepper pot lighthouses evidently proved totally inadequate to guide shipping, and 1840 saw the building of the very prominent lighthouse which stands on St Catherine's Point today. In due course the path begins to lose height then drops quite steeply to arrive at a road just south of the village of Niton (6).

Turn right onto the road, then very shortly left onto a path telling you Ventnor is 4 miles away, but I have to say it will seem longer. Follow the path, turning right at the end of the gravel drive then veering left and following the cliff-top path above the under-cliff with fields to your left and a fairly dramatic drop with thick vegetation to your right. You really do feel incredibly high up just along here, and you may be surprised when you find yourself climbing again, passing information boards and also a BT transmitting station. Having passed the latter, you need to look out for a signed path V81 leading off to the right, an important path turning which is easily missed. Follow the signed path down steep steps to reach Seven Sisters Road, then turn left onto this road and shortly right into Spindlers Road, arriving in the sprawling village of St Lawrence, noteworthy for having one of Britain's smallest churches, just 45 feet by 15 feet. You cross the main A3055 road onto Old Park Road, turn left along Woolverton Road then turn shortly right onto a path heading for Woody Bay; note, however, that you are signposted left round the inland side of Woody Bay Cottages, turning sharp right immediately beyond them to arrive back at the true cliff-edge. You pass Woody Point, from which you get your first view of Ventnor, and Orchard Point, going round the inland side of Orchard Bay House, then enter a hollow reminiscent of a meadow. From here, you go forward to a set of concrete steps to reach the edge of the 22-acre Botanic Gardens which boast 3,500 species including many subtropical plants. Turn right here and walk beside the garden fence, then when you reach a cricket field bear right down the steps to Steephill Cove. When you get to the bottom, bear hard left and hard right to proceed to the shore, go left again alongside Castle Cove. Walk up a concrete pathway and then go downhill on an obvious cliff path to reach the seafront at Ventnor (10). Known as the 'English Madeira' because of its subtropical climate, it was previously a fishing and smuggling village, but developed as a health resort. Its prosperity was assisted by the arrival of the railway in 1866 and the fact that a famous doctor, James Clarke, sang its praises. It is a large, sprawling town, built on a steep hill side, although walkers simply seeking a takeaway, ice cream or pie and a pint will not have to climb far, with the main street just a short uphill walk from the bandstand on the seafront. The waterfront itself is blessed with a plentiful supply of eateries and pubs including a splendid inn called The Spyglass. Besides the Botanic Gardens, there's also a museum of smuggling, lots of interesting shops including a fine second-hand bookshop very close to the front, and many Gothic Revival buildings in the town.

Having enjoyed your walk along the seafront, go forward to join the sea wall and now follow it for roughly a mile to the fishing and quarrying hamlet of Bonchurch. Turn left as signposted up steps, climbing behind a row of houses, and follow a metalled path through a copse to the Old Church; dedicated to St Boniface, it is said to have been built in 1040 by monks from Normandy, and is noteworthy for its medieval paintings on the north wall. Boniface was an eighth-century monk, and was reputed to have performed missionary work in the area. Turn right at the church and follow the path along the front of a sports field with Monks Bay to the right; pass the entrance to Carrigdene Farm and go into an area known as the Landslip on an obvious path continuing to rise, helped by stone steps on occasion. The twisty path proceeds past the Wishing Seat through thick woodland with only limited views to the sea, and seems to continue veering left away from the sea, but in fact (although you won't know it) you have passed another major headland and are now proceeding more resolutely northwards. The Landslip, another product of cliff erosion, was formed in the early nineteenth century, and yet again on your Isle of Wight coastal pilgrimage you will find a large swathe of collapsed cliff between you and the sea. You arrive at houses and pass through a kissing gate to enter a narrow lane which you follow downhill, heading now for the village of Luccombe and its chine; the lane begins to climb and becomes a footpath with good views ahead to Shanklin and Sandown. Walk out of the landslip emerging at the end of Luccombe Road, then follow Luccombe Road as signed towards Shanklin, descending and passing a magnificent hotel to reach a T-junction. Turn right here and, ignoring a sign to Rylstone Gardens, keep round to the right as signed to arrive at the beach; don't turn onto the high level promenade as this is a dead end, but descend to the promenade at the back of the beach and turn left to follow it. Looking to the right here, there's a good view back to the cliffs you have just come off. Heading for Shanklin now, you soon reach steps leading to Shanklin Chine, a deep wooded valley with rare flora of great interest, and now the town's principal visitor attraction, although you should note that there is a charge to enter it; note also that Shanklin's other attraction, the Old Village, is some way back from the coast. During the period following the Normandy invasions in 1944, there was a pipeline laid under the English Channel between Shanklin and Cherbourg, part of a series of pipelines supplying fuel to the Allied troops in France. Now continue along the promenade at Shanklin (13.5). The shops and other amenities of the town situated on the cliff-top can be reached on foot or by lift; there has actually been a lift between town and beach at Shanklin for the past hundred years, but you could be forgiven for regarding the lift as you see it today as something of an eyesore. Having reached the road at the end of the promenade, you can just continue along the sea wall and on to Sandown, although there is the option of a cliff-top promenade if you prefer, reached by turning left onto the road and following it uphill, bearing right onto the promenade itself. At the time of writing, a section of the cliff-top promenade had been closed for repair work, and with erosion an ongoing problem, further closures shouldn't be ruled out. Sandown (15) is a pure, unashamed holiday resort with no pretence to being anything else; the major attractions here are the Isle of Wight Zoo, Dinosaur Isle and the sands themselves, and you may feel somewhat out of place in your walking gear amongst the day trippers and sun seekers. The one saving grace is the view to Culver Cliff immediately to the north-east, which is your next objective. The zoo, with its much-hyped tiger island, and the dinosaur exhibition are both situated at Yaverland, which sounds like either a garish theme park or a fictitious American suburb featured in *The Simpsons* or *The Flintstones*.

# Day 34
# Sandown to Ryde 14 miles (534 miles)

**Difficulty rating:** Easy
**Terrain rating:** ▲▲
**Highlights:** Culver Cliff, St Helens Mill, Seaview

On arrival at Sandown the way forward is obvious, along past the pier which dates back to 1878 and is the only surviving pleasure pier on the island, then straight on along the front. You then continue beside the road out of Sandown, past Yaverland and it's attractions mentioned above. In due course you bear right onto an obvious path which leads away from the road towards Culver Cliff, and you follow the path leading to the cliff-top; aim for the stone needle which is a memorial to the Earl of Yarborough, the first commodore of the Royal Yacht Squadron, and pass immediately to the right of it. However, unless the weather has let you down, you should pause to enjoy views which will be tremendous, including not only large areas of the island but the Solent and mainland too. When you walk the section of coastline between Southsea and Eastney, and then the promenade on the south coast of Hayling Island, you should be able to identify the Yarborough memorial from the mainland.

You need to be careful when coming off the cliff; don't carry on towards the headland but aim direct for the chalets looking out on to Whitecliff Bay, and shortly you will pick up a path which passes to the right of the chalets and over some footbridges. Continuing on an obvious path, you proceed through a wooded area immediately to the right of school playing fields. Carry on along the cliff path, past the edge of Foreland Fields and through a little car park, then using path BB10 you pass to the seaward side of a couple of big houses; you turn left into the car park of the Crab and Lobster pub, then right past the coastguard lookout and inland to arrive at Beachfield Road. Proceed along the road and turn right at the end, walking through a modern estate and taking the second left, Forelands Farm Lane. Shortly turn right along the footpath and go straight ahead past the entrance to the Bembridge Coast Hotel, then walk along the Fishermans Walk above the beach to the lifeboat station and car park. Now you continue past the lifeboat pier and cafe and along to the end of the sea wall; it may be possible at low tide to walk along the shoreline all the way round to Bembridge Harbour, but unless you've checked and acted upon the tide tables in advance this good fortune cannot be guaranteed, and indeed the high tide route is the official one. This route bears left as signposted away from the shore along a road heading inland, and as you follow it you need to look out for a postbox on the right where there is a BB35 signpost pointing right. Follow BB35 to Love

Lane, then proceed along Love Lane until it bears left, and when it does so, you bear right, taking footpath BB5 to Ducie Avenue and Bembridge Point, thus arriving at the harbour at Bembridge (6.5). A deep water port was created at Bembridge in the late nineteenth century, but it suffered from silting, and the little town now prospers as a popular sailing centre. Its most notable feature, the windmill which is the only one to survive on the island and still works today, is set a long way back from the coast, but it may be worth taking time out to visit the maritime museum, crammed with artefacts including cannons recovered from local wrecks. If, however, through shortage of time or for any other reason, you have to stick to the coast path, you may well find Bembridge a bit of a disappointment, and will get the feeling of having walked extensively round its outskirts without ever having quite discovered its heart.

After the dreadfully dull, fiddly walking you have endured since coming down from Culver Cliff, you deserve some straightforward tramping and you duly get it, turning left to follow the main road clockwise round Bembridge Harbour past many boats, one at the time of writing offering B & B with en-suite facilities! You cross a bridge over the Yar, then just beyond the sign announcing your arrival at St Helens you turn right into Latimer Road. You shortly turn right again into North Quay and walk round to St Helens Mill, then observing the signposts you join the old Mill Dam Wall across the harbour, providing certainly the most enjoyable piece of walking since you left Culver Cliff. Having crossed the wall, you arrive at St Helen's Duver, an area of gorse and open grassland on a narrow sandy spit which is now a 'Site of Special Scientific Interest', attracting many migrant birds and around 250 different and rare wild plants. Keeping in the same direction, go forward to a tarmac road; although the coast seems accessible here, there's no path along it round the next headland, Nodes Point, so yet another frustrating inland foray is needed. Turn left onto the road and follow it past an old club house, bear round to the left and cross the road opposite the Old Church Lodge to join footpath R85. This proceeds uphill through a field, keeping to the right-hand field edge; after passing through some scrub you enter another field across which you walk diagonally left, aiming for a metalled gate which brings you out onto a road. Turn right onto this road, then after a couple of hundred yards turn left to join the Priory Hotel driveway.

You shortly arrive at rather grand gateposts and here you turn left onto a bridleway; at its end you turn right onto a gravelled track that goes down to Fernclose Road and the sea, then just before you reach the Seagrove Bay slipway take path R105 to the left. This goes forward to Pier Road which you follow to arrive at the village of Seaview (12) – no prizes for originality namewise there. Once the proud possessor of a salt industry that thrived on the marshes nearby, and a pier 1,000 feet long, it is a cheerful resort, smaller and more sedate than its sister Ryde just a couple of miles to the west; the AA Guide to Britain's Coast states that it 'still basks in nineteenth century charm'. It provides lovely views across the Solent and is a good place to view the granite forts in the Spithead area of the Solent itself, built in the 1860s on Palmerston's orders as defences against the French and described as 'pretty much indestructible'. Best of all, it offers the first en-route scones and clotted cream since Sandown 12 miles back. Turn right to follow down the High Street to the sea wall, and at the end turn left onto the Esplanade. Now, at long, long last, you are able to enjoy a proper seafront march again, and the going could not be easier as you proceed along the promenade past Seaview and Puckpool for 2 miles to arrive back at Ryde (14). As you walk, you can enjoy watching the huge variety of vessels in the Solent, trusting that your ferry back to the mainland is among them. It is only when you reach Ryde Pavilion that you're forced inland to follow the coast road, but in no time you're passing the Hovercraft terminal, crossing the railway and arriving back at the town end of the pier where you started. If you're feeling lazy, a train can transport you to the pier head for the Fastcat ferry back to Portsmouth. If you're feeling virtuous, walk along the pier – it's an enjoyable stroll with great views across the Solent. If you feel like going round again, just go back eleven pages and see you back at Ryde in four days time.

# HAMPSHIRE

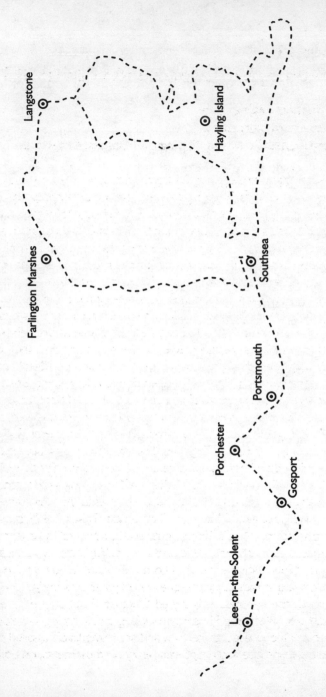

Langstone

Hayling Island

Farlington Marshes

Southsea

Portsmouth

Porchester

Gosport

Lee-on-the-Solent

# Day 35
# Portsmouth to Langstone 16.5 miles (550.5 miles)

**Difficulty rating:** Easy
**Terrain rating:** ▲▲
**Highlights:** Southsea, Farlington Marshes, Langstone

Assuming you are carrying on from Portsmouth Harbour station (either having come from Gosport or Ryde), follow the station approach road to arrive at a T-junction with the Hard. Turn right and follow this road briefly, then very shortly turn right into the Gunwharf Quays complex, and follow it to the waterfront. As you arrive at the waterfront you turn left to follow a waterfront walkway, but you could detour right to the Spinnaker Tower, which is definitely worth a visit. Follow the waterfront walkway round from the Gunwharf Quays complex, bearing right at its end to arrive at the Wightlink car ferry terminal, then turn left immediately and walk along the side of the car assembly area to Gunwharf Road. Turn right and follow this road as far as the fish market on the right-hand side, then bear right and walk down through the fish market to the water's edge; bear left here and go forward to Feltham Row, which you follow round a harbour area known as the Camber to a T-junction with Broad Street. Bear right here and follow Broad Street to its end, passing on to Spice Island from which there are superb views to the harbour area, with Spinnaker Tower looking particularly impressive. Turn hard left, almost doubling back on yourself, along first Bath Street, West Street, and then Tower Street, which are all quite narrow, until you reach a high red brick wall to the right; use the steps at the north end of the wall to climb onto the wall itself and begin your walk along the Millennium Promenade. This is a really splendid walk with great views to Old Portsmouth and its cathedral to your left, and the Solent to your right with Ryde on the Isle of Wight clearly visible across the water. Now, with the statue of Lord Nelson just below you to your left, go forward to cross a picturesque area of water by a bridge, and continue towards the conspicuously signed Clarence Pier. You are here entering Southsea, effectively Portsmouth's playground, having developed as a resort in the nineteenth century, and are immediately assailed by one of the most unsubtle and unappealing array of amusements, on both sides of your concrete walkway. Mercifully it's soon over, and you can proceed to enjoy an excellent open walk past firstly the hovercraft terminal – it's worth pausing to watch the hovercraft as it takes off amid a shower of spray – and then the huge Naval war memorial to the castle (2.5) which dates back to 1538. A little way to the north of the castle on Clarence Esplanade is the D-Day Museum which contains the Overlord Embroidery, a 272-foot tapestry depicting the events of 6 June 1944; it is certainly worth detouring off the promenade to visit it.

The walking is still easy as you continue along the promenade past South Parade Pier and forward to Eastney Beach, enjoying excellent views to the north-east part of the Isle of Wight. Now, as the main St George's Road (with signpost for 'Out Of City') goes away to the left, and you walk parallel with the quieter Esplanade past the Royal Marines Museum housed in Eastney Barracks, there's a big decision to be made. You may simply wish to continue up the Solent Way towards Langstone, in which case as the Esplanade leaves the shore you follow the road round to the left, turning almost immediately left into Driftwood Gardens and then shortly right into Halliday Crescent, arriving at a T-junction with Henderson Road. However, you could decide to continue along the shore and head for the extreme end of Portsea Island and effectively the entrance to Langstone Harbour. To do this, walk along the shore, being forced initially to shingle-tramp, but then as you pass a caravan park you're able to follow a good firm shore-side path beside the perimeter fence with the caravan park. As the park ends, turn left onto a rough track; when it ends, cross a track and go straight over a low metalled railing to follow a path through a rough grassy area, keeping the perimeter fence with Fort Cumberland immediately to your right. At the end of the path, turn right onto Ferry Road and follow it to the landing stage at the end of the spit, from which there is a frequent all-year ferry service to Hayling Island that lies just 250 metres across the water. You could decide to save a day's walking by using the ferry, and if you do this, you'll need to skip to page 163 to resume the narrative. However, by doing this you would actually be missing out on a large section of what is accepted as part of the south coast. If you decide not to take the ferry, retrace your steps back down Ferry Road, go straight on into Fort Cumberland Road through the Eastney district of

Portsmouth, and pass a potentially useful shop and cafe. Go straight over the crossroads beyond these amenities, now in Henderson Road, and pass Halliday Crescent coming in from the left, this being the road junction where the shorter route joins the longer one.

Continue westwards very briefly along Henderson Road beyond Halliday Crescent, but look out very shortly for a footpath going off to the right. If you find yourself at the junction with Bransbury Road you've gone too far. Follow the footpath through a park, bearing slightly left then right between houses – there is a Solent Way marker here – to reach Kingsley Road. Go straight over into Ironbridge Lane and follow it to a T-junction with Locksway Road; you are now in the Milton district of Portsmouth (7.5). Turn right and follow Locksway Road, in due course reaching a pub which is to your left; more or less opposite the pub a footpath goes off to the right, and very shortly arrives at the waterfront again. Now the going is really easy and enjoyable, with a clear path proceeding up the western shore of Langstone Harbour, and magnificent views across and beyond the harbour itself, particularly to the Kingley Vale Nature Reserve just north-west of Chichester. Previously the area covered by Langstone Harbour, stretching out so majestically in front of you, was a coastal plain, but this plain was flooded as a result of melting ice and rising sea levels. You go past a restaurant, incidentally the only amenity on the 9-mile stretch between Milton and Langstone village, then pass to the seaward side of an outdoor activity centre and to the landward side of an industrial works, keeping the A2030 close to your left. Cross a bridge over the harbour water as it thins out to the left. Beyond the bridge, you swing sharply right, now walking parallel with the A27, then soon bear right again to begin your negotiation of Farlington Marshes. This is a fairly sizeable peninsula sticking out into Langstone Harbour, but is particularly noteworthy for its nature reserve and its fantastic variety of bird life; the combination of marsh and meadow provides one of the best birdwatching reserves in Hampshire. The most important visitors are Brent geese, who return here every autumn from as far away as northern Russia to feed on the saltings and rough pastures and stay here till the spring. There are many other birds to see including the black-tailed godwit, dunlin, widgeon and teal and indeed the reserve supports more than 50 species of breeding birds.

Now follow the excellent path round the shore of the peninsula, the traffic noise potentially intrusive, but the views tremendous. You return to follow briefly parallel with the A27, heading just north of east; from here, still following an excellent harbour-side path, you walk just south of east, towards the Hayling Island road bridge which looks just a short distance away. However, this is deceptive, for on rounding a corner you find yourself forced away from the harbour up the left side of a channel past a sizeable industrial works. Shortly you go under a road bridge; immediately beyond it, bear left and climb to the road itself, then turn left (eastwards) and follow the road, Harts Farm Way, past the rather unsightly Broadmarsh industrial estate. Keep along the road, and just before a crossroads you can see clearly ahead, bear right onto a signed footpath which proceeds quite pleasantly back to the harbourside. The works do not enhance the beauty of the landscape but there is plenty of greenery around and you get the feeling that the authorities have tried to make an effort! On you go along the harbourside, but with the Hayling bridge almost within shouting distance you're again forced inland by a channel coming in from the left, and you have to follow this channel; it's not a long walk inland but it will seem longer at the end of a tiring day. Don't cross the first bridge you come to, but go on to the next and cross that, going forward into Mill Lane. Follow the lane to the point where it bears left and Harbour Side goes off to the right, and now go straight on along a path to the main Havant–Hayling road, the traffic noise from which is clearly audible; turn right to follow it, passing the Langstone High Street turning, to the Ship Inn which is on the east side of the road. Langstone (16.5), with its attractive houses and windmill, is a very pretty village and was once a port for Havant, with sailing ships calling here until the nineteenth century, while local barges could be seen here carrying coal, shingle and fertilisers.

Now you need to decide whether you're going to walk Hayling Island, which will add a full day to your itinerary but is to be thoroughly recommended and thus is included in the overall mileage. If you decide to skip it, cross the main road and walk into The Ship car park, then jump to page 167 where the narrative for your journey beyond The Ship continues.

## Day 36
## Hayling Island Circular 16 miles (566.5 miles)

**Difficulty rating:** Easy
**Terrain rating:** ▲▲
**Highlights:** Hayling Billy, Eastoke Point, St Peter's Church

If you wish to walk round Hayling Island, go on over the bridge crossing, keeping to the right-hand (west) pavement, then having crossed over on to the island, take the first right-hand footpath turn. The footpath initially stays parallel with the road, but very soon you turn right onto a path signed as the Hayling Billy route; from here you go forward to turn left onto the embankment of the 'Hayling Billy' railway line which linked Havant with the southern part of Hayling Island. It opened in 1867 and enjoyed huge popularity, bringing the island and its attractions within reach of the populace of the nearby towns and cities, but it shut in 1963 when the cost of necessary remedial work to the bridge linking it to the mainland was found to be too great. You could detour right when you reach the embankment of the old line in order to get a better view of the old railway bridge crossing of the harbour, but must then retrace your steps. From the point you initially joined the embankment, head south-westwards along the course of the old line. Soon you'll see land jutting out to your right and you'll be able to pick up a footpath that leaves the Hayling Billy line and follows alongside Langstone Harbour. This is lovely walking, with superb views across the harbour; soon you reach a saline lagoon and signboards tell you what bird life to look out for, which may include the common tern, little egret, oystercatcher and ringed plover. Again it may be worth detouring onto one of the embankments lining the lagoon and enjoying the great diversity of bird life as well as splendid views across to Portsmouth and Farlington Marshes, although the noise of the A27 is still quite intrusive. Keep to the harbourside path and follow it to be reunited with the Hayling Billy line, which you now stay on for rather longer, bollards directing walkers and cyclists to the left half of the path and horses to the right one! For a while you become separated from the harbourside by trees, but the walking remains delightful and with fields to the left it feels truly rural, with even the traffic noise on the A27 starting to fade.

In due course, and for the first time since you joined the Hayling Billy line, a large field appears to separate you from the harbourside, and you now have a choice of routes. The more conservative route continues along the old line to arrive at a T-junction with Station Road then bears right onto this road, and you follow the road westwards; as it bends half-left, bear right into Sinah Lane and follow it westwards, passing the south end of North Shore Road. A more interesting route, but not designated as a right of way, turns right to follow a path round the right-hand edge of the field, soon reaching and following the harbourside on a low cliff to the far end of the field, where the low cliff path ends. At low tide, you might think that it was possible to follow the shore on from here, but right of access is dubious, the going is potentially very slippery, the road/path journey (also preferred by the 'official' signed Langstone harbour waterside walk) is not unpleasant, and you're not going to get any better views of the harbour than at other points on your walk so far... so I don't recommend it. Instead, having reached the far end of the field, swing left, a little inland, then soon bear right into North Shore Road; follow this to a T-junction with Sinah Lane, turning right onto it to be reunited with the other route. Follow Sinah Lane westwards then when it bends sharply left go forward into Warren Close, almost immediately bear left onto a narrow path which follows a rather winding course to reach a T-junction with Ferry Road. Turn right to follow the road. In a few hundred yards you reach a right turn leading to a hotel and leisure complex; follow the hotel approach road, then soon fork right onto a road leading round the right-hand side of the hotel and providing access to the harbourside. Here you get the last really good views of Langstone Harbour, which has been your companion for so many miles, so make the most of it. Bear left and now proceed beside the harbour initially through the hotel grounds (public access appears not to be a problem) then along a shingly path, in due course veering back to Ferry Road along a firmer path on the east side of a little inlet called the Kench. Turn right onto Ferry Road and follow it just north of west to arrive at the Ferry Boat Inn, one of the oldest pubs on the island, by the landing stage for the ferry from Eastney. It is thus here that walkers who decided to miss Langstone Harbour by catching the ferry will be reunited with those who preferred the longer walk.

From the landing stage head for the Ferry Boat Inn, passing through the outside seating area of the inn on its harbour side, and go forward to join a harbourside path, heading for the harbour mouth. The scene has completely changed, with views over to the Isle of Wight ahead and the buildings of Portsmouth and Southsea across the harbour to your right, and you will note just how narrow Langstone Harbour is here compared to its great width a little further north. To your left is Hayling Golf Club, founded in 1883; it is one of the oldest golf clubs in the country, and one of the finest links golf courses on the south coast. As you approach the harbour mouth and veer left to follow the coastline proper, with open sea to your right, you've three options. These are a rather tame but firm path set well back from the shingle beach adjacent to the boundary fences marking Hayling Golf Club, an exhilarating walk along the sands, or a tough walk on the shingle bank. The sand option is, of course, dependent on tide but if available is the best; in due course, however, the walk along the sand is made much tougher by a line of breakwaters, and here you may feel constrained to join the shingle bank, the firmer path coming in to meet you at this point. Unless you want to follow a road behind a line of beach huts, you're then forced along a shingle platform as far as the Inn on the Beach pub, and, with the breakwaters relenting, there's then a choice between sand (tide permitting), shingle bank or coast road. The coast road is a long way back from the shore and in due course becomes separated from it by a miniature railway, so, unpalatable as it may seem, the shingle bank tramp is probably best if the sand is unavailable. To the left, there's a strange mix of rather tacky-looking holiday amusements, beach huts and an assortment of houses and flats including Norfolk Crescent, a very conspicuous grey stone block which was built in the nineteenth century. Another succession of breakwaters mean that sand walking is again rendered difficult, if not impossible, so it's up to the shingle bank and a real effort as you trudge past more beach huts; there's one all too short boarded section by way of a concession for those who think this is more than adequate penance for sins in this or a former life! Thankfully, as you become level with the car park, the shingle is a little firmer and shortly after you've passed a shark-fin-shaped sculpture (7) which is to your left, you arrive at an access point for the shops and cafes of Rails Lane. Here you pick up and follow a concrete seaside promenade. The luxury!

In just over half a mile the metalled promenade gives out and you simply proceed along the shingle round Eastoke Point. The views from here are absolutely stunning; the Isle of Wight, and the Yarborough memorial (see page 153), are still visible to your right, and straight ahead, you can see the Witterings, Bracklesham and Selsey Bill in West Sussex. Carry on round to walk inland beside the mouth of Chichester Harbour, having a choice between the shingle or a firm path along the back of the beach, and pass the lifeboat station. Beyond the lifeboat station you proceed along the shore parallel with and to the right (east) side of the concrete road leading to the Hayling Island Sailing Club straight ahead. Incidentally, Hayling Island claims to be the birthplace of the sport of boardsailing (another term for windsurfing) in 1958, when one Peter Chilvers, aged twelve, used a sheet of plywood and a tent flysheet attached to a pole with curtain rings to sail up an island creek! Pass to the right of the sailing club building and round the back of it, then aim for the left end of the roped-off dune area ahead, from which there are tremendous views to Chichester Harbour and the countryside beyond. Now follow the beach southwards, to the west side of the sailing club approach road, and go forward to join a road veering south-westwards away from the sailing club. Turn right to join this road and go straight on into Bracklesham Road which you follow to a T-junction with Sandy Point Road, turning right onto this road and following it to a crossroads with a parade of shops. Go straight over the crossroads into West Haye Road and follow this to a T-junction with Eastoke Road, turning left into this road and following it to a further T-junction with Southwood Road. Turn right into this road and follow it north-westwards, then in about a quarter of a mile turn right into St Hermans Road and shortly look out for a public footpath sign on the right. Bear right to follow the path, which soon arrives at an inlet of Chichester Harbour, and follow the left (north) side of this inlet, with a holiday park immediately to your left. The path is very clear and soon arrives at the mouth of the inlet, then swings north-westwards along the west side of Chichester Harbour. This is really lovely walking, with the harbour and all it's boating activity in the foreground, and a backcloth of hills including the South Downs stretching many miles to the east. You will also get a fine prospect of the eastern side of Chichester Harbour, including the area round Itchenor and West Wittering.

The path goes round a mini-inlet and continues north-westwards then veers just south of west to begin following around another inlet marked on maps as My Lord's Pond. Soon you pass a sailing club and are directed along a path between the boats, emerging at Marine Walk; turn right on to this road, going forward into Salterns Lane and following this to a T-junction with Rails Lane. At this junction look out for a footpath going off to the right, immediately to the left of a private driveway. Follow this clearly-defined footpath which in just a few hundred yards passes the end of a road and shortly beyond that arrives at a sign prohibiting further access. However, just beside the sign, you're able to bear left onto a legitimate footpath which continues northwards to arrive at the south end of Beech Grove. Go forward into Beech Grove and follow it northwards to a T-junction with Tournerbury Lane, turn right along this residential road, and just before reaching the golf club entrance bear left into Eastwood Close. Almost immediately, however, bear right onto a signed footpath which proceeds very pleasantly just west of north, with good views to your right past the golf course to Chichester Harbour and the hills above Chichester. At the end of the path you arrive at the Mill Rythe holiday complex approach road. Go straight over the approach road onto an unsigned but clear path which runs through a large field of rough pasture with just one plank bridge over a ditch to watch for. You pass into another field; carry straight on, aiming just to the left of the main part of the holiday complex, and, continuing on the path, climb up onto the embankment and turn left to follow it round what is another inlet of the harbour. You could in fact detour to the right for views out to the main harbour itself, with more superb views, but in due course you reach a dead end and make your way back alongside the inlet. Whether you've followed the detour or not, continue along the embankment beside the inlet, veering sharply right at the south-west tip of the inlet and proceeding along a narrow but clear path into a little marina-cum-industrial estate. There's no way forward alongside the inlet, so bear left into the industrial estate and follow the thoroughfare through it into Mill Rythe Lane. Follow this lane to a T-junction with the A3023, the main road through the island, and turn right to walk alongside this road; this is an extremely busy road, but very fortunately a pavement is provided, and you pass what may be a very welcome pub. A couple of hundred yards further on, bear right onto Yew Tree Road – there's another pub on the corner – and follow this road, passing a quite delightful timber-framed house which is on the right, to arrive at a T-junction where you turn right onto Copse Lane.

Follow Copse Lane briefly but look out for a signed footpath soon going off to the right. This leads to the shore and you can enjoy a very pleasant shore-side walk, albeit the views eastwards are restricted, but all too soon you are forced to bear left, away from the shore, up to a metalled lane. Turn left and then almost immediately right along Woodgaston Road, passing a garden centre which is on the right and which offers a welcome cafe. You reach a T-junction with St Peter's Road and follow this for just under half a mile; although it's more road walking, this is actually very enjoyable indeed, with a really splendid avenue of trees lining the road for most of the way. Shortly you reach the village of North Hayling, and look out on the right for St Peter's Avenue. Turn right into it and follow it as far eastwards as you can go; it then bends sharply right and looks to be heading into a yard, but just before the yard you turn left along a footpath which firstly heads southwards along a field edge then bends left and proceeds pleasantly and clearly to a flight of steps up an embankment. Turn left to follow a rough embankment path, enjoying beautiful views across Chichester Harbour to Thorney Island, East Head, Emsworth and the Downs above Chichester. You can also get a good view of the east-facing shores of Hayling, of which you will have had precious little sight. All too soon you reach a wooden barrier where you need to turn left down the steps and then along a clear path that takes you over the fields to Church Lane. Follow the lane to return to St Peter's Road by the very pretty church of St Peter (14.5), which is certainly worth exploring if you have a few moments to spare; it was built in 1140, escaped a great fire which swept through the surrounding village in the eighteenth century, and has a peal of three bells which is said to be the oldest in Hampshire. From the church, follow the road northwards to a sharp left bend at a junction with Northney Lane which leads into Northney Road. Taking this left bend, continue along Northney Road.

Watch out for house number fifteen on the right, then just beyond it turn right onto a footpath which passes a parking area and goes through a wooden gate. Go straight on along a good clear path initially through fairly thick vegetation but very soon passing into more open country, and shortly after it does so you will reach an information signboard which is to the right of the path. Look out here for a narrow path going off to the left almost opposite this signboard, which you take to continue progress back towards the mainland, but by detouring straight on along the main path you will find yourself back by the shore of Chichester Harbour. On a clear day the views from here to the surrounding countryside are stunning and include the spire of Chichester Cathedral and the Trundle. A clear path continues along the sea-wall and is well worth taking, despite the extra legwork, because of its beauty and tranquillity, but in due course you reach a dead end, with new housing across the rough grass to your right, and you are forced back to the signboard. Follow the narrow path to the left away from the 'main' path; this now follows an embankment alongside a marshy inlet of Chichester Harbour, leaving the waterside to pass through an area of scrub and emerging in the Langstone Hotel complex. Turn right to follow through a car park with hotel buildings to the left and the water to your right, then go forward into a further car park, aiming for the entrance to Northney Marina which is clearly visible ahead. Go into the marina complex past the barrier, and immediately bear right along a driveway which returns you to the waterside, then turn left along a metalled walkway with a car/boat park to your left and the harbour to your right. The walkway ends but you can continue by the harbour-side along an embankment path then, when this also gives out, you drop down to follow the shore, in due course rejoining the road on the northern side of the hotel complex and turning right onto the road. At high tide this shore-side path may be impassable; if so you can return to a metalled slip road, turning right to follow it, going straight on out of the complex and past the hotel and car parks to reach the road onto which you turn right to be reunited with the low tide route. Now follow the road beside the water just south of west to arrive at the A3023 again. Turn right onto the road, almost immediately reaching the bridge and crossing it to arrive at The Ship Inn, then turn right into the pub car park to be reunited with walkers who have chosen not to walk round Hayling Island. Walk through the car park and then through the outdoor seating area to the harbour side of the pub (16).

# WEST SUSSEX

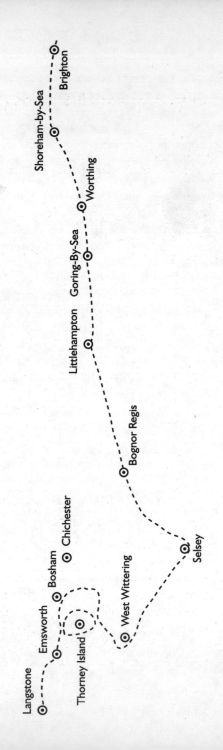

Langstone

Emsworth

Thorney Island

Bosham

⊙ Chichester

West Wittering

Selsey

Bognor Regis

Littlehampton

Goring-By-Sea

⊙ Worthing

Shoreham-by-Sea

⊙ Brighton

# Day 37
# Langstone to Bosham 15.5 miles (582 miles)

**Difficulty rating:** Easy
**Terrain rating:** ▲▲
**Highlights:** Emsworth, Marker Point, Bosham

At the far end of the pub seating area, you go forward to join a concrete path that runs along the waterside to reach the bottom of Langstone High Street. Cross over the street and go forward to pass The Royal Oak pub, which, like The Ship, was once a favoured haunt of smugglers, but now both pubs offer splendid hospitality. From The Royal Oak you continue along the shore-side, now part of Chichester Harbour, leaving Langstone behind; you follow the shore initially but soon you are directed left, inland, towards the pretty Warblington Church and a nearby castle ruin. Just before the church, bear right onto a clear path which continues very obviously and very attractively through lovely unspoilt countryside, passing through an area of woodland to emerge back at the shore. Note you are sharing your route at this point with what is the last bit of the Wayfarers Walk which has come all the way from Inkpen in Berkshire to end at Emsworth. You still have a little matter of 145 miles to do! Continue along the shore with the buildings of Emsworth to your left – looking back, you can still make out the Spinnaker Tower on the horizon – then immediately beyond Bath Road, which comes in from the left, go forward onto the Promenade which swings north to head directly for the centre of Emsworth and is a really lovely walkway with beautiful views to Chichester Harbour and Emsworth itself. Go straight on into South Street and follow it into the centre of Emsworth (2.5). Emsworth is an attractive little harbour-side town, full of pretty streets and alleys; it once boasted a flourishing oyster industry but is now better known as a yachting centre and host of a large and important food fair in September. To reach the station from the centre, bear left to the roundabout then straight over into North Street, the station a couple of hundred yards up on the left. To continue your coastal walk, bear right from the centre into Queen Street and follow it gently downhill to arrive at the A259, a road you will become very familiar with in the ensuing days, and turn right on to the A259. In doing so you finally leave the county of Hampshire.

You begin your walk through West Sussex by proceeding alongside the A259 out of Emsworth. If you've not broken your journey here you'll have reached the A259 from the town centre via Queen Street (the county border is at this junction); if you've started from the station it'll have been a walk alongside the A259 from the roundabout a little to the west to arrive at the county border. Immediately to your right having arrived in West Sussex you will see a millpond that served Slipper Mill, constructed in 1760, and still stands having been converted into flats. In front of you is a sign telling you that along the A259 Bosham is just 4 miles ahead, but your coastal route to Bosham will be some 9 miles longer. Putting all thoughts of cheating to one side, you reach the Mill Pond pub on your left, and here you turn right, away from the main road, down Slipper Road. The road soon peters out but you continue in the same direction across an area of gravel, soon arriving at a huge marina. Pass to the right of the harbour offices, then shortly you'll see a choice of paths, with right and left forks available. Fork right here, passing between the boats to get onto a track which you then follow to the right, soon reaching the waters of Chichester Harbour and turning left onto the waterside path. Chichester Harbour was formed after the last Ice Age by rivers of snow-melt and thawing permafrost; the gravel and stone carried by the rivers scoured out the harbour bed and as the sea level rose, the harbour was created. As you proceed beside the harbour, enjoy lovely views to Hayling, and try to visualise the steady procession of malt and flour-bearing vessels which once plied these waters.

To begin with there's a choice of ridge-top path or a wider lower path to the left, but both paths arrive at a formidable looking gate signifying your arrival at Thorney Island and its military base. To progress, you need to press a button and confirm your identity by intercom, and hopefully the gate will be opened for you. Thorney Island once really was an island but in 1870 a large acreage of land was reclaimed from the sea including a small area of land across the Great Deep channel which now joins Thorney to the mainland. The join helped to increase the island's population but it remained essentially a quiet agricultural community until an RAF base was installed in 1937. The RAF remained until 1976 and thereafter the island was to become an Army base. However, there are no difficulties in following the coastline around Thorney, as long as you keep to the path on the water's edge without being tempted to stray outside the line of posts provided. Look out for a fine variety of plants including glasswort, sea purslane, sea lavender, horned poppy and sea holly. At Marker Point you swing eastwards and then south-eastwards, and for the first time since you passed Eastoke Point on Hayling Island, this feels like proper coastal walking again. The path temporarily leaves the water's edge, going round the landward side of an area of quite dense vegetation, but soon returns to the sea and reaches the south-eastern tip of Thorney at Longmere Point. There are superb views north-eastwards from here to the wooded hills of the Kingley Vale Nature Reserve near Chichester, and seawards you can admire the great sand spit of East Head at the west tip of the Manhood Peninsula. Immediately in front of you is Pilsey Island with its spectacular array of bird life; look out for wild swans, brent geese, shelducks, curlews, dunlins, sandwich terns, ringed plovers, oystercatchers and many more. Moving northwards from Longmere Point, you pass the old runway, an obvious reminder of the RAF presence here, then go forward to pass the island's sailing club – at high tide you'll need to go to the landward side of the club buildings – and the impressive church of St Nicholas, Thorney's oldest building with an unusually large tower and parts that date back to the twelfth century. Straightforward walking takes you back out of the restricted area, and over the Great Deep out of Thorney Island.

You continue on to Thornham Point, past Prinsted Point and through the popular Thornham Marina, going forward to Prinsted (10), the village street coming down to meet the coast path. There are delightful views from here to the spires of Bosham Church and Chichester Cathedral. The village of Prinsted, it's name meaning 'place of pears', is most pleasant too, with thatched and timber-framed cottages along its lanes; although it has the appearance of a museum piece, traditional industries including agriculture and market gardening have flourished here, and formerly there was a plentiful supply of cockles and winkles in the bay. The going remains easy and straightforward, your solid embankment path proceeding on round an inlet between the Thorney and Chidham peninsulas. To your left as you follow the top of the inlet round is the village of Nutbourne, where there was a busy port in the Middle Ages, and a tide mill was built towards the end of the seventeenth century. It is still possible to identify the remains of the hard where barges used to come up to load and unload at the mill. Beyond Nutbourne you now embark on the Chidham peninsula towards its foot at Cobnor Point, and you can enjoy views back to Thorney, but once the path has passed Chidham Point and veers south-eastwards, you are forced onto the shingle and the going can be frustrating. Recent excavations show that man has been populating this part of the coast for 4,000 years; flint scrapers were discovered around here suggesting spear shafts were made in this locality, and other Iron Age finds show that these later people had built themselves primitive salterns using tiny lined pits in which sea water was trapped. It is with some relief that you arrive at a flight of steps which take you up onto a wheelchair-friendly path that rounds Cobnor Point, and from which it's a tantalisingly short distance across the water to the houses and boats of Itchenor. But you still have a long way to go by land to reach the village.

Beyond Cobnor Point you are briefly forced away from the coastline to go round the landward side of some houses, but soon you find yourself back by the water and enjoying lovely views to Bosham, your next port of call. At a tiny inlet you reach the metalled Harbour Way, bearing left and then shortly right; you could detour left at this second junction to visit Chidham, the most interesting building of which is arguably Chidmere House, a Tudor building which underwent restoration in 1930. Back on the main route you now continue first along and then parallel with the road to reach the A259. It is rather galling to observe a signpost saying Emsworth is just 3 miles back after your negotiation of these two big peninsulas, but that is coastal walking for you, and unfortunately it's not going to get any easier. Walk eastwards beside the A259 then as the road reaches the north-east tip of the next inlet, turn right via a flight of steps to join a shore-side path that takes you to Bosham; if the tide is high you may be forced to branch off along Westbrook Field rather than sticking to the shore but even then the way into Bosham is quite clear. Bosham (15.5) is the first real gem of the Sussex coast with so much to see. Architecturally its main attraction is Holy Trinity Church, some of which is pre-Norman, boasting a Saxon tower and chancel arch, an Early English east window of 1120 and a crypt that was built around the same time; its most famous worshipper was King Harold who received communion here before setting out to meet William in battle, and a fragment of the Bayeux Tapestry actually shows him on his way to the church. Although there are many pretty cottages in the village of red brick, stone and flint, dating back to the seventeenth and eighteenth centuries, it is the waterside setting of the village, and the beautiful Quay Meadow, which makes Bosham so attractive, particularly at high tide. It used to be a thriving shipbuilding centre and fishing port with one of the busiest oyster trades in the country, but sailing is now Bosham's principal 'industry' so to speak, and tourism has also assumed increased significance with many day trippers arriving by car at weekends and holiday times. If you pass by the village at high tide you may see some cars engulfed by the tidal waters that regularly catch unsuspecting motorists unawares; as a walker you wouldn't be human if you didn't permit yourself a touch of smugness!

# Day 38
# Bosham to Selsey 21.5 miles (603.5 miles)

**Difficulty rating:** Easy
**Terrain rating:** ▲▲
**Highlights:** Dell Quay, Itchenor, East Head

Having got a good cream tea inside you – or a few pints at the Anchor Bleu – set off along the raised waterside path (or the road if you prefer and are able). At low tide you may then use a causeway to take a short cut to continue your waterside walk but at high tide you will need to follow Shore Road right round, ignoring the Stumps Lane turning at the south-east corner. Short cut or no, you then stick to Shore Road heading south-westwards, passing some beautiful houses and enjoying great views across the inlet to Bosham; in due course the road bends left, away from the shore, but you are able to stick to the shore by means of a footpath, unless the tides are very high, in which case you may need to retreat to the road. Even if the footpath is available you're at length forced back to the road which you follow, now rejoicing in the name Smugglers Lane, for about a mile, your views to the harbour restricted by houses and by Combes Shipyard, famous for its work in restoring old vessels. At the end of Smugglers Lane there is a T-junction where you have to turn left into Hoe Lane, away from the harbour, with the exclusive Bosham Hoe private housing development separating you from the water. You follow Hoe Lane for about half a mile then turn right into Old Park Lane, following this to a T-junction. Old Park Lane bears left and at high tide, when the harbourside path this side of Fishbourne can flood (it's a good idea to check tide tables) you are advised to carry on along it into Fishbourne (2.5), joining the A259 onto which you turn right, then right again down Mill Lane to reach the harbour-side. If, however, you've done your homework, or are lucky, and the tides permit, you can at the T-junction bear right along the metalled lane which after half a mile comes to an end at Hook Farm; at the end of the lane you turn left onto a footpath which climbs gently and provides beautiful views across the next 'arm' of Chichester Harbour to Dell Quay and Chichester Cathedral. You cross a stream then bear right to follow a signed harbour-side path to the bottom of Mill Lane, here meeting the high-tide route. You can detour via Mill Lane and then left along the A259 and right up Salthill Road to view Fishbourne Roman Palace, or even bear right along the A259 and then left via a signed cycle path called The Centurion Way to Chichester, but either way it's quite a long walk and you may feel you want to press on.

You now embark on the biggest Sussex coastal peninsula of the lot, the Manhood. Resisting the temptation to follow a signed path stating 'Public Highway To The Sea' go straight on eastwards in the shade of trees, keeping a narrow channel to your left, then at the next footpath junction, don't continue eastwards over the footbridge but bear right along a boardwalk and continue along an excellent harbourside path. This is quite beautiful walking with lovely views in all directions, but the view to the north is particularly entrancing, the prospect of the harbour and the flat marshlands in the foreground contrasting starkly with that of the rolling hills behind. In due course, you cross over the river Lavant, and then continue beside the harbour, enjoying good views to the pretty village of Appledram (also spelt Apuldram) to the left; this village boasts most attractive gardens. a fine Early English church containing an organ originally made for Prince Albert, and Rymans, a stone built manor house with a tower dating back to 1410. Shortly you arrive at Dell Quay, formerly a very busy port and ranked in the eighth century as the most important port in Sussex. It emerged in the thirteenth century as the port for Chichester, was particularly busy in Elizabethan times, with three vessels sailing from here to fight the Armada; although it continued to prosper as a mercantile port in the eighteenth century, it had by the early part of the twentieth century declined in importance and is now principally a sailing and boating centre. If you lunch at the Crown and Anchor, an incredibly popular waterside pub said to be 400 years old, expect to be heavily outnumbered by boat owners.

You are temporarily forced inland, following Dell Quay Road past the pub then beyond Apuldram Cottage you bear right onto a permissive path which returns you to the water, and you can enjoy lovely views from the waterside to Chichester Cathedral and Dell Quay. You go forward through a patch of woodland known as Salterns Copse, then bear right at a T-junction of paths and pick up a concrete path taking you to the lock gates, noting to your left the huge Chichester Yacht Basin and marina, crammed with luxury craft. Cross straight over the lock gates, go past the marina offices and Peters' boat yard and then pass through the car park and to the left of the Chichester Yacht Club headquarters to arrive at another set of lock gates. This is Salterns Lock, and the channel you are about to cross here is actually Chichester Canal, part of the Portsmouth & Arundel Canal which opened in 1823 and provided a section of a canal network linking Portsmouth with London, although the section between Salterns Lock and the city of Chichester shut in 1906. Cross these lock gates and continue along the path, ignoring a right path fork by some modern houses, but then you are forced to bear sharp right along a path that leads you to Lock Lane. Join this road, heading south-westwards, and shortly arrive at Birdham Pool, the pool of Birdham tidal mill that opened in 1767 and shut in 1935, being taken over by the Birdham Yacht Club. You are close to the village of Birdham, not really worth a special visit, although it's worth noting that part of Birdham Pool became a marina in 1937 and was thus one of the earliest marinas in the country.

It is now very fiddly walking to the next village, Itchenor. Follow the road towards Harbour Meadow but soon fork left off the road along a path which skirts the right-hand edge of a large field; you skirt woodland to your right, returning to the water's edge at Westlands, but you are soon forced away from the water and up to a metalled drive. Turn right onto it, and go forward to a T-junction with a metalled lane, bearing right and following it for a few hundred yards to reach the buildings of Westlands Farm. Follow the path round to the left of the farm then at the next path junction bear right, diagonally across a field then through Westlands Copse to arrive at Spinney Lane; turn left onto it then in 200 yards bear right onto a path that returns you to the waterfront, and from here it's a mercifully easy waterside walk to the lovely village of Itchenor (10). Blessed with many fine houses, including Itchenor House that was built for the Third Duke of Richmond in 1787, the village is inexorably associated with shipbuilding, its heyday in this respect being around the eighteenth and early nineteenth centuries when a number of naval ships were launched from here. Although this industry declined, World War Two saw a number of small fast vessels and landing craft built here, and after the war the well-established Haines Boatyard concentrated on the production of pleasure craft including fast motor cruisers. Like Dell Quay, it is immensely popular with the sailing fraternity, some of whom you'll undoubtedly meet in The Ship Inn, the village's very popular watering hole.

From Itchenor it's possible to follow a waterside path almost all the way to West Wittering, with just one interruption after 2 miles where you are forced inland to reach a metalled drive, turning right and then just before Bricket Cottage right again onto a path that returns you to the waterside. This is lovely walking, if a little muddy in wet conditions, with magnificent views back to Hayling Island, Pilsey Island, Thorney Island, Cobnor Point... they seem like old friends and it's nice to look back and see just how much you've achieved. You pass a spit of land known as Ella Nore (no mention of Rigby) which provides a fragile but sustainable habitat for plants that include sea kale, sea campion, and yellow-horned poppy; you can sit on the seat provided and enjoy the view before the agreeable half-mile stroll to Snow Hill – no hill, unlikely to be snow and its green – where again you may be tempted to stop and enjoy the beautiful surroundings. You could instead, or in addition, detour left across the green and along Coastguard Lane to visit West Wittering, once the home of Henry Royce of Rolls Royce fame, and boasting a good pub and a number of shops. From the Snow Hill green, the coast route continues in a more south-westerly direction, heading now for the great spit of East Head, the south-western-most corner of the Manhood Peninsula; you are able to follow an excellent waterside path to the 'neck' of the spit, and from this neck you cannot miss a wide and popular path leading away to the right along the right-hand side of the spit. It does not, however, go all the way round, and you have a choice between taking a short cut to a path running down the west edge of the spit, perhaps using a board walk, or traipsing through the dunes to the top end. On a clear day your tenacity will be rewarded with views which extend to the Isle of Wight and the South Downs, and the whole area, owned by the National Trust, remains an important area for bird life including the lapwing, snipe and black-tailed godwit. At one time the spit pointed south-westwards leaving a gap of just 300 yards over the water – almost bridgeable!

Having joined the west-facing path on East Head you now proceed along a clear path south-eastwards, and at last you once more have the open sea to your right. It's been a long time! Be warned, however, that this path is obscenely popular in the summer and if you have the choice you should avoid summer weekends. The path becomes a delightful green carpet with clear views to Selsey Bill at the base of the Manhood Peninsula, but as you approach East Wittering, look out for Cakeham Tower on the left, a sixteenth-century hexagonal red-brick structure and a useful navigational aid for seamen. There are patches of shingle which makes this section of walk quite tough. Just beyond a large block of red-brick flats is a road that leads to the fleshpots of East Wittering (16), but assuming you wish to forgo (or have enjoyed) its amenities, continue along a track beside houses until you reach a gate indicating the way ahead is for beach-hut owners only. Turn left onto a track leading into Shingle Walk, go straight over at the crossroads into Charlmead, then at a T-junction turn right along a metalled road and go forward to a path that leads you back to the beach and shore of Bracklesham Bay. Now follow the shoreline using a narrow but firm concrete ledge, passing the uninteresting community of Bracklesham. Bracklesham Bay is, however, renowned for its fossils, with discoveries here of fossilised remains of turtles, crocodiles, sea snakes and large sharks dating back over 40 million years. Beyond Bracklesham the ledge peters out and it is now a laborious walk along the shingle bank, although the views to the hills above Chichester, including the Trundle and Goodwood, as well as to the Isle of Wight, are excellent. There's another big milestone for you to celebrate – 600, to be precise. You pass alongside the rather less appealing West Sands Caravan Park, are forced briefly away from the shore to get round a couple of residential properties, and continue along the shingle, passing Medmerry Mill; this structure, once used for milling flour, dates back to 1820, although other mills have existed hereabouts for over 300 years. The sails you see on it today were fitted as recently as 1977.

At length the going eases as you join a good path that takes you round the edge of low cliffs, the first cliffs you will have seen on your Sussex coastal walk. Bear right onto a gravel drive which goes forward into West Street, turn left along West Street then go first right into Clayton Road and second right into Danefield Road which takes you back to the shore. A shingle path now leads to the bottom of Hillfield Road providing easy access to the amenities of Selsey (21.5), the southernmost community in Sussex; it once stood on an island and at one time boasted a cathedral and a monastery, built by St Wilfrid who brought Christianity to this part of Sussex, although both buildings have long since fallen victim to rising seas. Its situation has made it particularly vulnerable not only to the elements – flood defences are a constant issue for its inhabitants – but to foreign invaders, and gun batteries were erected here during the Napoleonic Wars. The town has had and still enjoys a prosperous fishing industry but has never enjoyed (suffered?) the garishness of other South Coast resorts; its most recent claim to fame/notoriety was the tornado in January 1998 which caused a huge amount of damage despite its duration of just thirty seconds.

# Day 39
# Selsey to Littlehampton 16.5 miles (620 miles)

**Difficulty rating:** Easy
**Terrain rating:** ▲▲
**Highlights:** St Wilfrid's Chapel, Pagham Harbour Nature
Reserve, Climping Beach

Beyond Hillfield Road you now continue forward along a clear path towards Selsey Bill, the southernmost point in Sussex, perhaps looking back to enjoy final views of the Witterings. You reach a green at which you are forced to the landward side of buildings, joining a path just to the left of Bill Cottage which takes you back to the shore; you have now rounded the Bill and suddenly a brand new vista opens up with excellent views ahead to Pagham Harbour, Aldwick and Bognor Regis.

The going is very pleasant and easy for a while, past the Selsey Angling Club and the Selsey Lifeboat, and you should also look out for the memorial plaque to Eric Coates who was inspired by the view from here to write the theme tune to *Desert Island Discs*. Beyond the plaque the going gets tougher with some unwelcome sections of shingle, but becomes gentler again as views to Pagham Harbour open up to your left. Don't be fooled by the apparent proximity of Bognor Regis, for ahead of you is a tantalisingly narrow gap between two shingle embankments – until 1910 there was in fact a continuous embankment – and you are forced inland along a path that passes over some wooden sleepers and then beside the harbour waters. There are superb views; Chichester Cathedral can be seen from here, while nearer at hand is the red brick Norton Priory which contains both Saxon and medieval features. You reach a slip road leading to Church Norton, and it's worth a detour up this road to inspect the Mound, an earthwork which is believed to be a Roman coastal defence fort, and the thirteenth-century St Wilfrid's Chapel, actually the chancel of a rather larger church that once stood here, the remainder being removed to St Peter's in Selsey. It is possible that the chapel was built on the site of St Wilfrid's monastery, but whether or not this is so, the setting is still lovely. Returning to the harbourside, you continue close to the shore along what is a rather muddy and slippery path at times, but soon you reach an embankment path that takes you to the B2145 Chichester–Selsey road. Turn right and cross the harbour waters then bear hard right onto a path that now proceeds seawards beside the water, shortly reaching the course of the old Selsey Tram railway, noting the old embankment and bridge abutments to the right. Turn left to follow the course of the old railway which when operational was a remarkable line with no signalling, no crossing gates, an extraordinary number of halts and very old rolling stock; it enjoyed great popularity during the early part of the twentieth century but its fortunes declined and it shut in 1935. The path emerges at Mill Lane with the village of Sidlesham (5) close by to the left, and you need to turn right onto the lane and follow it, then as the road bends left, look for and join a path leading off to the right. That said, you may be tempted to detour a little way up the road to visit the hugely popular Crab and Lobster pub; it's an ideal place to stop for a drink and perhaps a meal, look out across the harbour and perhaps recall the days when nearby Sidlesham Quay was once a busy port, shipping out corn and importing coal, and smuggling was rife. In the late nineteenth century a great barrier was built across the mouth of Pagham Harbour, allowing the area to be farmed, but the defences were broken in a severe storm in 1910 and this breach created a new harbour. Its saltmarshes have become a wildlife haven, with the harbour becoming a nature reserve in 1964 and being noteworthy as a visiting place and breeding ground for the little tern, one of Britain's rarest breeding sea birds.

The footpath going away from Mill Lane proceeds agreeably beside the shore, although the going can be muddy and in fact at high tide it may be impassable and you'll then need to continue past the Crab and Lobster pub and bear right down Beggar's Lane, which leads to a footpath that returns you to the shore. In due course the surface does improve and you reach a T-junction of paths, turning right and shortly arriving at the embankment and sea defence known as Pagham Wall. You turn right to follow the wall, passing the old thatched Salt House immediately beyond which you turn right down a slipway to proceed beside the shore once more. Initially the path may be flooded at high tide; with no obvious alternative route it's best either to sit it out or to detour to visit the beautiful Pagham Church, with Norman and Saxon features, reached by continuing straight on past the Salt House and then bearing left into Church Lane, which takes you to the church. The shore-side path continues past the buildings of Little Welbourne and becomes much better defined, with excellent views to the hills around Chichester and also the spire of the cathedral. You follow the shore for a while then a stretch of embankment, passing the caravans of Church Farm Holiday Village, then beyond Pagham Lagoon bear left onto a shingle track, aiming for a gate at the right-hand end of a big car park. From here follow the embankment path past an old firing range and another lagoon, getting level with the harbour mouth, and you can look back with satisfaction to St Wilfrid's Chapel across the harbour and congratulate yourself that this long inland detour has been completed.

Now it is full steam ahead for Bognor Regis, starting with a walk beside Aldwick Bay, where a gun battery was erected in 1793 to guard against the threat of French invasion; unfortunately it's a shingle beach and the going is not easy, although you can mitigate the pain by getting as far down the beach as the tide will allow you and hopefully finding some firmer and/or sandier stretches. Sometimes at low tide it's possible to pick out a section of Mulberry Harbour that didn't make it across to France for the D-Day landings, but your energies will tend to go almost exclusively into making progress. The houses you can see to your left are part of Aldwick, regarded as the 'posher' end of Bognor Regis and where, at the now demolished nineteenth-century Craigweil House, George V stayed in 1929 when convalescing from illness. At length you reach a succession of breakwaters, and having negotiated these, you then have to pick your way round a huge wall of large rocks, using steps and a concrete path which may be submerged at high tide. After the rocks come a long line of beach huts, and when you draw level with the last you are able to scramble on to a concrete walkway known as the Esplanade; the walkway leads you unerringly to the seafront of Bognor Regis (9), which begging Selsey's pardon is the first real resort you will have encountered on your walk through Sussex. It was a Southwark hatter named Sir Richard Hotham who in the late eighteenth century, wanting to convert Bognor into an elegant seaside resort and encourage Royalty to visit, invested money in forty new buildings including the fine Hotham House set in lovely gardens.

Some speculators did invest in Bognor shortly after Sir Richard's death in 1799, with impressive buildings of the Steyne and Waterloo Square, but it was only with the arrival of the railway in 1864 that the town expanded significantly. A pier was built the very next year, many other entertainment centres were to follow, and the town had the accolade of 'Regis' being added to its title following the visit of George V and Queen Mary to the vicinity. It enjoys excellent sunshine records and good bathing, but it has a reputation for being a rather tacky place, not enhanced, perhaps, by the presence of Butlins. It features prominently in the *Crap Towns* guide, that warns 'if you take a pleasant evening stroll along the promenade in Bognor you are likely to be asked for drugs, mugged, or attacked by seagulls. Step into a local pub or club and prepare to be intimidated by a bevy of local lovelies dressed largely in skin-tight leopard print and knee high boots. Take heed, they may look harmless but they will happily gouge your eyes out with a false red nail if you so much glance in their direction.' Perhaps George V summed it up more succinctly, his dying words reputed to be 'Bugger Bognor.' All that said, the townspeople work hard to make Bognor Regis a more potentially appealing place to the would-be visitor, with the Birdman Rally and the summer Rox Music Festival now eagerly awaited and hugely popular annual events.

Beyond the pier you keep a good pace along the Esplanade, making up for time lost tramping beside Aldwick Bay, passing the sturdy red-brick Town Hall, the modern Alexandra Theatre, and then Butlins with its unmistakeable frothy white roof. You have now left Bognor Regis behind and to your left is Felpham, a sprawling residential area best known for its association with the poet William Blake who lived in Felpham for three years. You pass the sturdy flint-built Beachcroft Hotel, Felpham Sailing Club and beach huts, beyond which the surroundings become more genteel with trim suburban houses and gardens along the left-hand side of your route. At length the concrete promenade ends, being replaced by a dirt track and then a stonier path, going forward to a green beyond which a stony path brings you to the end of Sea Lane at Middleton-on-Sea. Now things get less straightforward. To continue along the shore you are forced down to the sands, there being nothing between sand and the high stone walls protecting the shore-side houses. Beyond the walls you may then retreat to a shingle bank and pick up a path along the back. Alternatively, you could stick to the sands, known as Elmer Sands, with a succession of rock-built groynes separating you from the sea, part of a coastal defence scheme that a plaque tells you was opened in 1993. There are tremendous views to Selsey Bill and, on a clear day, the Isle of Wight. If high tide prevents you gaining access to the sands beyond Sea Lane, follow this lane inland to a T-junction with Middleton Road, turn right to follow that road then at the mini-roundabout go forward into Elmer Road, following it to just short of a gate and then turning right onto a road that returns you to the shore.

It is now very easy going along a delightful path which leaves suburbia behind and passes through a precious countryside gap between the sprawls of Bognor Regis and Littlehampton. There is even a small woodland section at one stage. Emerging again into more open country you pass Bailiffscourt, a mock-Medieval house of warm limestone built in 1935, and a huge car park at the end of the road coming down from the A259 at Climping (or Clymping). The beach here is known as Climping Beach and is hugely popular in summer, so be warned. Beyond the car park you continue beyond the back of the beach, having to veer slightly left and scramble a little higher up the shingle to make progress; it's tough going for a while but the consolation is a great view towards the Downs and the castle and cathedral at Arundel. Things do get easier and you're able to follow a good path beside the dunes all the way to the mouth of the River Arun, or if you prefer you could follow the sands. The area is rich in bird life with visitors that include the kestrel, sanderling, finch, ringed plover and oystercatcher, and the sea offers crabs, whelks, cockles, shrimps and cuttlefish. Almost too suddenly, after enjoying such an unspoilt shore-side walk, you find yourself confronted with an area of metal fencing with the urban sprawl of Littlehampton straight ahead of you on the other side of the Arun, the first of four major river crossings you will have to negotiate in Sussex. You follow the west bank of the Arun with the option of either a road or sections of parallel path, the latter obviously pleasanter but a bit more fiddly. Either way, you end up at a T-junction with a road, turning right and going forward to a footbridge over the Arun; the present structure was built in 1981, replacing a swing-bridge that dated from 1908 which was once floodlit by 1,200 candle-powered lamps. Once over the bridge you turn immediately right into River Road then shortly right along an alleyway to join a new waterfront walk that takes you past impressive new housing developments along the east bank of the Arun, back towards the sea. In due course Pier Road comes in from the left (if you want to visit the town centre of Littlehampton (16.5), turn left to follow Pier Road to the shops); you now continue along the promenade between Pier Road and the river to reach the river mouth, passing a huge fun park and the Windmill Entertainment Centre before turning sharp left to pick up the seafront promenade. Littlehampton is now best known as a somewhat unsophisticated seaside resort and base for pleasure cruises up the Arun but there is considerable residential and industrial development in and around the town, and formerly it was an important base for shipbuilding. One particular milestone in the history of that industry in Littlehampton came with the construction here in the 1870s of the 532-ton ship *Trossachs* which took sheep and shepherds to the Falklands, helping to create what became the staple industry of these islands. As with so many other resorts on the south coast, it was really the arrival of the railway that triggered its popularity as a resort, and among visitors to the town in the nineteenth century were Lord Byron, John Constable and Samuel Taylor Coleridge.

# Day 40
# Littlehampton to Shoreham-by-Sea 14.5 miles (634.5 miles)

**Difficulty rating:** Easy
**Terrain rating:** ▲▲
**Highlights:** Goring-by-Sea, Worthing, Widewater Lagoon

Before striding out eastwards, take one last look out at Littlehampton's pier and also the lighthouse, built in 1948 to replace a mid-nineteenth century 'pepper-pot' lighthouse. Having done so, you head resolutely along the promenade with the open sea once again to your right and a broad expanse of green to your left, separating you from the centre of the town. You pass the Norfolk Gardens Pleasure Park, then a big sports complex, and the Rustington Convalescent Home, a fine Wren-style red-brick house dating back to 1897; looking back there are good views to the dunes on the west side of the Arun, and you may see the dome of Butlins making a guest appearance on the horizon. The promenade ends but you are able to continue along the pavement beside Sea Road. This road swings sharply to the left; if you wished to detour to Rustington, once the home of the composer Sir Hubert Parry and boasting a good little shopping centre and fine parish church containing many thirteenth-century features, you follow Sea Road inland, but to make progress along the coast continue along the seafront by way of a paved path across an area of green. The green ends and you then need to cross an area of shingle before picking up a further paved path which heads eastwards towards some beach huts. You're now embarking on a succession of greenswards – areas of immaculate green for public and recreational use which run between the very exclusive housing to your left and the sea to your right. Between here and Sea Lane, giving access to the useful amenities of Angmering, you can choose between the comfort of the greenswards, sometimes separated from the sea by tall vegetation, or the tougher shingle option. You bear slightly right onto Sea Lane then immediately left onto shingle, now passing East Preston, a sprawling and affluent residential area with a church dedicated to St Mary the Virgin which boasts an unusual stone spire and early twelfth-century north doorway. It's accessible via Sea Road, if you're interested.

Carry on along the shingle but then bear left to pick up another greensward with the houses of West Kingston and Kingston Gorse to your left. If the tide is out you've also the option of the magnificent sands punctuated by rocks, pools and channels; there is a small collection of black rocks, visible half a mile off-shore at low tide, that are believed to contain the remains of Kingston Chapel which was submerged by the sea in the seventeenth century. Two gates are followed by another greensward, another shingle tramp and then, thankfully, the paved Pattersons Walk which takes you past Ferring, another residential area and effectively the western end of Worthing, and boasting a neat Early English church. There are fine views from here to Highdown Hill with its Iron Age hill fort, and indeed it is nice to have a view northwards which for a change is uncluttered by building, but make the most of it, as you won't get another for many miles. If the tide is out, you could simply proceed all the way from here to Worthing along the sand, but if you are not so lucky, continue eastwards from Ferring across a green with Marine Drive to your left. You soon pick up a good path along the right-hand side of the green and this proceeds on past the next residential area, Goring-by-Sea, which was once a smugglers' haunt and for a while was the home of the naturalist Richard Jefferies. As you cross and move east of Sea Lane, from which there's a good view to the spire of Goring Church, your path becomes a proper concrete way, and the going is now extremely easy with good views to the South Downs beyond the sprawl of Worthing; there is the option of the shingle when the concrete way is separated from the sea by beach huts.

In due course the walkway widens to become a proper seafront promenade and it is very easy walking to Worthing (9), the largest town on the West Sussex coast. Just like Bognor Regis and Littlehampton, it was once a modest fishing village, but in the late eighteenth century and early nineteenth century a number of visits by distinguished personages sparked something of an expansion, and with the building of some fine houses, halls and terraces it acquired town status. Again, just like Bognor Regis and Littlehampton, it was the arrival of the railway in the mid-nineteenth century that precipitated its development as a traditional seaside resort, resulting in a pier being opened in the 1860s (the present one dates back to the early twentieth century), a cast iron bandstand being erected in 1897, and the Dome Cinema, which remains a distinctive feature on the sea front to this day, being opened in 1910. On the subject of Worthing and the arts, Oscar Wilde wrote his most famous play, *The Importance Of Being Earnest*, while staying in Worthing, and named one of the leading characters in the play after the town. Possibly the finest building in Worthing is its Town Hall, opened in 1933 and containing beautiful pastel coloured mosaics with maritime themes. Although Worthing's long fishing traditions have continued and were maintained by the existence of a fish market on the beach, the town is primarily a seaside resort, albeit rather more staid and reputedly of more geriatric appeal than its loud and garish neighbour Brighton. It suffered very badly from bombing during World War Two but is now a thriving town with flourishing societies and organisations for all ages and perhaps not really deserving of its unkind nickname 'God's waiting room'. You pass the pier, the Dome and the attractive Steyne

Gardens then go on past the Aquarena swimming pool, not far beyond which the promenade turns effectively into a pavement beside the busy A259. You can avoid the road noise by sticking to the beach as far as Western Road, but you are then forced back to the A259 by an area of private beach stretching right down to the mean low water mark. It's a depressing walk by the roadside out of sight of the sea but having passed Bessborough Terrace and Beach Lodge you can turn right onto a concrete path which returns you to the front. You have now arrived at Lancing (12) and as you continue along the front on a concrete walkway, South Lancing is immediately to your left; this is a modern and essentially uninteresting little resort, although in the nineteenth century it was a favoured haunt for smugglers, and coastguard cottages (since demolished) had to be built to combat their menace. Both the older and pleasanter North Lancing, and Lancing's grandest building, its College Chapel, are a considerable way inland and really too far out of your way for a detour.

Continue along the concrete path away from South Lancing. Your view to the sea is impeded by a line of beach huts for a while so you may prefer to detour to the shingle while you pass them. In due course your view to the sea from the path becomes uninterrupted again, and there are good views to the Downs and Lancing College Chapel to the left. You pass Lancing Sailing Club, a big caravan park, and then Widewater Lagoon, separated from the sea by a shingle bank but fed by seawater permeating through the cracks in the thin clay bed; it's now a nature reserve with a wide variety of plants such as sea anemone and sea campion, and birds that include redshank, grey heron and kestrel. Your path veers to the left and becomes West Beach Road, from where it's recommended that you join the shingle rather than stick to concrete. This is undoubtedly tougher going, but you can at least see the sea, the road nearest the sea (which changes from West Beach Road to Kings Walk and then Beach Road) becoming separated from the shore by a line of houses that form part of the Shoreham Beach Estate. Although the estate is comparatively modern it stands on the site of Bungalow Town, an unplanned collection of holiday homes once favoured by actors and music-hall performers. In due course you arrive at the far end of Shoreham Beach and can enjoy a grandstand view of the mouth of Shoreham Harbour and the River Adur; you will also see the rather sad-looking ruins of Shoreham

Fort, a brick-built fortification that was completed in 1857 and was rendered obsolete just thirteen years later.

Now begins the long and rather messy negotiation of Shoreham Harbour for a large part of which you're forced to forsake the waterfront. Having got to the end of the beach, retrace your steps a short way then bear slightly right and pass through a car park to enter a road called Fort Haven. Follow this to a T-junction and turn right onto Harbour Road which in due course becomes Riverside Road and follows the waterside for a while but then becomes separated from it by various industrial and residential developments including the impressive Emerald Quay. At the Waterside Inn bear right into Lower Beach Road and then right again to cross the footbridge over the River Adur into Shoreham-by-Sea (14.5); known as the Dolphin Footbridge, it opened in 1921 to replace a ferry crossing. Having crossed the bridge, you turn right onto the A259 to progress but you may want to stop and enjoy the town, officially New Shoreham (to distinguish it from Old Shoreham, which lies further inland) but marked on maps as Shoreham-by-Sea – albeit most people simply refer to the seaside town as Shoreham! It is the closest port to London on the south coast; historically the river was deeper and wider than it is today, thereby enabling boats to navigate further upstream, but silting made it necessary for a port to be built nearer the river mouth and Shoreham was the result. It became one of the leading ports of the medieval period, exporting wool, corn, salt and iron, and importing wine. The port dwindled in importance in the sixteenth century but the opening of the eastern arm of the harbour in 1855, and the laying of oyster beds within the river mouth, helped to bolster its fortunes once more and today it is still hugely busy; by the end of the twentieth century it was handling three million tons of cargo per annum. Architecturally only two historical gems remain despite the town's long history, one being the magnificent church of St Mary de Haura with twelfth century origins and boasting a splendid tower and choir-stalls, and the other being the Marlipins, a Norman building made of very distinctive chequerboard flint and Caen stone, and now a museum. Although one could hardly call the town a major tourist attraction, its centre is cheerful, attractive and popular with visitors; it has some excellent eating places so should be popular with you too!

# Day 41
# Shoreham-by-Sea to Brighton 9.5 miles (644 miles)

**Difficulty rating:** Easy
**Terrain rating:** ▲▲
**Highlights:** Shoreham Harbour, Hove, Brighton

It's a pretty grim slog alongside the A259 out of Shoreham past various retail and industrial units but at length the road does reach the water's edge, passing a lighthouse building that dates back to 1846. You leave the waterside once more and pass the redbrick Shoreham Port Authority building opposite Grange Road then shortly turn right where indicated by a sign pointing you to the beach via the lock gates. Following the signs to the beach, bear right and then having crossed the lock gates, continue on an obvious path to the seafront. The locks and surrounding developments are all legacies of massive reconstructions of this area in the 1950s. Having reached the front you could detour along it back to the eastern approach to the harbour, but impressive though the scene is here, with excellent views to the harbour and the Downs, and the crash of the sea against the rocks, I doubt your conscience or your sponsors will be greatly troubled if you just proceed eastwards now along the front, heading resolutely for Hove and Brighton. The concrete path along which you start turns itself into Basin Road South, with the eastern arm of Shoreham Harbour to your left separating you from the nondescript communities of Southwick, Fishersgate and Portslade. Pass along Basin Road South; the road is set well back from the shore and is occasionally obscured by walls, and you could opt for the shingle until a section of private beach forces you back to the road. You follow the road, passing the landward side of some warehouses at what is the very end of Shoreham Harbour's eastern arm, then when the road swings left beyond the harbour, turn right onto a minor cul-de-sac and pick up Hove Esplanade which starts here.

It's now plain sailing all the way to Brighton along a wide concrete promenade. Almost at once you pass Hove Lagoon, once a tidal reach of the Adur and now converted into a valued recreational facility, then walk parallel with Kingsway, here within striking distance of the centre of Hove (7). It's odd to think that in 1821 Hove had a population of just 300, but with the westward development of Brighton extending into the parish of Hove by this time, its population rose to 9,000 over the next forty years with some extremely fine buildings being created in Hove during this period, encompassing a variety of styles including Regency and Italianate. Later in the Victorian age the magnificent bold red-brick Town Hall, now sadly destroyed, was built, as was the particularly fine All Saints Parish Church in thirteenth-century French style. As more people populated Hove, the more attractive it became as a place not only to live but to visit, and it developed as a resort with parks, lawns and promenades springing up all around the town. Winston Churchill received part of his education in Hove in the 1880s, and during the following decade George Albert Smith and James Williamson began making films at Hove; they were among the earliest films ever made. Hove came through both World Wars relatively unscathed and still retains an identity of its own despite being effectively joined on to Brighton, even rejoicing in the soubriquet 'actually' after the supposedly snooty residents who if asked if they live in Brighton reply 'Hove, actually.'

Beyond Grand Avenue, easily identified by the fine statue at its sea end, you pass some of the best streets in Hove including Brunswick Terrace and Adelaide Crescent, then almost imperceptibly you enter Brighton, passing the Peace Memorial, dedicated to Edward VII and unveiled in October 1912. With the choice now between beach and promenade, you pass the ruins of West Pier, its doom effectively sealed by extensive storm damage and which has since been raised to the ground, then the luxurious Grand Hotel and the bland Brighton Centre. As you make your way towards the unmissable Palace Pier, numerous roads lead off to the left to provide access to the immense shopping centre of Brighton (9.5) with its many big stores, restaurants and cafes. Brighton as we now know it didn't start to develop till the latter part of the eighteenth century, it previously having been a busy but unremarkable herring fishing community known as Brighthelmstone. The founder of modern Brighton was Dr Richard Russell who in 1750 was practising as a doctor in Lewes and sent patients to Brighton to try a seawater cure; as a result of his recommendation, and that of a number of other promoters of health around that time, many distinguished people were drawn to Brighton including the Duke of Gloucester, the Prince of Wales, later Prince Regent, and Dr Johnson. As a result, efforts were made to erect larger houses and enhance older ones. In 1815 the Prince Regent appointed John Nash to build a palace to effectively replace the simple classical Marine Pavilion that had been built some years before, and the result was the stunning Royal Pavilion, easily the most distinctive building in Brighton. Many other splendid Regency buildings followed, some of the most outstanding examples being in Kemp Town (so named because it was built for Thomas Read Kemp), Regency Square, Belgrave Place, Russell Square and Clifton Terrace to name but a few. Other fine nineteenth-century buildings in Brighton include the Italian Renaissance style Grand Hotel and St Bartholomew's Church, at one time the biggest brick church in Europe. The coming of the railway in 1841 served as a catalyst for Brighton's development as a resort; Brighton's first pier had been built in 1823 (destroyed in 1896) and the West Pier and Palace Pier followed in 1866 and 1899 respectively. Another notable tourist attraction which arrived in the nineteenth century was Volks Electric Railway, and like Palace Pier it is still thriving today. Brighton suffered extensive damage during World War Two but many of its finest Regency buildings remain and the character and ambience of former times are preserved in the old narrow shopping streets known as the Lanes; although the present buildings on these streets are mainly nineteenth century they are built on the site of what was a labyrinth of medieval streets slightly set back from the sea, and populated by those who didn't depend on the sea for their livelihood. Now designated as a city with Hove, Brighton is a very bustling, garish, cosmopolitan place, many celebrities having made it their home, and not for nothing is it known as London-by-the-Sea with its huge variety of shops, bars, clubs and eateries. It is particularly noteworthy for its gay scene, hosting the very popular Gay Pride event each August. Whether as a walker you decide you love Brighton or you hate it, you can be sure you won't easily forget it.

**EAST SUSSEX**

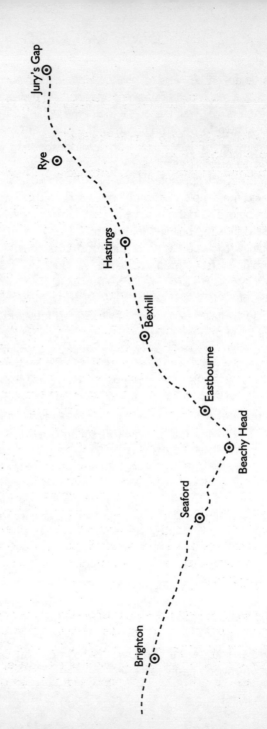

Jury's Gap

Rye

Hastings

Bexhill

Eastbourne

Beachy Head

Seaford

Brighton

# Day 42
# Brighton to Seaford 13 miles (657 miles)

**Difficulty rating:** Easy, moderate in places
**Terrain rating:** ▲▲
**Highlights:** Brighton Marina, Rottingdean, Newhaven Fort

From Brighton to Peacehaven the described route tends to use the cliff-tops, although for much of this part of the section an alternative under-cliff path is available. Beyond the Palace Pier the Esplanade continues and you keep following it, proceeding parallel with the Volks Electric Railway; where a small amusement park separates the concrete walkway from the shingle, you may in fact prefer the shingle, with good views not only to the sea but to the terraces of gracious buildings to the left. In due course you reach Black Rock Station on the Electric Railway and you now need to bear left to climb away from sea level to the cliff-top coast road, using a concrete slipway. The slipway rises to a tunnel which you pass through then ascend to the coast road; you proceed east alongside it, then once past a right-hand road turning you can continue along the south side of the coast road, soon enjoying the luxury of springy turf as you proceed along the cliff-tops. This is your first taste of proper cliff walking since you left the Isle of Wight! Looking down to sea level to your right is Brighton Marina, a major complex consisting of luxury homes, shops and boats, and there are tremendous views both to the marina and back to Brighton. You pass the Jacobean-style buildings of Roedean School, founded in 1885 and moved to its present site at the very end of the nineteenth century, and an eighteenth-century smock windmill, once used to store contraband and an important landmark for seafarers. In due course you drop down to Rottingdean (4).

Rottingdean first began to attract visitors during the nineteenth century, drawn perhaps by its charming valley setting so close to Brighton which was also greatly increasing in popularity at that time. Despite sprawling residential development to the north of the village, its centre is still very charming with its green, pond and buildings of flint, brick and timber. The flint church of St Margaret is of Saxon origin, and some pre-Norman work survives in the nave, while the earliest complete secular building in the village is the Black Horse, dating back to 1513 and popular with smugglers; smuggling was rife in Rottingdean during the late eighteenth century and their infamous trade was immortalised in verse by Rudyard Kipling who wrote some of his most famous work while residing in the village. Immediately beyond the High Street your coastal walk carries straight on beside the road, then just past the Marine Cliffs car park you turn right, back on the grass, to resume your cliff-top walking. Having climbed away from Rottingdean you descend to Saltdean, a sprawling residential village; there's then another big climb to a distinctive obelisk and weathervane, then as the ground begins to fall you're forced round the landward side of some waterworks and along the roadside. In due course you reach a pub immediately before which is a path that returns you to the cliffs. You now proceed along the cliff-top using a mixture of greenswards and wide, often stony, tracks. It's great to have the sea to your right, not so great to have the fearfully dull (compared with what some commentators say, that ranks as a generous tribute) residential sprawls of Telscombe Cliffs, Peacehaven and Peacehaven Heights to your left. Peacehaven (7.5) dates back to around 1915 and was originally intended to be called New Anzac-on-Sea until the debacle at Gallipoli during World War One persuaded the developers that this name might be insensitive. The only item of interest in Peacehaven which happily is right on the route is the George V memorial, erected in 1936, which marks Peacehaven's position on the Greenwich meridian, listing distances to all the outposts of the Empire.

The coast path continues on beyond Peacehaven, and you're now able to enjoy a very fine cliff walk, with excellent views ahead to Newhaven and Seaford. Continue along the clear cliff path – there are some undulations but the going is generally easy – but then keeping some chalets and new houses to your left, you rise to arrive at a mast. Pass to the right of the mast and continue along the cliff-top, but 150 yards or so beyond the mast you reach an area of bushes, with a choice between a path going steeply downhill to the right or one veering left into the bushes. Take the path veering left, which soon arrives at a gravelled path onto which you turn right and follow downhill. It bends left and passes a Castle Hill signboard, and as it passes this signboard you will see a coach park a short way across the grass to your right; leave the gravelled path and pass along the right-hand side of the coach park to reach the pedestrian entrance to Newhaven Fort. The Fort itself, with its excellent exhibitions of life in the two World Wars, is well worth visiting, but you need to turn left onto the metalled Fort Rise and follow it downhill to a T-junction with Fort Road. Your way here is left, but it's worth detouring right to go out to West Beach, with fine views across the mouth of the River Ouse and a popular spot for holidaymakers and locals. However, there is no way across the Ouse and you need to go inland alongside the Ouse estuary to make progress. Follow Fort Road back past Fort Rise (assuming you made the detour) then opposite the Marine Court flats, just beyond a toilet block bear right onto a road that leads you to a waterside walk through Newhaven Marina with its buildings and boatyards; this is a fascinating area which has only comparatively recently become available to pedestrians. At the time of writing the marina area is undergoing development which may result in some road or path closures and/or diversions, so follow signs carefully. There should in practice be no difficulty identifying a right of way leading riverwards off the main access road into the complex. At the top end of the marina bear right and go forward along a busy roadside to cross the swing bridge over the Ouse, which incidentally often opens to allow boats through, so you may have a bit of a wait! If you wish to explore Newhaven (10) you will need to bear left having reached the main road at the top of the marina. Previously named Meeching, the town at one time did not actually stand on the Ouse at all, but a change in the course of the river did bring it to the sea at Meeching, Meeching was renamed Newhaven, a Harbour Commission was formed in 1731 and by the middle of that century it was handling shipping of 150 tons. A ferry service to Dieppe started in 1825 and this is still thriving today. During the two World Wars, Newhaven became an important supply base but it is now a busy commercial and passenger port and with its marina is enjoying an expanding leisure industry. The town, the streets of which have an intricate street pattern in its centre, boasts a fine church with unusual blue and terracotta interior decor and a shingle spire. Newhaven's most famous visitor was Louis Philippe, once King of France, who stayed in the town incognito following his deposition in the French Revolution.

Having crossed the swing bridge you fork immediately onto Drove Road which goes over a level crossing beside Newhaven Town station; beyond the crossing you go first right into Railway Road, the road becoming Clifford Road and then Beach Road, but not getting any prettier. As Beach Road bends sharply to the left by the railway, look for a footpath which leads off to the right, and follow this path, staying parallel with (and to the land side of) the railway briefly then crossing the railway by means of a footbridge. Once over the bridge keep walking beside the railway but on its seaward side, now keeping Mill Creek to your right; in due course the railway goes off to the left but you stay on what is an excellent path with the creek still to the right. You cross a stile and continue along a dirt track to reach a concrete road onto which you turn right. This leads you back to the sea and on arriving at the shingle beach you simply follow it eastwards towards Seaford, looking back from time to time to enjoy fine views back to the cliffs above Newhaven Fort. Just before the beach you could turn left to follow a concrete road, but this is set some way back from the sea and you may prefer the shingle even though it's slower. In due course you arrive at Marine Parade, providing an easy walk along concrete on to Seaford (13), and although the centre of the town is situated a little way inland there are plenty of access options. Seaford was at the mouth of the Ouse before it transferred its allegiance to Newhaven, and in fact whilst at the mouth of that river it had been a busy port with a proud tradition of fishing and shipbuilding, and sent three ships to the Hundred Years War. Once the Ouse had been firstly rendered unnavigable by the forces of nature, and then lost altogether, Seaford remained in limbo, of no use as a port and undeveloped as a resort. Some entrepreneurs did in the mid-nineteenth century try to turn it into another Brighton, but despite the building of a seawall, the formation of an Improvement Committee, and the fine Esplanade Hotel which attracted King Edward VII in 1905, one is left today still with the impression of a seaside resort which never quite happened. There are some good buildings in the town including the fine medieval church of St Leonard, but many of the older buildings have been pulled down to make way for more modern development; perhaps the town's most interesting feature is its Martello tower, the most westerly of seventy-four such towers that were built along the south coast (so you can start counting them now) in 1806 as a response to the threat of French invasion. The Seaford one was restored in the 1970s and became a museum.

# Day 43
# Seaford to Eastbourne 10 miles (667 miles)

**Difficulty rating:** Moderate, strenuous in places
**Terrain rating:** ▲▲▲▲
**Highlights:** Seaford Head, Seven Sisters, Beachy Head

Now, in my opinion, begins the best section of walking on the Sussex coast. Keep along the promenade to the car park at its end, and begin a steady climb up onto the cliffs, with a choice of paths between the cliff-edge and the golf course to the left; eventually you make it onto Seaford Head, the site of an Iron Age hill fort, and continue along the cliff-top enjoying superb views to the Seven Sisters cliffs ahead of you. You now begin to descend on a clear path, eventually arriving at Hope Gap, a quite delightfully secluded spot in a valley between rising cliffs, then, veering left, rise again to get an excellent view of Cuckmere Haven, the valley between Seaford Head and the Seven Sisters through which the estuary of the Cuckmere River flows. You then turn right onto a clear track and descend to reach Cuckmere Haven, passing straight through a gate and proceeding along the shingle until you reach a channel of water. This is in fact a new cut of the Cuckmere River arriving at the sea, the cut having been created in 1846 to prevent flooding; there is no way of fording it, so turn left and proceed alongside it all the way to the A259 road at the Golden Galleon pub, bearing right onto the roadside and following it as far as the visitor centre at Exceat a few hundred yards down the road. More or less opposite the visitor centre you turn right by a bus stop onto a metalled track which you now follow back towards the sea, admiring the extraordinary meanders of the 'old' Cuckmere estuary to your right. This is one of the most unspoilt estuarine landscapes you will see on your south coast walk, and certainly the best in Sussex, with a huge variety of bird life including cormorants, herons, dabchicks, curlews, peregrine falcons, hen harriers and Canada geese.

After roughly half a mile the path swings quite sharply left away from the valley; don't swing left with it, but fork right onto a path signposted Seven Sisters, pass through a gate, then shortly fork left and proceed up a flight of steps, going forward to a fence. Keeping the fence to your right, press on uphill on a clearly marked path to arrive at the summit of the first of seven spectacular chalk cliff-tops known as the Seven Sisters, formed by geological activity between 50 and 100 million years ago. The depressions separating each 'sister' are the valleys of ancient rivers, formed when the chalk extended further seawards, but later cut off when the sea pounded the chalk away. The unspoilt chalk hills attract many birds including the fulmar, wheatear and jackdaw, and plants which include the cowslip and varieties of orchid, as well as several species of butterfly. Now just take each 'sister' in turn, enjoying the quite magnificent views back to Seaford Head and Cuckmere Haven until, the seventh having been conquered, you descend to the little hamlet of Birling Gap. There should be refreshments available at the Gap, a freak cleft in the South Downs with steep steps to the sea that were used by smugglers. Beyond the Gap, the way forward is obvious, with a choice of paths to take you back up to and along the cliff-tops, aiming for the old Belle Tout lighthouse. The lighthouse was built in 1830 but it proved to be less effective than hoped and a replacement was built below the Beachy Head cliff-top in 1902; indeed, owing to cliff erosion the now redundant lighthouse has actually had to be moved more than once, and may have to be moved again. The area of downland round its present site was once an Iron Age settlement and has been identified as a site of the ancient Beaker people.

You pass to the left of the old lighthouse then drop steeply to meet the road at a small car park, before beginning the assault on Beachy Head. It's a laborious climb, not helped by a big dip which sees you rapidly lose height you must then regain, but at least route-finding is no problem. The grass is lovely to walk on, and the views just get better and better. Finally you arrive on Beachy Head, 535 feet above the sea, and if you have a head for heights you may want to make for the cliff-edge and look down at the 125-foot lighthouse built as a replacement for the Belle Tout. Beachy Head is thought to derive from the French *beau chef* meaning 'beautiful headland' and on a clear day it certainly is beautiful with extensive views and a dazzling array of wildlife and plant life. Since 1990 it has become a breeding ground for falcons, it is one of the best places in Sussex to see the stone curlew, and plants include red valerian, sea radish, early gentian, harebell and orchid. On a more sombre note, the steep cliffs have proved a fatal temptation for many seeking to take their own lives, the treacherous seas below have resulted in many shipwrecks, and erosion is a constant problem, with a major cliff slip recorded as recently as 1999. There are numerous paths off the summit – you could avoid paths altogether and just walk over the grass – but you need to head for the cliff-edge to pick up a wide green track, which in fact is also the course of the South Downs Way; it drops down very steeply and from it there are really fantastic views to Eastbourne and the coastline all the way to Hastings. You rise briefly to meet a track onto which you turn right, the track becoming a metalled road and dropping down to a cafe (marking the end of the South Downs Way) beyond which you turn right into Duke's Drive and then, beyond Helen Gardens, right along a road that brings you to the Eastbourne promenade.

It's now an easy promenade walk all the way to Eastbourne. You pass the Wish Tower (another Martello tower) and its cafe, then from the Lifeboat Museum you have a choice of promenades and plenty of access roads into the town centre of which Devonshire Place, just past the huge Cavendish Hotel, is perhaps the best. Eastbourne (10) really developed in the mid-nineteenth century, when local landowners decided to create a resort less extrovert and garish than Brighton had become, but still stylish and attractive with plenty of grand avenues, fine parks, gardens and greenery. The result is arguably the most agreeable of all the Sussex seaside towns with its 3-mile esplanade, three-tier promenade, handsome villas and landscaped gardens; there is some fine architecture including the opulent Grand Parade and the majestic Cavendish Hotel, and there is an abundance of visitor attractions including several excellent museums, a pier with concert hall and pavilion, a bandstand, a butterfly centre and the ever popular Devonshire Park with theatre and tennis courts. One museum of particular note is the Sussex Combined Services Museum housed in the Redoubt, a massive brick building constructed as a defensive measure during the Napoleonic Wars.

# Day 44
# Eastbourne to Hastings 13.5 miles (680.5 miles)

**Difficulty rating:** Easy
**Terrain rating:** ▲
**Highlights:** Sovereign Harbour, St Leonards, Hastings

Continue along the promenade past the Redoubt as well as the pier, and going forward onto a concrete walk/cycleway, built up on shingle, you now pull away from Eastbourne, looking back for a fine view of the town and Beachy Head rising up behind it. You pass a large water treatment works then arrive at a roundabout where Prince William Drive meets Atlantic Drive; you're now entering the modern Sovereign Harbour development, a little reminiscent of Brighton Marina with its mixture of houses, shops, flats, restaurants and of course marinas. Turn left into Atlantic Drive, right along Santa Cruz Drive and right down Key West, crossing the harbour by means of the lock, then once over the lock bear right to pass the lifeboat station and then along a track that conveys you to the shore. Rights of way may change as the harbour area develops, and it is suggested you contact the Harbour Master's Office for further information before setting out.

Now keep walking along the shore, past the Pevensey Bay Sailing Club and the end of Timberlaine Road. You could leave the coast and detour via this road and then right onto the A259 to visit the historic village of Pevensey, with its magnificent Norman castle incorporating walls that date back to Roman times and refortified during both the time of the Spanish Armada and World War Two. It used to be a very busy port and became one of the Cinque Ports, a group of ports in Kent and Sussex that were granted special privileges through their provision of men and ships for the defence of the Channel, but silting caused it to go into terminal decline and it now stands well inland. If you do decide to visit it you should make time not only for the castle but the Early English Church of St Nicholas and the half-timbered Old Mint House which dates from the mid-fourteenth century. Back on the route, from Timberlaine Road you continue past the back of the nondescript village of Pevensey Bay and now follow the shore past the seaside communities of Beachlands, Norman's Bay and Cooden. Low tide is an enormous advantage as you can then follow the sand rather than the shingle, there being no promenade and the only relief being in the form of the metalled Herbrand Walk adjacent to the railway and Cooden Beach Golf Club on the other side of the tracks. Once this road disappears behind houses, however, it's back to shingle until a metalled promenade begins just beyond a particularly impressive mock Tudor house with its fine beach-facing lawn; the promenade peters out but after another brief shingle tramp you're able to bear left to follow a good wide promenade as far as the seafront at Bexhill (8). The old town of Bexhill was built half a mile inland and was developed as a resort by the Earls de la Warr, who owned the land between old Bexhill and the sea, in the 1880s. It enjoyed many Royal visits and in 1901 became the first resort in the country to permit mixed bathing. 1896 saw the opening of the Kursaal centre, offering traditional pier-type entertainment (the resort was never to acquire a pier) but was effectively superseded by the huge De La Warr Pavilion, built in the 1930s and today still the focal point of the resort with ballroom, concert hall and theatre. The town boasts some lovely gardens and good museums but never achieved the prominence as a resort that Brighton and Eastbourne enjoy, and is now a largely residential and retirement town with more than half its population being retired.

You follow the promenade past the very prominent clock tower and De La Warr Pavilion, and a green with a stone marking the finishing line of what in 1902 was the first international motor-racing meeting on British soil. The promenade ends at the Sea Angling Club and you may then choose between a bracing cliff-top walk using a good concrete walkway, or an equally good concrete path across the shingle below the cliff. If you decide on the cliff-top path, the views are obviously better including a grandstand view of a sprawling retail park across the railway to the left. The beach path peters out beyond the cliff and you'll then need to scramble over the shingle to join the path that's descended from the cliffs. Shortly a similar choice again presents itself – cliff-top or beach path, both again meeting up once the cliff is passed – and then it's a straightforward walk on a good firm path along the back of the shingle beach with the railway immediately to the left. At length you arrive at a T-junction of paths; turn right here, pass to the left side of a barrier and join a metalled road going forward to a parking area and then a stretch of shingle, and passing a row of chalets with private forecourts. Just beyond these chalets you're able to gain access to the metalled promenade which will take you all the way to Hastings past St Leonards. St Leonards (12) – the centre of which is marked by the Royal Victoria Hotel on the seafront – appears at first sight to be just a suburb of Hastings but it was designed as a completely separate development from Hastings by the architect James Burton. He bought an estate here and in 1828 set out to create a watering-place similar to Brighton, and inspired by his famous architect son Decimus, he created a number of fine buildings including not only the Royal Victoria but the Masonic Hall, part of which is based on a Greek Doric temple, and Regency and Gothic style villas. One infamous creation in St Leonards, certainly not Burton's work, is the monstrous Marina Court complex, designed in the 1930s to look like an ocean-going liner, but now simply a giant eyesore.

Beyond the Royal Victoria and the Marina Court complex you go past the verdant Warrior Square, consisting of a formal garden laid out in 1853 and regarded as the meeting point of St Leonards and Hastings, and on towards Hastings pier, built in 1872, with the fine White Rock pavilion, built in the 1920s, across the road. You could of course opt for the beach instead, but whichever route you take, continue on along the waterfront to the Breeds Place roundabout, attractively equipped with a fountain and offering convenient access to Hastings town centre. Founded by the Saxons, Hastings (13.5) was one of the original Cinque Ports (see Pevensey above) together with Dover, Hythe, Romney and Sandwich, and was already an important harbour town at the time of the Norman invasion. During the Middle Ages it regularly contributed ships to the Navy and although its importance as a naval town declined, it continued to be a bustling fishing port. The old town grew up in the valley between two sandstone ridges, East Hill and West Hill, and although the old harbour has long since succumbed to nature, there remain a host of historic buildings as evidence of the town's long and colourful history. These include the Norman castle ruins, the early-fifteenth-century All Saints Church, the late fourteenth-century St Clement's Church, and the many attractive town houses and shops around the Old Town whose quaintly named streets such as Tackleway and Rock-a-Nore Road invite exploration. The importance of Hastings' thriving fishing industry is reflected in the Fishermen's Museum near to the tall black-tarred wooden huts or 'net shops' where fishermen would store their gear and hang out their nets to dry. Hastings developed as a resort in the 1820s, with squares and terraces of seaside houses, many Regency in style, being built to the west of the old town. Both James and Decimus Burton, responsible for much of the architecture in St Leonards, were also responsible for the architectural highlights in Hastings; the Regency Pelham Crescent, Wellington Square, the Italianate Queen's Hotel and the Palace Hotel with its mixture of Renaissance and Baroque motifs are all good examples of this and worth seeing. It's fair to say that although Hastings attracts many holidaymakers today, it possesses neither the charisma of Brighton nor the charm and elegance of Eastbourne. However, there are many aspects that will appeal to the visitor, including not only the traditional trappings of a holiday resort but some fine exhibitions including the Hastings Embroidery housed in the White Rock Pavilion; a modern Bayeux Tapestry depicting 81 important events in British history.

# Day 45
# Hastings to Jury's Gap Bus Stop (for buses to Rye, Lydd and Camber) 15 miles (695.5 miles)

**Difficulty rating:** Moderate, becoming easy
**Terrain rating:** ▲▲▲
**Highlights:** Lovers Seat, Rye, Camber Sands

To leave Hastings, begin by following the main seafront road (A259) which bends sharply at its junction with Rock-a-Nore Road. Take the next right, along East Bourne Street, then turn left up All Saints Street and right into Crown Lane, rising steeply; where the road swings left, go straight ahead up a steep flight of steps which take you onto East Hill, the site of an Iron Age hill fort, and now a pleasant green. Follow the right-hand side of the green, close to the cliff-edge fence, and go forward to a proper path. You are now in Hastings Country Park, much of which has been designated a 'Site of Special Scientific Interest'; it is also extremely beautiful, with deep wooded glens, heather-clad hills and fine sandstone cliffs consisting of some of the oldest rocks in the south-east. Keeping the cliff-edge fence to your right, you drop down into Ecclesbourne Glen, a wooded valley which 200 years ago was popular with smugglers and provides ideal nesting territory for tits and warblers. You rise from the glen but are soon descending to Fairlight Glen, carpeted in spring with bluebells and wood anemones, while a stream runs between large boulders under the trees. Following the signs for Lovers Seat, you again climb steeply to reach the tremendous viewpoint of that name, then following signs for Warren Glen and Firehills you descend to Warren Glen, less thickly wooded than the previous two but still populated with oak, hazel, beech and ash. Then climb yet again to the heathland area known as Firehills, watching and listening for the yellowhammer or stonechat and enjoying yet more superb views. Keeping to the cliff-edge path, enjoy a magnificent cliff-top walk before descending on a wide stony path as far as Shepherds Way; turn left along it, then right into Bramble Way, going forward into Rockmead Road and right at the T-junction into Lower Waites Lane, and right into Sea Road. Proceed towards the gate, just before this you bear left onto a cliff path which you follow uphill, this being your last cliff climb in Sussex. At length the path levels out and descends, then at the foot of the hill turn left onto a drive; this at once reaches a T-junction with a road onto which you turn right, now entering the appropriately named village of Cliff End (6.5). Follow the road to the Smuggler Inn, walk through the pub car park and go past the church, and you're then able to pick up a promenade which gives way to an embankment path.

Continue along the embankment path, enjoying views to the left firstly of the Royal Military Canal (see Hythe below) and then across a wide flat expanse of reclaimed marshland known as Pett Level; criss-crossed by drainage ditches and canals it widens into the immense Romney Marsh which you will meet when you enter Kent. You will also see the disused windmill at Hog's Hill which forms an impressive landmark. There are shortly views ahead to the lovely hilltop town of Winchelsea, and looking to your right across the beach you may at low tide see the 7,000-year-old roots and stumps of the remains of a forest, once a Stone Age settlement. Roughly 2 miles beyond Cliff End, you pass the straggling Winchelsea Beach (8.5), hardly worth stopping for, but by dropping down to the parallel Pett Level Road and detouring along it for about a mile from Winchelsea Beach, you can enjoy the old town of Winchelsea. The old town was one of the Cinque Ports and stood on a shingle spit at shore level, but it was virtually destroyed by a storm in 1287 and a 'new' town was built on the hilltop, using a distinctive grid street pattern – medieval town planning, if you like. Although attempts were made to develop it as a port, nature again took a hand and it became effectively cut off from the sea. The town has many fine features including the Church of St Thomas with much surviving fourteenth-century work, the Court Hall which is thought to date from the early days of the rebuilt town, and three medieval town gates.

Beyond Winchelsea Beach the embankment path ends. At low tide you can just continue along the sand, but at high tide you must choose between the shingle or the parallel road linking Winchelsea Beach with Rye Harbour. The road bends away from the sea to proceed towards the village of Rye Harbour; if you have followed the sands you will be forced inland too, onto the shingle bank, by the last Sussex river obstacle, the East Sussex Rother, which is emphatically not fordable. Fortunately, a concrete path then does become available to provide easy access to the road which you now need to follow alongside the west bank of the Rother to a junction by a huge Martello tower. Turn right here then bear left into Harbour Road and pass through the centre of the pleasant but unremarkable village of Rye Harbour. The village grew as a result of its position close to the mouth of the Rother, and it flourished as a port in the nineteenth century due to dredging work keeping the harbour entrance clear; following a bad storm in 1882, however, the entrance became practically blocked, and although a timber firm helped revive its fortunes by building a wharf and warehouses, it now has the feel of being a rather poor relation to the 'proper' town of Rye further upstream. That said, it does boast a fine nineteenth-century Gothic-style church, and to the west of the village there is a nature reserve consisting of 1,800 acres of tidal saltmarsh, creeks and shingle built up by the force of the sea. It is on a major bird migration route and is an important wintering place for seabirds.

Having followed Harbour Road through the village, you now stay on it all the way to its junction with the A259 on the edge of Rye itself, and a pretty ghastly walk it is too, with no pavement and a lot of traffic; it is indeed a relief to reach the junction and turn right to arrive in Rye (11), the loveliest town you'll meet in Sussex. This hilltop town, formerly a hill fort, became one of the Cinque Ports in the mid-fourteenth century and, standing as it did at the confluence of three rivers, was once a port of considerable strategic importance, exporting wool and iron to the Continent. However, it suffered badly at the hands of the French during the Hundred Years War and its fortunes as a port suffered severe decline from the sixteenth century as a result of silting; today, the town's principal industry is tourism, with thousands of visitors drawn each year to Rye's picturesque cobbled, narrow streets, crammed as they are with historic houses, many timber-framed, tile-hung or weather-boarded. The town's focal point is St Mary's Church which has a remarkable clock that is said to have the oldest functioning pendulum in England. Other interesting features in Rye include the fourteenth-century Landgate; the last remaining of Rye's original fortified gates, the Ypres Tower; dating back to the thirteenth century and once a prison, the Mermaid Inn in the cobbled Mermaid Street, with it's thirteenth-century features; the Old Grammar School in the High Street with distinctive Dutch gables; the fifteenth-century timber-framed Flushing Inn; the eighteenth-century arcaded Town Hall; the three-storey fifteenth-century timber-framed Fletcher's House; and the magnificent Lamb House, an eighteenth-century building in West Street and sometime home to the novelists Henry James and later E. F. Benson, two of very many writers who have lived in the town. It is a lovely place to wander round and enjoy at leisure, secure in the knowledge that from the highest point of the town you can gaze out at Kent, the last county on your south coast journey.

To leave Rye, it's suggested you follow the High Street north-eastwards to a little viewpoint with a telescope as the road begins to swing left and drop downhill. Just past the telescope look out for and descend a steep flight of steps to the A259 bypass; cross over this road, bear left and walk up to a mini-roundabout, turning right here and going forward to cross the bridge over the Rother. Immediately beyond the crossing you turn right and immediately right again through a gate to gain the embankment path beside the Rother heading seawards. In due course the path passes to the right of a lake then veers left to reach a metalled track, onto which you turn right and which you follow past Rye golf course; although this is to your left, you should watch carefully for golfers driving from a tee situated to the right of the track. It wouldn't do to be knocked unconscious by a golf ball so near to journey's end! Go forward to a gate, now on the course of an old railway, the Camber Tramway which functioned between 1895 and World War Two, providing rail transport from Rye for golfers and holidaymakers going to Camber Sands. Sections of the track were concreted over during World War Two to provide easy access to supply dumps in the Rye area, and it was decided that the costs of re-laying the track after the war were prohibitive. Beyond the gate, fork right onto a path that continues on the left bank of the Rother estuary until, on approaching the mouth of the river, you find yourself on Camber Sands. This is a superb expanse of gently-ridged golden sand, stretching out to sea for half a mile or more at low tide, complemented along the back of the beach by extensive sand dunes among which marram grass has been planted to preserve the special qualities of the sands from the effects of the wind. Passing the village of Camber (14.5) you now proceed along the sand, unless the tide is high in which case you may be forced onto the dunes and, when these end, you can choose between the shingle or a metalled promenade alongside the road linking Camber with Lydd. Camber Sands imperceptibly become Broomhill Sands, and at a spot known as Jury's Gap, the Camber-Lydd road strikes out inland. Although the border with Kent is still a little way ahead, you may feel, if you have decided to limit yourself to a Sussex coastal tramp, that this is the obvious place to end it, since the border between Sussex and Kent is inaccessible by public transport and there's a useful bus stop at Jury's Gap (15). For you, then, congratulations – rummage in your pocket for your last reserves of loose change for the bus, and enjoy your celebratory tea and hot jam doughnuts in Rye. But if you will not be satisfied until the official border has been reached, or are now pressing ahead into Kent, you need to read on and walk on.

# Day 46
# Jury's Gap to Folkestone 17 miles (712.5 miles)

**Difficulty rating:** Easy
**Terrain rating:** ▲▲
**Highlights:** Dungeness, Dymchurch, Folkestone

Jury's Gap, though a useful staging post with its bus-stop, is hardly the centre of the universe, and you'll be anxious now to forge on into Kent, the final county you pass through on your south coast walk. However, within literally yards of here along the shoreline, a major logistical problem presents itself, namely an Army training area known as the Lydd Ranges which lies to your left; indeed, the area has been used for military training for over 150 years. Lydd Ranges are still used for live firing with a 'Danger Area' extending out to sea and access even along the shingle is prohibited when red flags are flying. You really should try to plan your walk along this section for a day when no firing is scheduled; weekends and holiday periods offer your best hope, but for further information on live firing times you need to ring one of the contact numbers shown in the list at the end of this book. If you're out of luck, you'll have to follow the road from Jury's Gap all the way to Lydd – not an especially attractive town, although it does boast an interesting fourteenth-century church – then return along Dungeness Road to the coast at Lydd-on-Sea, again using the road.

Assuming all is well, proceed along the metalled track towards the MOD installation which marks the start of the restricted area. Beyond it, you could stay on the track or drop down to the shore, and I suggest that you at least begin along the track, from which you get a good view of the sea, the Ranges and also the vast expanse of Romney Marsh. The area was originally a saltmarsh but was reclaimed from the sea long ago and is now a mixture of arable land and grazing pasture, home to the white-faced Romney Marsh sheep; the area is exceedingly rich in bird life, and you should look out for wintering lapwings, golden plovers, bewick's swans, lapwings, migrant fieldfares and redwings, swallows, wagtails and nightingales. Before long the shingle bank to your right becomes too tall to view the sea properly, so use one of the paths across the shingle depression to your right to access the bank and then make your way to the shore. Imperceptibly, you pass from Sussex into Kent. The mix of sand and shingle is quite firm so you can make progress without difficulty, unless the tide is right up in which case you may be forced onto the bank and this will prove a tiresome slog. Eventually, some 5 miles of shore walking from Jury's Gap, and with 700 miles now clocked up from Land's End, you draw level with the Dungeness nuclear power stations, although if you are walking along the shore you will only be able to see the topmost funnel from the shoreline.

For what is a small place on the map, Dungeness (5) is actually a fascinating area. The great shingle spit here, deposited by the sea over a period of 400 years, is 4 miles deep, increasing all the time and is the largest shingle bank in Europe; its flora is surprisingly varied with over 400 recorded species, notably the carpets of thrift, stonecrop, sea-kale and sea campion. The shores around Dungeness provide a significant migration watchpoint, with many rare birds to be seen including Palla's warblers and red-breasted flycatchers, and as well as smew, terns and grebes, there are crowds of gulls to be observed including the rarely seen dark-hooded Mediterranean gulls. Architecturally, Dungeness is dominated by its lighthouse and two power stations. The modern lighthouse, opened in 1960 (though the first lighthouse to be built here was in 1615), is a most impressive construction, worked from complex control panels in its base; the power stations, meanwhile, were both built in the early 1960s, the later one planned to be the most powerful nuclear power station in the world. In World War Two, Dungeness housed one of the two northern terminals for PLUTO, an acronym for Pipe Line Under The Ocean, an underwater oil supply pipe carrying petrol from England to northern France in the wake of the D-Day landings. You may recall the one at Shanklin on the Isle of Wight – what a long way back even that will seem now. Lastly, Dungeness is the southern terminus of the 13-mile Romney, Hythe and Dymchurch Railway, one of the best known and best loved steam railways in the country, built as a tourist attraction in 1929; its engines are miniature replicas of London North Eastern Expresses and the rails are just 15 inches apart.

When you draw level with the power station, clamber up onto the shingle bank. At a stroke, the vista changes completely and on a clear day you will get a marvellous panoramic view of the Kent coast as far as Shakespeare Cliff between Folkestone and Dover. Now you literally turn the corner, your direction of travel going from just south of east to north, to be rewarded by a tough shingle tramp, your walk made no easier by the many ropes and wires surrounding the boats planted on the stones; there are some firmer sections but you have to look hard for them! Aim for the very conspicuous RNLI station, the tarmac forecourt briefly providing some easier going, but once you've passed the station to the seaward side you then face more shingle walking. Finally you arrive at, and perhaps patronise, The Pilot pub and enter the straggly village of Lydd-on-Sea, meeting the road coming in from the left which swings north-eastwards at The Pilot to become a coast road; you are now reunited with the inland route via the town of Lydd which may have been necessitated by firing on the Lydd Ranges. From here past the next, and no prettier, village of Greatstone-on-Sea you could follow the coast road or trudge along the shingle bank to the right of the road. You should bear in mind that some areas of this shingle are privately owned, and you may not be popular if you try to cross them, but, tides permitting, there's the possibility of following the sands; during the days of smuggling the sand dunes here offered good cover for those occupied in the trade. Continue beyond Greatstone-on-Sea to Littlestone-on-Sea, a greensward just beyond the lifeboat station providing relief from the shingle, but apart from the unusual pink granite Diamond Jubilee fountain there is little to stop for at Littlestone, which became a popular residential resort in the 1890s. However, it is possible to detour here onto the B2071 which in just over a mile brings you to Romney, one of the original Cinque Ports and boasting an attractive main street, an exceptional Norman church, and many fine old buildings including the splendid brick-fronted Assembly Rooms and Priory House. Ironically it is now not even by the sea at all, its harbour having been destroyed by a storm in the thirteenth century.

Beyond the greensward at Littlestone the going gets extremely easy, as there is now a proper concrete coast path running all the way to St Mary's Bay. You pass a very conspicuous late nineteenth-century tower, and Littlestone golf course, from which it has been claimed you can see the coast of France; though the chances of this are slim, the views across to Hythe, Folkestone, the North Downs and Shakespeare Cliff just west of Dover are superb. Passing the houses of St Mary's Bay – the village was once the home of Noel Coward and also Edith Nesbit, author of *The Railway Children* – you continue along an impressively wide promenade which gives you wonderfully easy marching all the way to Dymchurch, and it's a very short walk down the slip road to the many amenities this village has to offer. Dymchurch (12) was once a smuggling port, and more prosaically the meeting place of the Lords of the Level who looked after the drainage of the Romney Marshes; it enjoys the protection of a huge sea-barrier known as Dymchurch Wall which was first constructed by the Romans. Dymchurch is now predominantly a seaside resort, crammed with visitors in holiday periods, with safe bathing, good shore fishing and shrimping, and a quota of tacky shops and eateries on offer. It boasts a Martello tower, now an English Heritage site with many exhibits showing preparations to deal with prospective Napoleonic invaders, a church which contains some Norman work, and the eighteenth-century New Hall opposite the church with its old Court Room containing the Royal Arms of George II.

Leaving Dymchurch, you continue along a good concrete path by the back of the beach, making excellent progress. In just under 2 miles you reach the Dymchurch Redoubt and the entrance to the Hythe Ranges, blessed with three scheduled Ancient Monuments and used for live firing for nearly 200 years. The Danger Area extends out to sea, and when firing takes place the area is out of bounds; to enquire about live firing times, contact one of the numbers listed at the end of the book, and again hope that you're able to coincide your walk with a non-firing day. If the ranges are open, proceed round the beach side of the MOD buildings, walking across slippery stones to join a track that continues for 2 miles along the back of the beach with good views to the ranges and street mock-ups. Beyond the ranges a Martello tower blocks the way straight ahead, and when you reach it, go down onto the beach then almost at once scramble back onto a concrete path taking you forward to Hythe (15); the path bypasses the centre of Hythe and if you wish to stop to visit the town you will need to bear left up St Leonards Road which takes you into the centre. If firing is taking place, you will need to walk from the Redoubt to the adjacent A259 and follow it all the way past Pennypot into Hythe itself, forking right off Dymchurch Road into Portland Road and then first right into St Leonards Road, which takes you down to the concrete path. The detour will add a good extra mile to your journey but will give you a good excuse to visit Hythe which, like Romney, was one of the five original Cinque Ports but is now somewhat set back from the sea as a result of silting and the build-up of shingle. It stands today at the eastern end of the Royal Military Canal, built in 1807 as a response to the threat of invasion during the Napoleonic Wars; the canal, popular with fishermen, is lined with trees and flowers, and a water pageant has been a regular feature here in recent years. The town, the eastern terminus of the Romney, Hythe and Dymchurch Railway, contains many other delightful features. There is a long narrow High Street, with a pretty grid of streets and lanes between the High Street and the church of St Leonard which dates back to the twelfth century (although the present tower is much later); the church has possibly the grandest chancel of any non-monastic church in the county, built in about 1220, and buried in the churchyard is Lionel Lukin, who invented the lifeboat. Other buildings of interest include the eighteenth-century Old Manor House, the early nineteenth-century Hill House, and the Town Hall which dates back to 1794.

Continue along the concrete path, passing the Hotel Imperial and a golf course, now heading for the Sandgate and Folkestone conurbation, the going is still very easy. About 2 miles beyond Hythe the A259 comes in from the left and as you reach a garage you find yourself walking along the roadside pavement into Sandgate at the western end of Folkestone, still with the beach to your right. However, in a little over half a mile the A259 becomes separated from the beach by buildings, and you now leave the A259 to follow another concrete path along the back of the beach. Soon to your left you will see Sandgate Castle, one of a series of castles built by Henry VIII around 1540. During the early years of the nineteenth century, in response to the perceived threat from the French during the Napoleonic Wars, its central core was converted into a gunfort, and it became effectively a Martello tower. In 1820 a landing was carried out close to Sandgate Castle involving 300 smugglers, leading to a pitched battle with excise officials. One famous resident of Sandgate was H. G. Wells who had a seaside hide-out at Spade House in Radnor Cliff Crescent, and indeed his book *Kipps*, which inspired the musical *Half A Sixpence*, was set in and around Folkestone. Sandgate has also an excellent reputation for its fish, with regular catches of plaice, conger and codling.

Keep along the concrete path, now heading for Folkestone, noting the rocks of Mill Point and the paraphernalia of an elaborate flood defence scheme. As your path bends slightly to the left you can now see more of the buildings of central Folkestone, and to your left is the funicular railway linking the seafront with the very popular Leas area (see below). Shortly the concrete path gives way to a large open area where markets are regularly held and a little beyond that are some rather antiquated fairground attractions. You are now approaching a dead end so you need to turn left and pass between the amusements to join the harbour-side road onto which you turn right; very soon it swings sharply left, marked on maps here as the Harbour Approach Road, and suddenly you find yourself facing the town's harbour and surrounding buildings. Walk beside the water and soon reach a cobbled area on your right where there are often stalls selling seafood, and to continue your coastal walk you will need to bear right into this area. The centre of Folkestone can easily be reached by crossing over via Harbour Street and going forward into Tontine Street. Historically, Folkestone (17) consisted of little more than an accumulation of fishermen's cottages by the harbour and a few houses round the church. Although the town was granted a licence for its own port in 1629, and became one of the Cinque Ports, Folkestone's real prosperity began with the arrival of the railway and the growth of the cross Channel passenger service in the nineteenth century. It became an extremely popular seaside resort, with good beaches, all the traditional seaside attractions and, along the top of the cliffs, a very special area known as the Leas, consisting of an expanse of lawns and flower gardens separated from the sea-level promenades by a tangle of broom and pine trees. Folkestone's most famous son was the biologist William Harvey who discovered the circulation of the blood, and there is a statue of him in the Leas, holding a heart in his hand. Architecturally Folkestone is not outstanding, but it has its moments. The church on the hilltop, an Early English building, has an unusual dedication, to St Mary and St Eanswythe. It stands amid attractive weather-boarded and Georgian redbrick buildings, and there is a certain charm about the narrow, steep High Street. The most significant development in Folkestone's recent history has been the siting of the Eurotunnel terminal here, opened in 1994, although it's situated some way inland.

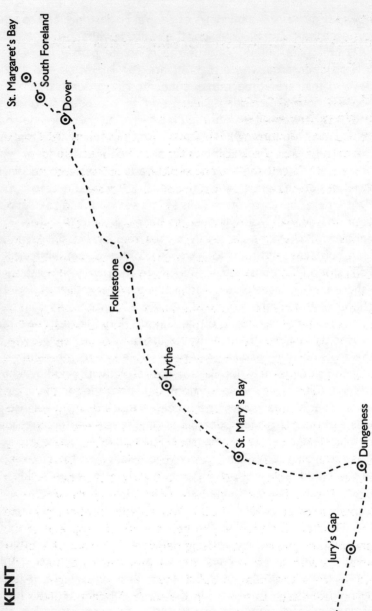

KENT

St. Margaret's Bay

South Foreland

Dover

Folkestone

Hythe

St. Mary's Bay

Dungeness

Jury's Gap

# Day 47
# Folkestone to South Foreland 15.5 miles (728 miles)

**Difficulty rating:** Moderate
**Terrain rating:** ▲▲▲
**Highlights:** Shakespeare Cliff, Dover, South Foreland lighthouse
*The mileage stated presupposes that you will continue to St Margaret's Bay. If you end the walk at South Foreland the mileage for this day section is reduced by 1.5 miles.

To continue your coastal walk from the harbour at Folkestone, turn right through the cobbled area off Harbour Street to join the Fish Market, itself a cobbled street which passes under the redbrick railway arches and beside further fish sellers and attractive redbrick houses. Go past a sign pointing to East Cliff and The Warren; the cobbled street becomes a concrete path which keeps close to the beach, and as you follow this path you will enjoy fine views to the cliffs ahead. Shortly beyond a cafe and toilets turn left as signposted up a flight of steps to reach an area of green on the cliffs, then turn right to walk along the green, passing to the cliff-side of a building prominently marked THE PAVILION. You soon join a metalled track and shortly arrive at a signpost pointing you left to the Martello Tower Visitor Centre and Warren Birdlife Trail; bear left as signed, and return to the cliff-edge, then keeping the cliff-edge immediately to your right, continue forward across the green area, going downhill and to the right of some enclosed greens. Shortly beyond is the site of a Roman villa which was occupied from AD 100 and 350. You ascend, continuing in the same direction, but then as you get towards the top end of the green walk diagonally left, passing below and in front of another Martello tower, to arrive at a narrow metalled road; turn right onto the road and follow it uphill, then, as it bends right, join a narrow path which carries on in the same direction. Follow this path steeply uphill.

This is tremendous walking; below you is the Folkestone–Dover railway, and to your right is the Warren, a landslip basin and extraordinary wilderness area between the cliffs and the sea, rich in plant and bird life, formed by a series of landfalls over the past 4,000 years caused by chalk movement and shingle drift. Continue uphill to reach a T-junction at which you turn right, here reaching the North Downs Way national trail which you will follow to the outskirts of Dover. Go forward along the path to arrive on the cliff-top, and permit yourself a pause to enjoy the view before bearing resolutely left (north-eastwards) to continue towards Dover; the going is now very easy as you follow the North Downs Way using the waymarks. Almost immediately you notice to your left the very impressive Battle Of Britain Memorial, completed in 1993 and serving as a navigational aid, then simply keep to the cliff-top path, and avoid paths leading down into the Warren. The only slight deviation from the cliff-top comes when about a mile and a half beyond the memorial you are forced a little inland to bypass some buildings, but even then you are soon reunited with the cliff-top and continue resolutely on. This is tremendous walking, with glorious sea views and the Warren immediately below you. As you continue, look out on the right for Samphire Hoe, a broad chalk platform formed from 4,000,000 cubic metres of chalk dug from the Channel Tunnel workings; it stands on the foreshore behind a new seawall and has been landscaped, with rye grass and other local plants being encouraged to grow around the site. The picturesque church you can see over the fields to your left is the Norman church of St Lawrence the Martyr at Church Hougham, once used by smugglers for concealing contraband.

Looking to your left, you will see the main A20, which has been close at hand for much of this cliff walk, as you descend towards Dover, and you will also see part of the town ahead of you. Before plunging down into this immensely important and interesting town, you must negotiate the last and best-known cliff on this section, namely the sheer Shakespeare Cliff, so named because it was the site of a famous scene in *King Lear*. Having made your way over this final cliff-top you descend, now enjoying sumptuous views to Dover and its surroundings. As you reach the bottom of the cliff, still quite a way above the sea, you will notice the North Downs Way signposted as going off left beneath an underpass below the A20; don't take this route, but instead continue parallel with the A20 and very soon you reach a flight of steps going down to your right. Take these steps which lead you over the railway and down to the beach then turn left to follow the shingle beach towards Dover. Soon, however, a concrete path is available, and the going becomes easier; follow the path until you can go no further, the way ahead effectively blocked by the Western Docks, part of Dover's huge harbour complex which befits its status as the world's busiest passenger port and England's principal cross-Channel port. Turn left and go forward to reach a roundabout where you take the signed A20 Folkestone exit, which fortunately has a pavement, as this is a very busy thoroughfare for motor traffic entering and leaving the Western Docks. Soon you reach the Limekiln Roundabout where you turn right to follow beside the A20, the main waterfront road, using the pavement on the harbour-side. You will then reach a third roundabout, marked on maps as the Prince of Wales Roundabout, and here you turn right into Union Street, using the cycle path. In a few yards you arrive at the waterfront proper, and you turn left to follow the Esplanade, with the Outer Harbour to your right. Although your coastal walk continues along the front, by way of the Esplanade, Waterloo Crescent and Marine Parade, you will surely want to use one of the roads or walkways leading off to the left hereabouts to detour to Dover's centre.

Although you are so near the end of your walk, you must make time to explore Dover (10.5), Britain's nearest point to mainland Europe. The Romans, not in fact the first settlers here, called the town Portus Dubris, and in about AD 50 they established a beacon or 'lighthouse' in what was to become the grounds of the Norman castle. The 62-foot high lighthouse, or 'Pharos' as it is known, is one of the oldest surviving Roman buildings in the country, the lower part of the lighthouse having been magnificently preserved; the other outstanding Roman building still to be seen in Dover is the Roman Painted House, built in around AD 200. The main attraction of Dover is its Norman castle, renowned for its magnificent and richly-decorated keep, built by Henry II in the 1180s with walls that are 17 to 22 feet thick, later requisitioned by Oliver

Cromwell in the English Civil War and subsequently strengthened to counter the threat from Napoleonic forces. From the castle keep there are extensive views which on a clear day can extend to the French coast. During World War Two, the elaborate network of tunnels under the castle, built during the time of the Napoleonic wars, was used as the control base for the Dunkirk evacuation, and another piece of history within the castle grounds is the really fine Saxon church of St Mary in Castro. When you tire of the castle and its attractions, there are plenty of other features of interest in Dover, including the assembly of Napoleonic Wars fortifications on the Western Heights, the thirteenth-century St Edmunds Chapel in Priory Road, consecrated in 1253 and believed to be the smallest church in regular use in the country, and Maison Dieu House, opposite this chapel and now the Public Library, which dates back to 1665. If that's not enough history for a weary walker, the chiefly nineteenth-century Dover College in Effingham Crescent incorporates the remains of St Martin's Priory, which was founded as long ago as 1131, and the Victorian Town Hall in Biggin Street incorporates the medieval Maison Dieu hospital and the old town gaol. The impressive museum in Market Square offers a wide range of exhibits that bring Dover's past to life, including a Bronze Age boat, while the White Cliffs Experience provides a more interactive introduction to Dover's history and surroundings.

Back on the route, continue north-eastwards along the waterfront until you reach the Premier Travel Inn, just beyond which you bear left to a pedestrian crossing over the A20; cross here and join the East Cliff road immediately opposite, which proceeds quite sharply uphill, starting as a narrow road but widening as you continue. As it opens out you keep to the left, going forward past Athol Terrace to join a path which now goes quite steeply uphill, with some sections of steps, passing under a bridge carrying the A2. You reach the crest of the hill, and as you do so look out for a Saxon Shore Way signpost which points to the right along a grassy path, and turn right here to follow the Saxon Shore Way as indicated. Keeping a car park to your left, just follow the path and now enjoy a magnificent cliff-top walk; you are now literally on top of the White Cliffs of Dover and looking down at the bustle of the Eastern Docks with its huge variety of shipping and cargo. There are lots of paths to choose from initially – the simplest advice is stick to the one nearest the cliff-edge, thus gaining the best views – but as you gain height, the options diminish and you can enjoy a straightforward, very enjoyable, cliff-top march with no route-finding dilemmas. Now proceed confidently along the cliff-top to South Foreland, which could be described as the most south-easterly point of the British Isles; beyond South Foreland the coastline is east rather than south-facing, and this therefore could be said to mark the official end of the south coast of Great Britain. Well done! As you proceed along the top of the chalk cliffs, some 300 feet above the sea, look out for the South Foreland lighthouse (14) to your left, which you should detour to visit; built in 1843 to guide sailors past the notorious Goodwin Sands nearby, the lighthouse has important associations with the Italian inventor Marconi. In 1898 he made history by sending a message in Morse code from here to a ship 12 miles offshore, and three months later succeeded in sending a wireless signal from South Foreland across the Channel to France. You may think back all those hundreds of miles to the Lizard Peninsula in Cornwall and recall the Marconi monument near Poldhu commemorating the great man's first radio transmission across the Atlantic in 1901. The lighthouse is owned by the National Trust and on a clear day it is possible to view the coast of France from its parapet.

You now have to find your way back to civilisation. You could simply backtrack to Dover, and if time is short and you have urgent appointments with trains, buses, boats, loved ones or fish and chip takeaways in the town, this may be the best option. However, for the sake of completeness, I recommend you finish your walk at the water's edge, and to do this, you need to carry on for another mile and a half to the next village, St Margaret's Bay, which could be said to be the settlement closest to the eastern tip of the south coast of Great Britain. Leave the cliff-top along the Saxon-Shore-Way-marked path, then just beyond the end of a fence to your right, turn right to access a rough driveway. Follow the driveway past some residential properties, passing a fine weather-boarded smock mill, then just past the windmill, and beyond the surrounding vegetation, turn right through a gate to resume your cliff-edge walk. There are now lovely views ahead to the village of St Margaret's Bay. Now you begin to descend, dropping to a gate where you are forced to turn left, away from the cliff-edge; you go down quite steeply along a track, then at the T-junction bear right along Beach Road into the village of St Margaret's Bay (15.5), passing the St Margaret's Museum which at the time of writing housed a welcome tearoom, and also quite delightful Pines Gardens. In order to get down to the sea, continue on past the museum to the next T-junction of tracks where you bear right again, almost immediately arriving at a road on a sharp bend beside South Sands House. Turn right onto the road, and drop down to the car park and Coast Guard Inn, which boasts that it is closer to France than any other pub in Britain; you will be following in illustrious footsteps, as both Ian Fleming and Noel Coward lived by the sea here for a time. Go and ceremoniously dip your toe in the waters of St Margaret's Bay before enjoying a celebratory drink at the Coast Guard, mission now very definitely accomplished – and then think about transport back to Dover.

If you have walked all the way from Land's End, you will probably have mixed feelings en route from South Foreland or St Margaret's Bay to Dover for road, rail or possibly even sea connections back to your home. You will doubtless feel extremely tired and weather-beaten. You will not relish the thought of returning to reality, and either – if you're returning to work – the prospect of a hideously full e-mail inbox, or – if you're not – the even worse prospect of a return to a daily diet of Noel Edmonds and Anne Robinson. And you will probably feel a huge sense of anticlimax, now that the adventure which was so long in the planning is now finally over. But as you doze in front of *EastEnders*, trying to work out how many murders, weddings and unplanned pregnancies you've missed since you watched the last episode all those weeks ago, get on to your PC to download photographic prints of your adventures, and reach in your file for your sponsor form and calculate just how much five pence per mile from each of your twenty work colleagues will have raised for your own particular good cause, you can think back on a truly wonderful experience, with so many contrasting and captivating images.

Whilst you may not have followed in the footsteps of John Merrill or Richard and Shally Hunt and gone all the way round, by walking the whole of the south coast you will still have achieved something quite special and you'll have had a taste of everything you could expect to see were you to have tackled the west, north and east coasts as well – from the spectacularly unspoilt cliff-scapes at the Lizard, Worbarrow or the Seven Sisters to the grotesque rock formations of Kynance and Cadgwith. From the incredible panoramic views at the Needles and Portland Bill to the magnificent castles at Falmouth and Dover. From the extraordinary modern architecture of the Spinnaker Tower and Dungeness Power Stations to the lovely old towns of Fowey, Dartmouth and Lyme Regis. From the picture postcard villages of Polperro, Beaulieu and Bosham to the cheerful resorts of Torquay and Bognor Regis. From the massive harbours of Poole and Langstone to the unashamed affluence of Hamble and Itchenor. From the fish restaurant in Plymouth where you had the most perfectly cooked sole to the B & B at Sandown which you got locked out of when you weren't back in by 10 p.m. You'll also realise just how much your walk will have taught you about yourself. If you've made it to the end, you'll have learnt you're stronger and fitter than you perhaps thought you were; you'll have learnt to keep going, whatever the weather; you'll have learnt not to give up, however tired and demotivated you may have felt during parts of your journey; you'll have learnt to nurture a new respect for the sea and our noble island shores... and you'll have learnt that if your mobile battery has gone you need more than one twenty-pence piece to use a BT call box.

Congratulations. You did it!

# Useful Information

## Accommodation

There is a vast range of accommodation on the south coast, from luxury hotels to campsites, from guest houses to farmhouses, from B & Bs to youth hostels. Where you choose to stay will be dictated largely by your budget, but also by the rather more fundamental question of availability. To try and list available accommodation in a book like this would be an impossible task, so I won't try. Far and away your best bet is to go onto the Internet and Google-search tourist information centres; local centres will be happy to provide relevant lists of accommodation of all types, including the location of campsites. If you don't have Internet access, just contact your local tourist information centre by telephone or in person, and they can put you in touch with the centres local to the area you're checking out.

## Amenities

The south coast is dotted with settlements of tremendously varying size, from great cities such as Plymouth, Southampton, Portsmouth and Brighton & Hove, to tiny fishing villages. Below is a list of larger towns/cities on the south coast which provide the full range of amenities including shops, banking facilities and good public transport (bus, coach and rail) links, and smaller towns and villages on the south coast where you should find a shop, cafe, or pub, or possibly two or three of these, but limited public transport. Those with an asterisk (*) are served by rail. For further information on all public transport availability, which as with lists of accommodation can never be either exhaustive or up to date, check the Internet or contact local tourist information centres as suggested above.

### Cities/Larger Towns

Cornwall: Penzance*, Falmouth,* Fowey, Looe*.

Devon: Plymouth*, Salcombe, Dartmouth, Brixham, Paignton*, Torquay*, Teignmouth*, Dawlish*, Exmouth*, Budleigh Salterton, Sidmouth, Seaton.

Dorset: Lyme Regis, Weymouth*, Swanage, Bournemouth*, Christchurch*.

Hampshire: Lymington*, Hythe, Southampton*, Lee-on-the-Solent, Gosport, Portsmouth*, Southsea, Emsworth* (note that Hayling Island has numerous amenities dotted all around it, but no network rail service).

Isle of Wight: Ryde*, Cowes, Ventnor, Shanklin*, Sandown*.

West Sussex: Bognor Regis*, Littlehampton*, Worthing*, Shoreham-by-Sea*.

East Sussex: Hove*, Brighton*, Newhaven*, Seaford*, Eastbourne*, Bexhill*, St Leonards*, Hastings*, Rye*.

Kent: Hythe, Folkestone*, Dover*.

## Smaller Towns/Villages

Cornwall: Mousehole, Newlyn, Marazion, Praa Sands, Porthleven, Mullion Cove, Lizard, Cadgwith, Coverack, Porthallow, Helford, St Mawes, Portscatho, Portloe, Gorran Haven, Mevagissey, Pentewan, Charlestown, Par*, Polruan, Polperro, Seaton, Downderry, Portwrinkle, Cawsand, Kingsand.

Devon: Wembury, Noss Mayo, Bigbury-on-Sea, Inner Hope, Torcross, Stoke Fleming, Kingswear, Shaldon, Dawlish Warren*, Starcross*, Topsham, Beer.

Dorset: Charmouth, Seatown, West Bay, West Bexington, Abbotsbury, Fortuneswell, Osmington Mills, Lulworth Cove, Kimmeridge, Worth Matravers, Studland, Boscombe, Mudeford.

Hampshire: Barton-on-Sea for New Milton*, Milford-on-Sea, Keyhaven, Bucklers Hard, Beaulieu*, Exbury, Calshot, Ashlett, Fawley, Netley*, Hamble*, Warsash, Hill Head, Eastney, Milton, Langstone.

Isle of Wight: Wootton, Whippingham, Gurnard, Porchfield, Newtown, Shalfleet, Yarmouth, Colwell, Freshwater Bay, Brighstone, Chale, Niton, St Lawrence, Bonchurch, Bembridge, Seaview.

West Sussex: Bosham*, Fishbourne*, Birdham, Itchenor, West Wittering, East Wittering, Bracklesham, Selsey, Sidlesham, Felpham, Middleton-on-Sea, Climping, Ferring, Goring-by-Sea*, Lancing*.

East Sussex: Rottingdean, Peacehaven, Cliff End, Winchelsea Beach, Camber.
Kent: Lydd-on-Sea, Greatstone-on-Sea, Littlestone-on-Sea, St Mary's Bay, Dymchurch, Sandgate, St Margaret's Bay.

## Route obstacles

Below are listed some contact numbers for information on availability of ferries, and path closures for firing purposes. These may not be readily available from tourist information centres.

Helford ferry: 01326 250770
Falmouth–St Mawes ferry: 01326 313201 (summer): 01872 862312
St Mawes–Place ferry: 01326 372703
Falmouth–St Mawes-Place water taxi: 07970 242258
Fowey–Polruan ferry: 01726 870232
Cremyll–Stonehouse ferry: 01752 822105
Sutton–Mountbatten ferry: 07930 838614
Wembury–Noss Mayo ferry: 01752 880079 or 07817 132757
Avon ferry: 01548 561196
Salcombe–East Portlemouth ferry: 01548 842364 or 01548 842061
Dartmouth–Kingswear ferry: 01803 752342
Starcross–Exmouth ferry: 01626 862452
Topsham ferry: 07779 370582
Lulworth Ranges: 01929 404819
Sandbanks ferry: 01929 450203
Mudeford ferry: 01202 429119
Hythe–Southampton ferry: 023 8084 0722
Hamble–Warsash ferry: 023 8045 4512
Gosport–Portsmouth ferry: 023 9252 4551
Lydd Ranges: 01303 225518 (office hours) or 01303 225467 (out of hours)
Hythe Ranges: 01303 225879 (office hours) or 01303 225861 (out of hours)
Sovereign Harbour Master: 01323 470099

# Top Ten Weekend Walks

**Best heritage walk**
Day 30 – LEE-ON-THE-SOLENT TO PORTSMOUTH
Includes the impressive fortifications round Gilkicker Point and Gosport and the vast range of sights and attractions in Gosport and Portsmouth including the magnificent Spinnaker Tower. (1 day)

**Best wild walk**
Days 3 and 4 – PORTHLEVEN TO HELFORD
Two days of unforgettable 'away from it all' walking in deepest Cornwall with miles of remote and completely unspoilt coastal scenery, the highlights being the astonishing Kynance Cove and the most southerly headland in Great Britain. (2 days)

**Best nature-lovers' walk**
Day 26 – BARTON-ON-SEA TO LYMINGTON
The Keyhaven Nature Reserve is a paradise for birdwatchers, and there are constantly changing views throughout, with added interest in the shingle bank walk to Hurst Castle, the closest mainland point to the Isle of Wight. (1 day)

**Best challenge walk**
Day 23 – LULWORTH TO SWANAGE
A very long and tough but immensely satisfying rollercoaster walk on some of the steepest cliffs on the south coast. (1 day)

**Best cliff walk**
Day 18 – SIDMOUTH TO LYME REGIS
Part of the Jurassic Coast, there is an amazing variety of cliff scenery from uncompromising steep cliffs between Sidmouth and Branscombe

to the amazing landscapes produced by the cliff slips along the eastern section of the walk. (1 day)

## Best scenic walk
Day 8 – FOWEY TO LOOE
A walk of pure joy, with lovely unspoilt cliff scenery, and the beautiful Cornish seaside settlements of Fowey and Polperro. (1 day)

## Best walk for views
Day 32 – YARMOUTH TO BRIGHSTONE
The views start good and just get better, with the climax at the Needles where on a clear day you can observe the entire south coastline between Swanage and Southampton. (1 day)

## Best diverse walk
Day 28 – BEAULIEU TO SOUTHAMPTON
There is something for everybody: a historic abbey, motor museum, gardens, a country park, sands, a sixteenth-century castle, tremendous views, a Victorian pier, a ferry journey, big ships and a bustling port. (1 day)

## Best family walk
Part of Day 45 – RYE TO JURY'S GAP
This section of Day 45 starts with a beautiful old town and incorporates a walk beside a river then along broad golden sands – and there is a good bus service back to the start. (Half day)

## Best pub walk
Day 37 – LANGSTONE TO BOSHAM
This walk round Chichester Harbour on the borders of Hampshire and West Sussex offers a variety of excellent pubs close to or on the route, with two at the very start and further good pubs at Emsworth, Chidham and Bosham itself. (1 day)

# Bibliography and Further Reading

Ayto, J and Crofton, I *Brewer's Britain and Ireland* (2005, Weidenfeld and Nicolson)

Bathurst, David *Walking the Coastline of Sussex* (2002, SB Publications)

Bathurst, David *Walking the Kent Coast from End to End* (2007, SB Publications)

Carne, Tony *Cornwall's Forgotten Corner* (1986, Lodenek Press)

Cherry, B and Pevsner, N *Pevsner Buildings of England Series: Devon* (2002, Yale University Press)

Dawes, Bill *AA Exploring Britain's Long Distance Paths* (1992, AA Publishing)

Dewhurst, Robin *Philip's County Guides: Hampshire* (1993, G. Philip)

Dillon, Paddy *The South West Coast Path* (2003, Cicerone)

Edwards, Anne-Marie *Pub Walks Along the Solent Way* (2002, Countryside Books)

Holder, John and Shurlock, Barry *Explore Hampshire* (1987, Hyperion Books)

Hunt, R and S *The Sea on Our Left* (2000, Summersdale)

Jordison, S and Kiernan, D *Crap Towns II* (2005, Boxtree)

Livingston, Helen *AA Leisure Guide: Hampshire* (2002, AA Publishing)

Merrill, John *Turn Right at Land's End* (1989, Hyperion Books)

Newman, J and Pevsner, N *Pevsner Buildings of England Series: Dorset* (1997, Penguin)

Pevsner, N and Radcliffe, E *Pevsner Buildings of England Series: Cornwall* (1996, Penguin)

Reynolds, Kev *Classic Walks in Southern England* (1990, Oxford Illustrated Press)

Various authors *AA Book of British Villages* (1980, Drive Publications)

Various authors *Hutchinson Encyclopedia of Britain* (1999, Helicon)

Various authors *Illustrated Guide to Britain* (1977, Drive Publications)

Various authors *Ordnance Survey Guide to Devon and Exmoor* (1996, AA Publishing)

Various authors *Readers Digest Illustrated Guide to Britain's Coast* (1996, Reader's Digest)

Various authors *The Rough Guide to Devon And Cornwall* (2007, Rough Guides)

# THE
# BIG WALKS
## OF GREAT BRITAIN

including South Downs Way, Offa's Dyke Path, The Thames Path,
The Peddars Way and Norfolk Coast Path,
The Wolds Way, The Pembrokeshire Coast Path,
The West Highland Way, The Pennine Way

## DAVID BATHURST

# THE BIG WALKS OF GREAT BRITAIN

David Bathurst

£9.99    Paperback    ISBN: 978 1 84024 566 0

From the South West Coast Path to the Great Glen Way, from the Cotswold Way to Hadrian's Wall, and from the Yorkshire Wolds to Glyndwr's Way, there are big walks here to keep you rambling all year round. And what better way to discover the landscapes of Great Britain, from green and gentle dales to majestic mountains and rugged cliffs?

An indefatigable walker, David Bathurst has unlaced his boots to produce this invaluable companion to the 19 best-loved long-distance footpaths. His appreciation of the beauty and history of the British countryside and his light-hearted style will appeal to experienced and novice walkers alike.

- The definitive guide to the national trails of England and Wales and the Scottish National Long Distance Walking Routes

- Detailed descriptions of the trails and a wealth of practical information, including amenities available

- Recommends historic and geographic areas of interest on or near the paths, from ancient burial mounds to flora and fauna

- Routes range in difficulty from the gentle 73-mile Great Glen Way to the massive 628-mile South West Coast Path

# The Best of
# British Festivals

Food · Music · Theatre · Comedy · Dance · Kayaking · Drumming ·
Carnival Workshops and much, much more...

## Barney Jeffries

# THE BEST OF BRITISH FESTIVALS

Barney Jeffries

£9.99   Paperback   ISBN 978 1 84024 656 8

Ah, the great British festival – crawling out of a tent and squelching through foot-deep mud to enjoy a burger for breakfast... But British festivals aren't all moshpits and partying – there's a host of other experiences on offer. You could:

- Soak up some culture at the Edinburgh festivals, where you'll find experimental theatre, comedy, street acts, music, books, ballet and opera
- Chase a giant cheese down a hill at the Stilton World Cheese Rolling Championships
- Watch performers from all over the globe in the heart of the picturesque Welsh countryside at the Llangollen International Eisteddfod
- Take the kids out for adventure playgrounds, activities and workshops galore at the Outsider Festival or Larmer Tree festival.

*The Best of British Festivals* is a fun-seeker's guide with a difference, giving you the low-down on the best events taking place up and down the country in every month of the year.

# the sea on our

## left

A couple's ten month walk around Britain's coastline

# the

# sea

Shally Hunt

SUMMERSDALE TRAVEL

# THE SEA ON OUR LEFT
## A Couple's Ten Month Walk Around Britain's Coastline

Shally Hunt

£7.99    Paperback    ISBN 978 1 84024 105 1

This is the best-selling story of a husband and wife team walking clockwise for 302 days around the coastline of England, Wales and Scotland. It gives a lively account of the progress they made, and describes with humour the strains imposed on them, the varied scenery they walked through, the problems they encountered and the people they met along the way.

'Although many dream of it, few achieve it. Both aged 52 and at the peak of their careers they gave up their gentle lifestyle to spend the next 10 months trudging 4,300 miles'                EVENING STANDARD

'Living like a tortoise, carrying the whole world on your back, can reduce you to a tortoise's pace, as Shally and Richard found . . . they have worn through three pairs of boots each, fought blisters and stomach cramps, fended off Highland midges, heaved their rucksacks up mountains – and come close to destroying their marriage'                SUNDAY EXPRESS

'This book leaves you wondering why you haven't got the nerve to do it'
ADVENTURE TRAVEL

'An intrepid adventure'                                EVENING  STANDARD

'A remarkable trip of endless diversity and surprises... a unique travelogue'
EARTH MATTERS (Friends Of The Earth)

www.summersdale.com